McGowar.

Donald Hauka

NEW STAR BOOKS

VANCOUVER

2003

Publication of this work is made possible by grants from the Canada
Council, the British Columbia Arts Council, and the Department of
Canadian Heritage Book Publishing Industry Development Program.

Printed and bound in Canada
First printing, November 2003

New Star Books Ltd.
107 - 3477 Commercial Street
Vancouver, BC   V5N 4E8
www.NewStarBooks.com

NATIONAL LIBRARY OF CANADA CATALOGUING IN PUBLICATION

Hauka, Donald J.
  McGowan's war / Donald Hauka.

Includes bibliographical references and index.
ISBN 1-55420-001-6

  1. McGowan, Ned, 1807–1893. 2. British Columbia — History —
1849–1871. I. Title.
FC3822.H38 2003   971.1'02   C2003-905344-X

Contents

Acknowledgements

I would like to acknowledge the following people, who helped make this book possible: First, Rolf Maurer, whose patience and perseverance have finally paid off; Terry Glavin, who thought it was worth telling; Audrey McClellan, who edited the manuscript so deftly; Dr. Gerd Asche, who made Dr. Max Fifer flesh and blood (even though we agree to disagree about McGowan's character); Helen D. Harris, who dug up the dirt on Peter Brunton Whannell and found his descendants; Nola Buzza, that descendant, who filled in great blanks in her eccentric forebear's life for me; Cole Harris, whose advice and encouragement were crucial in seeing me through; and finally, my family, Donatella and Nicolas, who have sacrificed much so I could spend my time typing quietly away in the basement. And to everyone else who I wearied with each new detail I unearthed, thanks for your patience. Here's a chance to read the whole thing . . .

McGowan's War

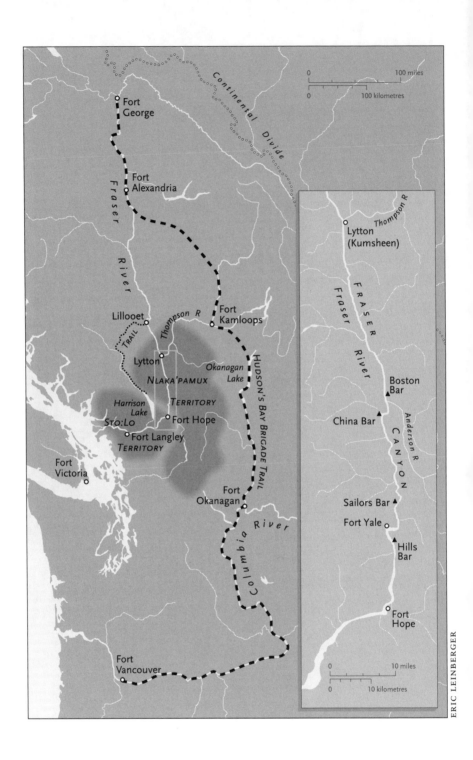

Fort George

Continental Divide

Fraser River

Fort Alexandria

Lillooet

TRAIL

Thompson R

Fort Kamloops

Lytton

Okanagan Lake

NLAKA'PAMUX

TERRITORY

Harrison Lake

STO:LO

Fort Hope

HUDSON'S BAY BRIGADE TRAIL

Fort Langley
TERRITORY

Fort Victoria

Fort Okanagan

Columbia River

Fort Vancouver

0   100 miles

0   100 kilometres

Lytton (Kumsheen)

Thompson R

FRASER RIVER

Boston Bar

China Bar

Anderson R

CANYON

Sailors Bar

Fort Yale

Hills Bar

Fort Hope

0   10 miles

0   10 kilometres

ERIC LEINBERGER

Introduction

John Drummond Buchanan Ogilvy, Hudson's Bay factor for Fort Hope, walked quietly into the frigid dawn of January 17, 1859, his snowshoes softly crunching on the hard, crisp snow. Ogilvy was leading a force of Royal Engineers and volunteers along the west side of the Fraser River to Fort Yale. A few yards to his right, on the east bank, was the settlement of Hill's Bar, the epicentre of the Fraser River gold rush. Ogilvy knew that the bar was the headquarters of Yankee renegades who were plotting to overthrow British rule by drawing American army forces, stationed just south of the still-disputed border, into the newly founded colony of British Columbia. He moved warily, for the Americans weren't amateurs. They were led by Major Tom Dolan (a veteran of the Mexican-American War and soldier of fortune) and the notorious outlaw Ned McGowan, who had eluded the Vigilance Committee of San Francisco before fleeing to the Fraser River gold mines.

Ogilvy glanced behind him. The Engineers and the Cornish volunteers were now coming out of the trees and into the open by the river. They were but a stone's throw from the campfires of the American sentries, ranged in a semi-circle by the river bank. This was the crucial moment. With no cover and day's light growing stronger, the Engineers' dark great coats stood out against the white snow, making them easy targets for American sharpshooters. But they had to get past this spot to reach their commander, Colonel Richard Moody, at Fort Yale.

Halfway across the clearing, a twig snapped underfoot. An American sentry shouted into the gloom. They had been spotted. Would the Yankees let them pass unmolested? Ogilvy walked on, quicker now and with no heed to the noise he was making. Then one of the Americans fired across the river. Instantly, the entire American force began shooting wildly at the British troops. Ogilvy marched steadily ahead. Those were their orders. If even one Engineer stopped to return fire, a bloody melee would ensue and the Americans would have the international incident they'd been praying for . . .

This was the pivotal moment in "Ned McGowan's War." Almost forgotten now, the "war" threatened to deliver B.C. into American hands on the eve of the U.S. Civil War. Dolan and his chief, Judge Edward McGowan, had the men and arms to do it, vastly outnumbering and outgunning the small detachment of British troops. It was only the efforts of three English gentlemen — a colonel, a lieutenant and a judge — HBC men like Ogilvy, and McGowan himself that prevented a war between Britain and America. And it was thanks to the work of Governor James Douglas, who was as astute politically as he was commercially, that they had a British Columbia to save in the first place.

How close did B.C. come to being hijacked by American fortune seekers in 1858 – 59 when the Fraser Canyon was transformed from an ancient cradle of civilization into a near-lawless El Dorado of the North? Would Californian desperadoes have dared march on Fort Yale to provoke an invasion by the United States military? How much of the trouble was the fault of Richard Hicks, Douglas's trusted man on the gold fields, who proved so faithless? Was the feud between Hicks and his fellow official Peter Brunton Whannell the main wellspring of McGowan's War? Are B.C. politics so weird and, well, *Californian* because of the precedent-setting miners' political meetings in the gold fields? Or is it because of the unorthodox methods used by Douglas, a practical man who bucked authority and led from the heart as well as a crafty mind to secure Canada its doorway to the Pacific? Just who was McGowan anyway, and why did he get the blame for that quixotic incident commonly known as Ned McGowan's War?

Answering these questions from the past gives us insight into how B.C. works today. Further insight lies in the canyon itself, for to walk along the narrow banks under the sheer rock faces is to wander through the heart of the history of this place, which beats and churns like the rapids that boil through Hell's Gate. At a now-deserted spot on the Fraser's east bank above Hope is Hill's Bar, where the gold rush started. Farther up the river on the opposite bank is Yale, where McGowan and Judge Matthew Baillie Begbie faced each other in a log-cabin courtroom and helped to determine the course of B.C.'s political history. Running in the midst of it all and binding it together is the river, which helped one culture flourish on salmon and jump-started another by giving of its rich deposits of gold.

To make order of the chaos that marked the birth of British Columbia, it's best to begin with one central premise: Modern B.C. was born of a political crisis created by a sudden rush to exploit a rich natural resource and by the need to keep the territory out of the hands of the Americans. In the nearly 150 years since that initial dilemma, not much has changed.

ONE

Idylls of the Mulatto King

Dinner was over. Amelia Douglas and her daughters cleared the china and fine crystal from the linen-covered table as the officers of the Hudson's Bay Company outpost of Fort Victoria pushed their chairs away and sipped after-dinner brandy or Madeira. All eyes were on Amelia's husband, James Douglas, "Old Square Toes," who was holding forth at the head of the long table. Douglas was the chief factor of the almighty Company as well as the governor of the fledgling colony of Vancouver Island, which on that evening in 1857 was little more than a hamlet huddled about the palisades of the trading post.

The dark-skinned, dour Douglas controlled virtually everything in this, his domain, including after-dinner conversation. He frowned on sharing personal anecdotes unless distinguished guests like another chief factor or a chief trader were dining with him. Sometimes he would choose a subject picked out of a suitable (if somewhat dated) publication like *The Times*, but on this night Douglas had something more exciting than a newspaper clipping for the men under his command to discuss. John Sebastian Helmcken, Douglas's son-in-law and the HBC doctor, was at the governor's elbow as Douglas held up a small soda-water bottle full of fine gold and wove a fantastic tale that was met with incredulity by his audience.

"The Governor attached great importance to it and thought it meant a great change and busy time," Helmcken later remembered.

"He spoke of Victoria rising to be a great city — and of its value, but curiously enough this conversation did not make much impression."[1]

Helmcken assumed his penny-pinching, ever-entrepreneurial father-in-law would use the gold to encourage a modest-sized rush, counting on the ensuing excitement to boost the price of town lots. But no one gathered around that table, least of all Douglas himself, realized that the governor held in his hands the instrument of the destruction of their safe, comfortable world. The gold set in motion a chain reaction that threatened to deliver the personal fiefdom of Old Square Toes into the hands of the Americans, caused suffering and death for the territory's First Nations peoples, laid the foundations of B.C.'s peculiar brand of politics and ended with Douglas doing the un-thinkable: severing his seemingly unbreakable ties with the Hudson's Bay Company.

To understand the significance of these changes, you have to understand James Douglas himself. Diligent, hard-working, he "turned parsimony into an art form"[2] and made the fur trade his life, devoting himself to the Hudson's Bay Company, which had given him a wife, a fortune, and a chance to rise to the top. Although he was an illegitimate mulatto from the colonies, he took the standards of English society to heart and imagined himself a gentleman. He looked down on Americans, but had sympathy for the First Nations people he dealt with as an HBC trader. Imperious, a virtual despot, answerable only to the Company's committeemen[3] or the colonial secretary in London, with power of life and death over those he ruled, he had to smoke in the garden because Amelia forbade him to do so inside their house.

The Rise and Rise of James Douglas

To get to the head of the mess table, Douglas had overcome huge handicaps, starting with his birth in 1803 on a sugar plantation in Demerara, British Guiana. He was an illegitimate mulatto, son of John Douglas, a Scottish plantation owner, who had three children with a Barbados-born black woman named Martha Ritchie, the daughter of a "free coloured woman." When John Douglas returned to Scotland, he left Ritchie behind and married a Scottish lass. However, in 1812 he sent for James and his brother Alexander and enrolled them at a prep school in Lanark, Scotland. James was bright and quick to pick up French, but he also had a fearful temper. When angry, he would frown frightfully, and a horseshoe-shaped mark would appear on his forehead. Later in life, his employees and his political opponents learned to fear the appearance of that wrathful horseshoe.

Career options were few for a man of mixed blood in Britain's rigid class structure, so James set his sights on the New World, where the vast territories north and west of Rupert's Land were a battleground for rival fur companies. Douglas entered the service of the Northwest Company when he was not yet sixteen years old and sailed for Quebec in 1819. Sent to Fort William on the north shore of Lake Superior, he learned the fur trade from the ground up. When the Northwest Company merged with the Hudson's Bay Company in 1821, Douglas switched allegiance to the HBC. By 1825 he was posted to New Caledonia, the northern Interior of what is now B.C. In 1828 he married Amelia Connolly "by the custom of the country." Amelia was half-Cree, half-Irish, the daughter of William Connolly, chief trader[4] for Fort St. James, and his Cree wife, Suzanne. James and Amelia legally married nine years later in 1837. They had thirteen children. Only six reached adulthood.

Amelia saved her husband's life one day in 1828 when Douglas's temper got the better of him. He was chasing down a Native man who had murdered a Hudson's Bay employee five years before at Fort George. Finding the alleged murderer in a Dakelh village close to the post, Douglas and a handful of men apprehended him and beat him to death then and there. The next day, Kwah, chief of the Nak'azdli people of the Dakelh First Nation, led a force of men into Fort St. James, captured Douglas, bound him and threatened to kill the young clerk with a dagger. Amelia started throwing trade goods — tobacco, blankets and clothing — into the crowd of Nak'azdlit'en from a second-storey window of the main building. The goods proved an acceptable ransom and Douglas was freed.

The infamous horseshoe mark of anger on Douglas's forehead

appeared less frequently after the episode with Kwah. He had learned a valuable lesson, not only in anger management, as we would call it today, but also in the art of patience and in using a show of force rather than violence to resolve disputes. In 1853, when pursuing the murderer of an HBC shepherd, Douglas outwaited two hundred Cowichan warriors by sitting on a camp stool on the beach, calmly smoking his pipe, a cutlass in one hand, a pistol in the other and a pile of presents at his feet. Douglas got his man.

In 1830 Douglas was transferred to Fort Vancouver at the mouth of the Columbia River in the Oregon Territory and took up his duties as a clerk. There he came under the wing of Dr. John McLoughlin, chief factor of the Columbia Department (which included New Caledonia). McLoughlin was a huge, white-haired lion of a man who became Douglas's mentor and patron. Under McLoughlin's tutelage, Douglas learned how to dispense patronage, the importance of marriage in cementing bonds of loyalty and how to move stealthily through the byzantine world of HBC politics. He was promoted to chief factor in 1839.

Douglas could have stayed happily at Fort Vancouver to the end of his days, but Manifest Destiny and the Oregon Treaty of 1846 cost the HBC its territory south of the 49th parallel. Hudson's Bay policy was to discourage settlement in its lands, so there were no British citizens in the area to offset the flood of American settlers, which gave de facto possession of the Oregon Territory to the United States. When James K. Polk won the U.S. presidency in 1844 with the slogan "54 – 40 or fight," it was only a matter of time before the Stars and Stripes would fly over Fort Vancouver.

"There was something grand and majestic about Douglas — in the first place, he was broad and powerful and had a wooden hard face when necessary, which said very plainly, 'I am not afraid but noli me tangere'" (Don't touch me — or else). John Sebastian Helmcken's assessment of his father-in-law was born of long experience. James Douglas's own long experience would serve him well during the crisis of 1858–59 — a crisis that he inadvertently helped to engineer.

The Colony of Vancouver Island

Foreseeing the inevitable eviction from Oregon, in 1842 the HBC ordered Douglas to find an alternative to Fort Vancouver. He chose a sheltered harbour with serpentine waterways at the southern tip of Vancouver Island — Fort Victoria. To get the Company's grant of monopoly past a reluctant House of Commons, the HBC agreed in 1848 to establish a Crown colony on Vancouver Island, though it had no intention of spending money to encourage settlement. The Company's strategy was simple: Vancouver Island would be "a protective shield for its coastal and continental fur trade."[5] The mainland of British Columbia, New Caledonia, remained the vast, private economic empire of the HBC, off-limits to everyone else and almost untouched by Europeans, while the colony of Vancouver Island would pay its own way and not become a burden to the shareholders.

The parsimonious Douglas was, in the Company's eyes, the ideal man to carry out this grand design. In 1849 he left Fort Vancouver to become chief factor of Fort Victoria. He had served a long apprenticeship in the wilderness and was by far the most qualified man for the post of governor of the new colony. But while the Company urged the colonial office to give Douglas the job, the mandarins in London balked at the idea. Worried the public would think the HBC all-powerful in the new settlement, they decided to appoint Richard Blanshard, a young lawyer with no ties to the Company, to fill the post. It took the thirty-two-year-old Blanshard a year to arrive at Fort Victoria. When he did, he found that Douglas had not yet bothered to build him a residence. Virtually everything in the colony was either run or owned outright by the Hudson's Bay Company, and James Douglas, who was keenly aware he'd been passed over for the governorship in favour of a man he considered completely unsuited for the job, was the HBC.

While he might not be governor in name, Douglas had the very real power of the Company behind him and knew how to use it. He made Blanshard's stay as unpleasant as possible. The new governor was indignant to discover he was being charged top rate for his personal purchases from the HBC stores because, as Douglas patiently explained, His Excellency was not a Company employee and therefore not entitled to a discount.

If Blanshard had hoped to win the hearts and minds of non-Hudson's Bay settlers, he was again sorely disappointed when he discovered that the Company had learned nothing from the Oregon Territory fiasco. It did not want just any old riffraff populating its Pacific shield, so rather than encouraging hordes of settlers to establish Britain's claim on the Island, the HBC insisted that men of substance and property settle the new colony. Land on Vancouver Island cost five dollars an acre, and colonists were expected to bring their own labourers to work it. In contrast, just south of the line, U.S. settlers got their 640-acre pre-emptions for nothing.

As a result of HBC policy, Blanshard found he had but a single settler in his charge. And what a settler he was. Captain Walter Colquhoun Grant was an officer in the Scots Greys (the famous regiment that committed celebrated suicide at Waterloo) and had arrived as the first non-HBC settler in Victoria in the summer of 1849, so destitute that the Company had been forced to pay for his passage west. A bank failure had cost Grant his fortune but not his English gentleman's attitude towards other people's money and his own debts. When he arrived, his "essentials" included cricket gear and two small cannons.[6] (Personal property was always more important to Grant than mere cash. It was said that during one battle, when his horse was shot out from under him, Grant took care to remove the bridle and saddle from his dead mount before retiring from the field, despite being under heavy fire.)

For lack of any better entertainment, Grant used to hold forth in the fort's bachelor quarters, a square log house with a main room twenty feet by twelve. The walls were unfinished cedar planks, and a few cedar mats were hung on them to keep down the draft. In the middle of the room was a large, dilapidated wood stove made of sheet iron, which provided scant warmth. Above the heads of the single men in the Company's employ were the loose floorboards of the children's dormitory, replete with cracks and chinks. It was here that Grant amused himself and the HBC men by demonstrating his prowess with a sabre. When he showed them how to use a sword to snuff out a candle mounted on the back of a chair, the display ended with sizable chunks carved out of both candle and chair. Not surprisingly, there were no volunteers when Grant offered to demonstrate how to cut a button off a coat. On one particularly boisterous occasion (and under the influence of a considerable dose of rum and brandy), Grant declared it was time to "escort Her Majesty to Windsor Castle." Pretending to be cavalry, the revellers followed Grant around and around the hall, jumping kangaroo fashion, laughing and shrieking like banshees. The riot came to an end when one of the young girls who was listening sleeplessly overhead poured the contents of her chamber pot through a crack in the floorboards above, showering the cavalry and halting the procession abruptly.

Grant named his land near Sooke "Mullachard" after his ancestral estate in Scotland. It was a grand name for a shanty. He also established a long-standing British Columbia tradition of spending the winter in Hawaii. Further and further in debt, Grant eventually signed his lands over to the HBC in 1853 and left for Oregon, then finally returned to England and rejoined the Greys, fighting in the Crimean War and the Indian Mutiny. He died of dysentery in India in 1861 at age thirty-nine.

A slow trickle of somewhat less colourful colonists gradually added to the non-HBC population, but the powerless Blanshard stuck it out in his hopeless position for less than a year. Douglas did not make things easy for him, constantly finding more important work for the men who were supposed to build the governor's residence, delaying its completion until five months after Blanshard arrived. Miserable, Blanshard resigned and was forced to pay for his passage home, but he left Douglas with a farewell present that the chief factor and future governor would curse: the beginnings of representative government.

On August 27, 1851, just four days before Douglas was to replace him, Blanshard appointed a governor's executive council. He could not leave the powerful Douglas off the council, nor could he avoid appointing John Tod, the chief factor's long-time friend and loyal Company servant. But Blanshard balanced these by naming Captain

James Cooper to the august body. Cooper was a former Company employee, master of the HBC ship *Columbia*. He had run afoul of Douglas for trying to do a little bit of independent trading in his spare time. Cooper wanted to ship cranberries from the mainland to San Francisco, but the mainland was the Company's private preserve, and Douglas forbade the scheme. Besides, the HBC was engaged in a similar business. Cooper resigned from the HBC to become an independent settler and had been Douglas's implacable foe ever since. Now he had political clout.

No Taxation without Representation

With this good-bye gift in place, Blanshard left Victoria in September 1851, and Douglas officially became governor of Vancouver Island. The colony he presided over was very small and growth was slow. Handfuls of new colonists arrived, supplemented by former HBC employees like Cooper, who opted to try and make their own way and resented the Company's interference in their affairs.

Another former HBC employee who decided to try his hand at colonizing was James Yates, who had arrived in Victoria in 1849 aboard the *Harpooner* as the ship's carpenter. Born in Scotland in 1819, Yates was a dark-complexioned, powerfully built, cantankerous man with a broad, pugnacious face and a huge handlebar mustache. His entrepreneurial spirit was frustrated by HBC rules and its custom of paying employees in Company "scrip," which had no value outside the Company stores, rather than in cash. Yates ran away to the California gold rush in 1850. When he returned, he was imprisoned in the fort's bastion for a month before being released. Yates quit the HBC and went into business with Cooper as a wine and liquor merchant. He was soon one of the wealthiest men in Victoria. Nursing his grudge against the HBC, he was a constant thorn in Douglas's side, agitating for, among other things, representative government. But there was no representative government, only the governor's council, which Douglas easily dominated.

Always anxious to please the HBC's committeemen in London, Douglas looked for ways to make the colony pay for itself and not become a drain on the Company. He soon found a measure that appealed to both his parsimonious and puritanical natures. On March 29, 1853, Douglas summoned his appointed council: Tod, Cooper and Roderick Finlayson, a reliable HBC employee who had filled Douglas's seat. They met in the bachelors' quarters, and there the governor presented plans for a liquor tax of $500 a year that would pay for general improvements and for colonial officers. Cooper was aghast and vehemently disagreed with the proposed tax — the HBC was supposed to pay those costs. More importantly, it would hit him and his partner, Yates, right in the pocketbook.

The debate went back and forth all day and into the evening. Douglas decided reason, argument and an appeal to Cooper's morals were of no use. But he knew his opponent's weakness. As dinner was cleared away, Douglas ordered Madeira and tobacco be brought in. Over their pipes and a never-ending stream of glasses of wine, Cooper's opposition gradually softened. Helmcken describes what happened next with some relish.

> *Captain Cooper, who liked a glass of good wine (and in those days the wine was of the very best) took more than one, and then altho the room was smoky, he began to see more clearly the subject was not without some reason and so his determination weakened a little — a glass or two more — "Pass the decanter, gentlemen" — the wine is good and generous (the Governor took but little himself, and was always very abstemious, but could smoke a great deal and deliberately) so Cooper took some more, and from being disagreeable became amiable and at length subsided, saying he would not consent — consented. There was a little more wine and friendship after this and then the first Council adjourned — having passed the first law — the "Licence Law."*[7]

With the new tax passed by unanimous consent, Cooper made his unsteady way to Yates's tavern to explain things to his business partner. Yates was furious, and after another liberal dose of liquor, so was Cooper, who could no longer see why he had assented to such a "tyrannous" measure. Cooper soon had everyone in the tavern agitated as he ran about shouting, "No taxation without representation! Down with tyranny and the governor, beware the first tax!" Cooper took his diatribe out into the muddy streets of the village to convince passersby of the unjustness of the tax, but the dramatic impact of his argument was somewhat spoiled when he went sprawling face-first into the mud outside the saloon.[8]

The tax brought in £400, or about $2,000, not an inconsiderable sum. But the governor's victory was not without consequences. The tax had to be approved by the colonial office in London, and the British government was very sensitive to the complaints of settlers like Yates and Cooper, whose cry of "no taxation without representation" was all too familiar. So while the colonial administrators held their noses and let Douglas have his way, they also insisted an elected House of Assembly be instituted at once to prevent further disputes or a Victoria tea party (or, in this case, a rum, brandy and ale party).

For a man who had ruled with the absolute authority of a czar in the wilderness, the very idea of elected government appalled Douglas. He was a staunch imperialist and anti-democrat who had known only the exacting discipline and hierarchy of the Hudson's Bay Company as a model for conducting both business and social affairs. For three years he was able to procrastinate as the colonial office did not pursue the matter, but in February 1856 Douglas received orders to hold elections for a House of Assembly to help him govern.[9] He wrote London about the "feeling of dismay" these orders awoke in him: "I am utterly averse to universal suffrage, or making population the basis of representation."[10]

Vancouver Island would have anything but universal suffrage. The governor set the standards for the franchise high. Only men with twenty acres of land could vote. To be elected, a representative had to have property worth over £300. There were seven seats: three for Victoria, two for Esquimalt-Metchosin, one for Sooke and one for Nanaimo. There were almost as many candidates as there were electors, with about fifty men qualifying to vote.

The only real race was in Victoria. Here, the foundation of B.C.'s polarized politics was laid with two irreconcilable camps vying for power. The anti-HBC forces were led by Yates, who was joined by the like-minded Edward Edwards Langford as a candidate. An army officer, Langford had sold his commission and arrived in the colony in 1851 to manage Colwood farm for the Puget Sound Agricultural Company, a subsidiary of the HBC. Langford and his wife entertained lavishly and he borrowed just as lavishly, some years spending up to eight times his annual salary. In 1853 the Langfords went through 237 pounds of tea and 70 gallons of brandy, much of it consumed by guests. Even more booze was consumed on the hustings in Victoria, where rum and whiskey were liberally applied in an attempt to secure votes. Fisticuffs were a common form of debate.

When the dust cleared, Yates, Langford and another HBC foe, Captain C.E. Stewart of Nanaimo, were elected, along with two disgruntled HBC employees, Thomas Skinner and John Muir, the member for Sooke, who was the original backbencher. Helmcken remembered him as "one of the led," who "said aye or nay, when present." They were opposed by two Company men, including Helmcken, who had won in Esquimalt-Metchosin, and Joseph Despard Pemberton, the town surveyor.

The First Assembly

The new assembly convened on August 12, 1856, in the rat-infested bachelors' quarters where Grant had once led his bacchanalian revels. A somewhat more sober crowd gathered to do the business of representative government for the first time in B.C. history. They sat around a plain, homemade wooden table in seven matching wooden chairs for Douglas's speech opening the first session. There was no mace, no coat-of-arms, not even a penknife or a postage stamp. Helmcken observed that a "respectful distance away" from the table were two wooden benches without backs for the use of any who wished to see the people's elected representatives at work. All the furniture belonged to the HBC, so there was no need to spend public funds on furnishings.[11]

Douglas gave a high-minded speech to the small assembly, exhorting members to remember the public duty. At the heart of that duty was ensuring that the colony was "self-supporting and defraying all the expenses of its own government." He warned the "poverty of the country and the limited means of a population struggling against the presence of numberless privations must necessarily restrict the amount of taxation." He also appealed to the members to do their business with a sense of honour and propriety. "The interests and well-being of thousands yet unborn may be affected by our decisions, and they will reverence or condemn our acts according as they are found to influence for good or for evil the events of the future."

With that admonition out of the way, the assembly got down to business. The HBC faction secured the election of Helmcken as Speaker. The good doctor then presided over a bare-knuckle session aimed at unseating two of the sitting members. The profligate Langford's qualifications to sit as an elected representative were challenged, based on his well-known indebtedness. A similar charge was levelled at Stewart. Some malcontents threw their lot in with the HBC interest and in swift order, Langford was disqualified and replaced by Joseph William McKay, a steadfast HBC man. Stewart's replacement was John F. Kennedy (a doctor and no relation to the later JFK), another stout Company loyalist. With Helmcken, Pemberton, McKay and Kennedy now sitting, the Hudson's Bay Company was assured a narrow, four-three majority.

The effect of these machinations was far-reaching. Voters in B.C. have seen many "business friendly" administrations in the province's history. W.A.C. Bennett boasted that his Social Credit administration was "the first business government that B.C. has ever had," but in 1856, government *was* business and business was government. What was good for James Douglas and the Hudson's Bay Company was good for the colony.

The elected assembly's debates initially centred around vital issues like whose turn it was to light the fire in the stove. As Helmcken described it, there was "no chaplain, no prayers, no Sergeant-at-Arms, no reporters, no nothing to add grace and dignity to the floor, which could not boast either of carpet or cleanliness." The only attendant on the body was "Dick the Indian boy," who was also the servant to the bachelors of the HBC. There was no smoking allowed and no booze to be had. The MLAs received no pay. Their guide, initially, was an American rules of order used in the California legislature. Helmcken summed it up this way: "Imagine, then, half a dozen honest, upright, intelligent, well-informed, well-mannered gentlemen, meeting to discuss any important or unimportant question, whether in the House or out of it, and you will form a very good idea of the debates in the House of Assembly."[12]

Disaffected voters today can only dream of having the opportunity for direct democracy that the chamber pot-equipped children living above the legislators' heads enjoyed back then. Because members were unpaid, the assembly's record of sitting was patchy. They met and adjourned on "any old day"and "very often had to be drummed up." Eventually the assembly moved to a room in Judge Pemberton's hotel, which served both as a jail and a lunatic asylum. Their contact with Douglas was, at first, in writing. Later Helmcken arranged to have formal interviews with Douglas, but the governor gave him little information.

Eventually, even the stalwart Company men of the assembly started to turn on Douglas. The key issue was, of course, money. The only revenue the assembly had was the tax on liquor licences, which amounted to $2,000 a year. All other monies raised were taken in by the HBC, including cash from the sale of land. The House resolved that, until all revenues were placed under its control, it would not vote for any supply nor undertake any public works. This suited Douglas well, for, in effect, the assembly had rendered itself powerless. Douglas was now completely in charge of the purse strings, and the assembly he despised was of no further trouble to him. Thereafter, the assembly did little more than pass resolutions condemning Douglas for exercising his powers.

One thing the assembly did accomplish was the passage of the Franchise Bill and other related acts, which allowed it to commit electoral suicide by setting down the exact means of holding another election. On November 9, 1859, Helmcken informed Douglas there was no more work for the assembly to do and it awaited official dissolution. But this only came after a long period of wrangling between

Douglas and Helmcken over holding another vote. From time to time the Speaker would approach the governor about dissolution and a new election.

"About prorogation, Your Excellency?" Helmcken would ask politely.

"Give the members plenty of time, Mr. Speaker, plenty of time!" Douglas would reply with an imperious wave of a hand.[13]

Thus Douglas ruled almost absolutely and by decree. Wearing his twin hats of governor and chief factor, he served two masters, but there was never any doubt which one was dearest to his heart and his balance sheet.

Under these conditions, the growth of the little colony was painfully slow. It remained divided into two camps. On the one hand was the HBC social pyramid, with Douglas at its apex. Beneath him were the officers of the Company, chiefly Scots. Below them were the working class of French Canadians, Kanakas (Hawaiians) and others. In the other camp were the new colonists, former HBC employees like Yates and the Langfords, the Skinners and the Mckenzies. Hardly nobility, they nonetheless considered themselves a cut above the families of the HBC employees. They were the landed gentry, and although many came from the direst of circumstances, they were social snobs. Even the humblest settlers from England found it intolerable that Douglas was above them in social status, since in their eyes he was an upstart, bastard mulatto with a half-breed wife whose children of mixed heritage they sneeringly referred to as "Improved Scots."[14]

Despite this private scorn, Douglas was still very publicly the First Man in Victoria. After a lifetime of constantly moving at the behest of the HBC, he and his family had found stability and a measure of peace. His affection for the place made exile from his beloved Fort Vancouver easier. When settling on the site of Fort Victoria, Douglas's soul was moved by its beauty. He described his "perfect Eden" as having "dropped from the clouds." The term "Lotus Land" is often misused by the rest of Canada to describe all of what is now British Columbia. The original Lotus Land on the West Coast was and remains Victoria and its environs on Vancouver Island.[15] Victoria was very different then, of course. All around James Bay, roses, red currant, mock orange and spiraea were in abundance. A fringe of pine and fir trees (some over 200 feet tall) sheltered the area from icy blasts off the Olympic Mountains across the Strait of Juan de Fuca. Outside the fort were fields of wheat and pastures for cattle.

Douglas built his house a mile from the fort (where the Royal B.C. Museum now sits), on the other side of the tidal flats that were later filled in to become the causeway. The house was surrounded by its own stockade and by a garden in which he planted grape vines that had come from Oregon. Douglas helped establish that smug attitude exemplified by the annual flower count, which Victorians insist on holding in March, when the rest of the country is still in winter's grip. Witness Douglas's postscript at the end of an official missive to Arthur Blackwood, a senior official in the colonial office, written December 27, 1858.

> *The weather is at present fine, and the opposite hills still retain their hue of green; a single Castille rose, somewhat faded, was picked yesterday, and the humble Daisy-heart's Ease, and wall flower, growing exposed in my garden, have not yet entirely lost their bloom. Those few facts will perhaps give a clearer idea of the climate than any description.*

By the time Douglas wrote these words to Blackwood, the bloom had already gone off the rose of Victoria's quiet existence at the furthest edge of empire. Changes were coming that would put an end to the safe comfortable world of Old Square Toes. For Douglas himself was about to let a golden djinn out of the bottle.

TWO

The Glorious River of Gold

By 1857 and the night of that fateful dinner with the golden soda bottle, there were no more than a thousand white settlers in Her Majesty's colony of Vancouver Island, scattered from Fort Victoria to Nanaimo. They were surrounded and outnumbered by tens of thousands of Natives belonging to a dozen different (and sometimes hostile) nations. Spreading out from the fort, Victoria was a quaint, level village of stump-studded fields and whitewashed cottages with crooked chimneys. In their gardens, the English settlers planted flowers from home to ease their sense of isolation. There was no running water or central reservoir. Water came from Spring Ridge, several miles away. Slowly, schools, churches, sawmills, stores and houses were being built outside the stockade's walls.

As chief factor of the HBC, most of Douglas's attention was focused on the Company's commercial interests on the mainland. Here the white man's tread upon the land had been light indeed. There were but a handful of HBC forts established along the banks of its major rivers and no white settlements.

Although New Caledonia appeared empty and undeveloped to the recent arrivals, however, it was no wilderness, especially in the Fraser Canyon. For millennia before the arrival of Europeans, the Sto:Lo, Nlaka'pamux, and other people of the canyon lived in a complex world of riches based on salmon. High rocky cliffs sheltered the densest population of non-agricultural beings on the planet. Winter villages were a mile or two apart, and summer fishing camps lined the shores. The rock faces were laced with burial shrines, and painted totemic figures stared out over the river below. The level land was occupied and trails led off into the mountains over a well-known geography. First Nations groups from all over the Pacific Northwest made annual trips to the canyon for its rich salmon runs. There was no room for newcomers without displacing the existing population.

Douglas worked with the First Nations to earn the HBC a handsome profit, employing them in almost every aspect of the HBC's operations. The Native peoples, in turn, were not passive bystanders, but active and aggressive partners who helped expand the Company's trade from furs to salmon, lumber and other products. It was a cooperative and profitable arrangement.

If there was a shadow hanging over this cozy business partnership, it hovered just south of the ill-defined border in the shape of a grasping American eagle. While the 49th parallel had been named as the border in the Oregon Treaty, Great Britain and the United States were only now getting around to surveying it, and they could not agree on just where it met the Pacific. Further complicating matters was the fact that southern Vancouver Island dipped well below the agreed-to line. Great Britain (and Douglas) was pressing for a boundary that would preserve not just Vancouver Island, but also the southern Gulf and San Juan islands for the Crown. The Americans countered with a proposal that would see both island archipelagos under the Stars and Stripes, and they had sent two hundred troops to escort their boundary surveyors and strengthen their position. The dispute was a worry, but business went on in Douglas's quiet colonial outpost, which was — despite the obstacles put in its path by the Company — slowly growing.

Best-Laid Plans

Growth had to be funded, however, and not out of HBC coffers. By 1857, Douglas devised a modest economic stimulus: a gold rush.[1] Small-scale rushes had been money in the bank for Douglas before. There had been a short-lived stampede to the Queen Charlotte

Islands in 1851 and 1852 after gold was discovered there, and small amounts of gold were occasionally discovered by Natives, who traded them at Hudson's Bay posts. A party of three miners were working at Foster's Bar on the Fraser River in 1857.[2] But when the Nlaka'pamux discovered a rich find of the precious metal above the Fraser Canyon, near the confluence of the Fraser and Thompson rivers, in 1857, Douglas began to see real dollar signs.

Douglas ordered his officer in that area, Donald McLean of Fort Kamloops, to hire Natives and start digging. Once he was satisfied that there was a large enough strike to draw a considerable number of gold seekers, Douglas set about formulating his scheme down to the finest detail. He left, he thought, nothing to chance. A new fort would be established at The Forks, where the two rivers met, and it would be stocked with shovels, picks, flour and all the supplies the expected rush of miners would need. Douglas drew up elaborate plans for provisioning the fort, given the imposing obstacle of the Fraser Canyon.

By February 1858, Douglas's scheme kicked into high gear. With the site for the fort settled and the trade goods on their way, it was now time for a little advertising. He took out ads in papers and journals in Oregon, proclaiming that anyone who happened to be interested in gold mining in HBC territory needed to purchase a licence and beware the First Nations populace. He calculated that this would suffice to prompt a small-scale rush to New Caledonia, but two things conspired to escalate the situation. One was Douglas's own planning. The other was his timing.

Douglas can be forgiven for thinking that his modest scheme would cause no more than a minor stir in a quiet corner of the British Empire. Britain was still putting down the Indian Mutiny and was preparing for the Second Opium War against China. The colony of Canada was in the grip of a severe depression.

Things were just as bad south of the disputed border in the United States, and it was into this maelstrom of economic malaise that Douglas sent another stroke of pure Hudson's Bay hucksterism. In February 1858 he shipped nearly a thousand ounces of gold to San Francisco aboard the Company steamer *Otter*. The *Otter*'s captain took the gold to the city mint and made no secret of where it had been found. The superintendent of the San Francisco mint was duly impressed.

Shortly thereafter, in early March, a group of volunteer firemen were sitting around Engine House Number Eight in San Francisco, resting and shooting the breeze after practice. As fate would have it, one of those firemen was the superintendent of the San Francisco mint. He spoke glowingly about the quality of gold brought in by the Hudson's Bay steamer.

"Boys, the next excitement will be to the Fraser River," he declared.[3]

The superintendent's audience was easily infected with gold fever. San Francisco had gone bust. The city had forcibly ousted its elected government (dominated by Democrats) in a business-backed coup and was run by the Committee of Vigilance. In an early version of Proposition 13, the committee had slashed taxes for business so severely that the city had to close several schools and could not afford to buy hoses for volunteer fire companies, like the men gathered at Engine House Number Eight. Prospects for recovery appeared dismal. But now the superintendent was talking about the stuff that dreams are made of, and desperate men follow their dreams.

Among the young firemen gathered in the hall that warm spring evening was James Moore, then twenty-five years old. Adventure, mining and prospecting were in Moore's blood. Born in Ireland in 1832, he had run away to sea at age seventeen. After plying the coastal routes of the British Isles, Moore took passage to California by way of Cape Horn. He worked as a quartermaster on a steamer until 1853, when the lure of the gold fields drew him to Tuolumne County, California, where he met with mixed success.

Moore was working at a bonded warehouse in San Francisco in 1858 when he found himself listening to the superintendent spin his tale of riches in New Caledonia. That was enough for him. It was also enough for his fellow firemen, many of them former gold miners. The group moved with lightning speed to take advantage of the superintendent's insider tip and formed a company to go prospecting up the Fraser River. The little party consisted of Moore, Edward Hill, W. Ferris, Ted Sweeney, Ned Campbell, Con Mooney, John and Tom Kelly, Harry Garrison, Bill Heffner, Pat Cosgrove, Sandy Glennon, Tom Nolen, Sam Jack and George Perrier (who later figured prominently in McGowan's War).

Hill's Bar

The fifteen men left San Francisco on March 12, 1858, taking a steamer to Port Townsend in the Washington Territory, where they caught another boat to Fort Victoria. They took their own small boat across the Georgia Strait to the Fraser. Moore and his American compatriots were struck by the unspoiled beauty of what was to become the urban and industrial sprawl of the Lower Mainland.

"When we entered the Fraser I shall never forget my first view of this magnificent river — the snow-capped grandeur of the mountains which held it in place — the thickly timbered valley through which it swept was awe-inspiring," Moore wrote in his *Reminiscences*.

Their welcome at the Hudson's Bay post at Fort Hope a few days later was anything but inspiring. Donald Walker, the dour factor, gave the Yankees a chilly reception. Walker's warehouses were full of valuable furs ready for shipment, and he suspected the American party of being a band of brigands: a natural suspicion, since it was rare to have a troop of white men who were not in the employ of the Company roaming the territory. Walker refused to answer their questions about the nature of the canyon above Fort Hope and sent them brusquely on their way. The Americans spent the night camped outside the stockade, puzzled by the hostility. The next morning they pushed on, headed for the Thompson River, ignorant of the terrain ahead. They never made it to their destination.

They spent the morning battling the Fraser's current and making just ten gruelling miles. Ahead of them, below Fort Yale, the Fraser came bursting out of the canyon, a daunting obstacle. The party paddled up the shallows of the east bank, avoiding the full force of the river's main channel, then stopped for lunch on a wide gravel bar. The spot was known to the Sto:Lo as "Hemhemetheqw," which means "Good place to make sockeye salmon oil." The Natives used large boulders on the banks as "pecked pots" to collect oil. Given the right conditions (lots of sockeye running, hot weather and a strong wind to keep the flies off), the oil oozed out of the fish and into the naturally occurring bowls in the boulders.

As the Americans ate their beans among the gravel and rocks, Edward Hill noticed flecks of gold in the moss at his feet. Hill abandoned his lunch plate for his gold pan and discovered he'd been eating lunch on top of a rich deposit of placer gold. The rest of the men got out their pans and realized they'd stumbled on the jackpot. They didn't know it, but the spot they named Hill's Bar would become the richest claim in the Fraser River, the epicentre for what was to come. And it was on this spot that James Douglas's carefully laid plans started to go awry.

Moore and company were not supplied for a long stay, having only mounted a prospecting expedition. While most of the men set to work constructing rocking boxes and excavating the bar, a party set off to purchase supplies from the Hudson's Bay post at Fort Langley. The Americans received much the same welcome as they had at Fort Hope, and the foragers returned with only a small amount of flour and tea. But while there, they told the Hudson's Bay men all about their discovery at Hill's Bar. Word that a band of Americans had struck gold just below the canyon travelled along the Company network. The news soon reached James Douglas in Victoria and also spread up the canyon among the Native people.

Moore and his American mining partners soon had company on the bar: a large contingent of men, women and children from what he called "the Yale tribe." But Moore was mistaken. While some of the Natives may have been Sto:Lo from around Yale, others were Nlaka'pamux from Spuzzum, led by their chief, Kowpelst, known to the whites as Copals and well acquainted with Douglas. Kowpelst and his people were operating in what was technically Sto:Lo territory, and that may account for their willingness to share the bar with Moore's party. Other Yankee gold prospectors had not been so lucky. The previous year, the Nlaka'pamux had expelled several American gold seekers from their territory; an event that Douglas

mentioned in his official correspondence with the colonial office —
with some sympathy towards the Natives.

> *The native Indian tribes of Thompson's River . . . had lately taken*
> *the high-handed, though probably not unwise course, of expelling*
> *all the parties of gold diggers, composed chiefly of persons from the*
> *American territories, who had forced an entrance to their country.*
> *They have also openly expressed a determination to resist all*
> *attempts at working gold in any of the streams flowing into*
> *Thompson's River, both from a desire to monopolize the precious*
> *metal for their own benefit, and from a well-founded impression that*
> *the shoals of salmon which annually ascend those rivers and furnish*
> *the principal food of the inhabitants, will be driven off, and*
> *prevented from making their annual migrations from the sea.*[4]

It should also be noted that these were not "noble savages," ignorant
of the ways of capitalism. The Hudson's Bay Company employed
Natives as loggers, farm hands, stevedores, sailors and mill workers.
And, of course, they were part of the HBC mining operation on the
Thompson River that had brought the Yankees to Hill's Bar in the
first place. Kowpelst and his people knew a good thing when they
saw it, and they wanted their fair share of the gold.

The two groups worked at opposite ends of the bar, which hugged
the shore of the Fraser. It was half a mile long, sixty feet wide and no
more than five feet deep. At first the competing camps were friendly.
The Americans allowed the Nlaka'pamux to use their shovels and
picks, and the cooperative arrangement continued for several weeks.
The Americans were making fifty dollars a day per man, incredible
wages for the time. Kowpelst's people had similar results. There was
plenty for everyone.

In early April, the American and Native miners had yet another
visitor to Hill's Bar. William T. "Billy" Ballou, a former California
express man, had moved to New Caledonia and started up a business grandly titled Ballou's Pioneer Fraser River Express. Ballou was
described in a contemporary account as "a wild waif, a hare-brained
adventurer of French descent, who since 1846 had been floating

around the mountains and shores of the Pacific."[5] Ballou was delighted to find so many customers on the Fraser River who were eager to pay the then-outrageous sum of one dollar each way for letters. The miners sent letters and gold samples to their friends down south. Reports that there was gold on the Fraser River in abundance spread as fast and furiously as the river's current.

So far, Douglas's plan was working well enough. True, Moore and his party had not quite made it to the chosen "Gold District" and had not bought any goods from the designated centre at The Forks. But they had made it partway along the path laid out for them. Douglas knew they would not be the last to abandon everything for the mines. He also knew that others, closer to home, would be tempted by the prospect of easy riches and could leave the HBC without labourers. To forestall this, he sent a trusted agent on a secret mission to San Francisco to drum up more miners and find some much-needed manpower.

Arrival

The end result of the mission came to light on Sunday, April 25. It is a famous scene in British Columbian history, but not always painted in its entirety.[6] The morning church service had just finished, and as Douglas exited the small, wooden building with his family, thanking the Rev. Edward Cridge for his sermon on the evils of drink, a Voltigeur,[7] one of Douglas's few militiamen, pushed his way through the crowd of worshippers. Dressed in buckskin pants and wearing a blue cap and sash, the colourful messenger had urgent news for His Excellency. The side-wheeler *Commodore* had just docked and hundreds of men were pouring off the vessel looking for supplies and transport to the Fraser River.

Douglas led a procession of surprised and apprehensive Sunday worshippers (including Helmcken), dressed in their best, to the slope overlooking the harbour. There on the dock were four hundred men: American, British, German, French, Italian and Canadian. Many wore the miner's uniform of red flannel shirt and boots and carried shovels, picks, and gold pans: the tools of the mining trade. Douglas noted even from a distance that each and every one of them was armed with at least a pistol and a knife.

This moment traditionally marks the beginning of both the Fraser River gold rush and the crisis that transformed British Columbia into a colony of the Crown. Douglas is usually described as being as surprised as his fellow churchgoers at the spectacle, but I imagine he had a sly, quiet smile of satisfaction on his face, for this was all part of his plan. What is more, few accounts mention that another group on the dock stood out entirely from the flannel-clad miners. Douglas, Cridge, Helmcken and the rest of the crowd also saw over fifty black men standing on the dock, heads bowed and voices raised in a loud prayer of thanksgiving.[8]

Again, a combination of circumstance and Douglas's meticulous planning (not to mention his penurious nature) led to this seminal moment. He had foreseen that even a small rush to the gold fields would place a tremendous strain on the colony's limited manpower. (In fact, at the height of the gold rush, deserters from all ranks in the HBC and even the Royal Navy were so numerous that an embarrassed Douglas, on being ordered to build a barracks for the small group of British surveyors that made up the Boundary Commission, marking the border with the U.S., was forced to tell his colonial masters that there was no labour for hire save native Indians, who were "a rather unruly force, requiring very close and constant superintendence.") Douglas mulled his options. He'd thought of bringing in a few "Sandwich Islanders" or Kanakas from the HBC post in Hawaii, but this would cost the Company money. What he needed, ideally, was a pool of labourers who would gladly pay their own way to Vancouver Island and, perhaps, buy some of those town lots he hoped to sell at inflated prices.

The solution was handed to Douglas on a platter by a United States that was tearing itself apart over the question of slavery. On the eve of the Civil War, California was a supposedly free state, but decidedly friendly to slave owners. In March 1858, Bill 339, "An Act to Restrict and Prevent the Immigration to and the Residence in this

State of Negroes and Mulattos," was introduced in the state legislature. It would not only bar further immigration of blacks and mulattos to California, but would also deport those already living there.
Those blacks who did not leave at once of their own volition (and at
their own expense) faced virtual enslavement. Sheriffs charged with
their removal were authorized to "hire" them "for such reasonable
time as shall be necessary to pay the costs of the conviction and
transportation from this State, before sending such Negro or mulatto
therefrom." It also imposed stiff penalties for any white person who
dared harbour or help blacks or bring them into the state with the
intention of freeing them.

The bill died on the order paper when the spring session
adjourned, but no one doubted it would become law when the legislature resumed sitting later that year. It caused an outcry in San Francisco's prosperous and educated black community, which mobilized,
holding a series of meetings to discuss options, starting on April 6,
1858, at the Zion Methodist Episcopal Church on Stockton Street.
Having declared that all free blacks in California were "degraded by
the enactment of such an unjust and unnecessary law against them by
their own countrymen," the assembly moved on to the main agenda.

Those who wished to leave California had received two offers of
refuge: one from Panama, the other from Governor James Douglas
of Her Majesty's Colony of Vancouver Island. Seated on the stage,
with maps and charts of Vancouver's Island on his lap, was Douglas's agent, Jeremiah Nagle, skipper of the *Commodore*.[9] Nagle
answered questions from the audience about the colony's climate,
governance, and so forth. There was only one dissenter, who preferred the idea of Panama, but a majority of people at the meeting
wanted to move to Victoria and to move as a community, and soon it
was full steam ahead for the British possession. Wellington Delaney
Moses was one of a threesome elected to lead an advance party to
seek out Douglas and discuss their prospects.

On April 20, 1858, at four o'clock in the afternoon, the advance
party of about fifty black men led by Moses went down to the pier
where the *Commodore* was docked. It was not a quiet passage. A
huge crowd of men packed the dockside, trying to get aboard the

vessel. Here and there hung maps of the Fraser River and posters proclaiming the riches of the gold fields in the territory of the "Coteau" Indians. Moses and his party pushed their way towards the steamer, jostled by the crowd and the apple and orange vendors, who were doing a swift business. Once aboard they were greeted by Nagle, who was going to make a killing off this sailing. Having encouraged the black vanguard to book passage, he had also helped spread the news of the wealth of the Fraser River diggings. The *Commodore* was full to overflowing with both paying customers and stowaways. The deck was crowded with miners bearing their tools, provisions, guns and whaleboats. At 5:30 p.m., the gangplanks were pulled away and the *Commodore* steamed off for the New El Dorado with the first party of gold diggers in force and the first contingent of hundreds of blacks, both seeking a new promised land.

The passage aboard the *Commodore* was no pleasure cruise for the black advance guard. The large number of stowaways consisted mainly of white bully-boys who intimidated the blacks, hurling insults and kicking over their pans of food. But when it came to stealing articles from the baggage in the hold, the bullies weren't fussy about race. The voyage itself was miserable, beset by storms and foul weather.

Promised full rights of citizenship and freedom from persecution by Douglas, Moses and his party quickly fell under the spell of Victoria, and in a glowing report they urged the community in San Francisco to move en masse to the colony. "To describe the beauty of the country my pen cannot do it. It is one of the most beautifully level towns that I was ever in . . . I consider Victoria to be one of the garden spots of this world . . . the climate is most beautiful; the strawberry vines and peach trees are in full blow," wrote Moses. "All the coloured man wants here is ability and money . . . it is a God-sent land for the coloured people."[10]

Ultimately, about four hundred black families, over a thousand people, made the move north. They formed their own Masonic lodges and other groups, and organized the Victoria Pioneer Rifle Corps (a.k.a. "Douglas's Coloured Regiment," or "The African Rifles") in 1859 after its members were prevented from joining an all-white fire brigade. The blacks in B.C. had their own holidays. Until Lincoln's emancipation replaced it in 1863, they celebrated the emancipation of the slaves of the West Indies on August 1. On that day, black-owned businesses would shut down and a parade would wend its way through the streets of Victoria. Sometimes as many as two hundred people on horseback or in carriages headed for Cadboro Bay for a picnic, returning to the hall of the Victoria Pioneers to end the celebrations.

All that lay in the future. For now the blacks were taken in by the Reverend Cridge, and the white miners set about transforming Victoria in their own way. The single boatload disgorged by the *Commodore* had more than doubled the size of the village overnight. At first, there was almost a carnival atmosphere. The miners erected hundreds of grey cotton tents the length of the harbour front. To Douglas's satisfaction, they bought supplies and clamoured for passage to the gold fields. His plan was working splendidly.

The *Commodore* was soon followed by steamers arriving at Victoria and Esquimalt: the *Seabird*, *Panama*, *Surprise*, *Republic* and *Sierra Nevada*. When the *Cortez* and the *Orizaba* landed 1,900 miners between them on a single day, it became apparent that the modest-sized rush had turned into a flood.

Out of Control

In San Francisco, men left their jobs and their families to strike it rich in the diggings. In the general economic gloom that afflicted North America, New Caledonia was suddenly the bright spot, the beacon of hope for tens of thousands of people dreaming of easy riches. Worse still, from Douglas's point of view, some of them were merchants who had the audacity to bring goods with them and dared to sell them in the HBC's own private preserve.

On May 8, 1858, Douglas wrote to the colonial secretary, Henry Labouchere, to describe the scene.

Boats, canoes and every species of small craft are continually employed in pouring their cargoes into Fraser's River, and it is supposed that not less than one thousand whites are already at work, and on their way to the gold fields now. Many accidents have happened in the dangerous rapids of that river; a great number of canoes having been dashed to pieces, and their cargoes swept away by the impetuous stream, while the ill-fated adventurers who accompanied them, many have been swept to eternity. The others, nothing daunted by this spectacle of ruin, and buoyed up by the hope of amassing wealth, keep pressing onwards towards the coveted goal of their most ardent wishes.

The same day he penned this letter, Douglas, perhaps a little unnerved by now at the size of the rush and certainly annoyed that private merchants were operating in Company territory, issued a proclamation that was published in newspapers in both Oregon and Washington territories. It bluntly stated that New Caledonia wasn't open for settlement and also asserted the trade monopoly the Hudson's Bay Company enjoyed among the Native Indians. The decree threatened stiff penalties for anyone who tried to set up commerce on the Fraser River without a licence from the Company.

To exercise his authority, Douglas ordered the twenty-one-gun steam corvette HMS *Satellite* to anchor off the mouth of the Fraser River to collect the licence fees. Within a few weeks, Douglas had to agree to pay the *Satellite*'s crew a bonus of a dollar a day to keep them from deserting their posts for the far more lucrative prospects on the gold fields.

Douglas enforced his proclamation as vigorously as he could. Shortly after it was issued, the HBC seized $2,000 worth of goods belonging to Samuel McCaw of Steilacoom, an American merchant at Fort Langley, and also took a vessel, the *Black Duck*, from a pair of merchants named Tilton and Gibson. This raised the ire of free-trading Americans and caused a diplomatic stir in Washington, D.C., where the British minister to America, Lord Napier, referred the matter to the home government in London. Unfortunately for Douglas, there had just been a change of government in England. John Henry Temple, third Viscount Palmerston, had been ousted as prime minister in February 1858 after a vote of non-confidence and been suc-

COURTESY BC ARCHIVES, PHOTO# A-00260

A steam corvette of 1,462 tons, the Satellite *was supposed to be assisting the Boundary Commission surveying the 49th parallel. But its twenty-one guns and crew of 206 men (including a complement of Royal Marines) made it an ideal enforcer at the mouth of the Fraser in 1858. Charged with preventing gold seekers from going upriver without a mining licence, the vessel's crew members were given a pay raise to discourage them from deserting for the gold fields. Commanded by Capt. James C. Prevost, the* Satellite *was stationed in Esquimalt between 1857 and 1860.*

ceeded by the Earl of Derby, whose administration was less friendly to the HBC. The diplomatic stir in Washington played into its hands.

Unaware of the international machinations, Douglas and a small party of Royal Navy marines from the *Satellite* arrived in Fort Langley in late May on their way to inspect the gold fields. While there, he received letters from Donald Walker, chief factor at Fort Hope, about the mining operation on Hill's Bar.

"Letters from Walker, Fort Hope, report that Indians are getting plenty of gold and trade with the Americans," he noted in his journal. "Miners working two miles below Fort Yale who are making on average one-and-a-half ounces a day each man. The place is named Hill's Bar and employs eighty Indians and thirty white men."

From Fort Langley, Douglas and his men pressed on, travelling in canoes powered by Native paddlers and accompanied by the gig from the *Satellite*. His progress was slow and the Americans on Hill's Bar had another visitor before His Excellency finally got to Ground Zero of the gold fever explosion in his mainland backyard.

A few days before May 31, Moore and company were mildly surprised to see a heavily laden boat labouring up the river. At first Moore thought an independent merchant selling supplies had finally made his way to the diggings, but when the boat landed, they discovered its cargo consisted entirely of liquor. The boat's owner was Mr. Taylor, an American booze-runner. Even if Taylor's brew was as good as the "English Brandy" sold by the Hudson's Bay Company, it would have been foul. More likely it was composed of those unique ingredients Yankees continued to sell to Canadian First Nations until they were run out of Fort Whoop-Up fifteen years later: a vile concoction of watered-down whiskey laced with everything from tobacco and Tabasco sauce to gunpowder.

Moore sourly notes the Natives were eager customers of the bootlegger. He does not mention whether his own group purchased any of Taylor's wares. The party that followed the arrival of the rotgut whiskey unnerved the Americans. Moore describes in his memoirs how many of the Natives got drunk and ended up "howling all night with their guns and walking up and down the bar." Sleepless in their tents, the miners decided they had to do something about Taylor.

In a bleary, red-eyed dawn, the ever democratically minded Yankees held one of the first of many meetings to be conducted by American miners on the gold fields. After a lively discussion, they first tried buying their way out of the problem, offering to purchase Taylor's entire cargo if he would leave. But Taylor refused to sell wholesale. Moore's party then voted to take the law into its own hands.

"Next morning we held a meeting and concluded to confiscate all of Taylor's liquor, knock the heads of all the kegs out and dump the contents on the bar," wrote Moore. "And the first Prohibition Act in the country came into effect without delay. We gave Taylor no compensation, but offered him a present of a hempen neck-tie if he chose to remain in the camp for more than twenty minutes."[11]

The bar's gravels were then christened with the brew, and empty barrels were strewn on the river bank. Faced with a quick lynching if he remained, Taylor fled the rough justice of his countrymen.

There was more trouble ahead. Moore blames the difficulties that occurred soon after Taylor's ouster on the Natives, but Douglas, who talked to Kowpelst and heard his grievances, concluded "the quarrel arose out of a series of provocations on both sides, and from the jealousy of the savages, who naturally feel annoyed at the large quantities of gold taken from their country by the white miners."

As Moore tells the tale, one Native, known to the Yankee miners as White Cap, "one of the bad Indians of the Yale tribe, had been a heavy purchaser of Taylor's firewater. And after the supply was so suddenly shut off he appeared to become more sullen than before."

Whatever the cause of this sullenness, there was a confrontation between White Cap and one of the American miners. On May 31, 1858, White Cap borrowed a pick from Cornelius "Con" Mooney, as was the habit of the Natives working the bar. When Mooney wanted the tool back an hour later, though, White Cap refused to surrender it. Mooney "lost his patience and broke a shovel handle on Mr. White Cap's head."

It is not known how seriously White Cap was injured. What is clear is the depth of anger that blow stirred among Kowpelst's people.

"This precipitated a row in camp. The Indians congregated in their camp and their muskets came into evidence. The chief made a forum of a stump and harangued his followers but as none of us could understand the language we were totally ignorant of the tenor of his speech," wrote Moore.

The Americans feared the worst. Fleeing was out of the question. If they took to the river, they figured they'd be caught and slaughtered by the Natives pursuing them in their swift canoes. As for the canyon, its steep walls closed about them like a coffin. There was no escape. The American party was forlorn in the wilderness, just fifteen men utterly beyond help against dozens, possibly over a hundred, Native warriors, many of them armed with muskets. The Yankees loaded their weapons and readied for battle with little hope, "prepared for the worst and prepared to sell our lives dearly if necessary," Moore recalled.

Suddenly there was a shout from the river. James Douglas arrived at the moment usually reserved in Westerns for the U.S. cavalry, coming around the bend of the river with the *Satellite*'s gig, accompanied by a half-dozen blue-jacketed sailors and Native paddlers in their canoes.[12] Douglas quickly sized up the situation.

"On the arrival of our party at 'Hill's Bar,'" he wrote, "the white miners there were in a state of great alarm on account of a serious affray which had just occurred with the native Indians, who mustered under arms in a tumultuous manner, and threatened to make a clean sweep of the whole body of miners assembled there."[13]

The Americans welcomed Douglas ashore with a salute of gunfire. Douglas, with his usual aplomb, imperiously demanded to know just what was going on. Paul Furness, one of the Yankee miners who had been elected leader, told Douglas about Taylor's visit and the ensuing fracas. Douglas then spoke with Kowpelst and convinced him to abandon Hill's Bar, sealing the decision with a gift of ship's biscuit and molasses. A little patronage didn't hurt either: faced with trouble, Douglas hired Kowpelst as a magistrate for his people. "[I] took the leader in the affray, an Indian highly connected in their way, and of great influence, resolution, and energy of character into the government service, and found him exceedingly useful in settling other Indian difficulties."[14]

As it turned out, Douglas's arrival was not the dramatic salvation the miners thought it was at the time. Unbeknownst to the Yankees, Kowpelst was not working his warriors up to a fever-pitch in preparation for battle. Moore admits in his reminiscences that later he was told the chief was urging moderation, not murder. "We learned afterwards however that he was a pacifist and had urged his people into the paths of peace."

Moore makes no mention at all of the stern lecture Douglas then gave the Yankee miners about trespassing on British soil.

"I lectured them [the miners] very soundly about their conduct on that occasion," wrote Douglas. "... I also spoke with great plainness of speech to the white miners, who were nearly all foreigners, representing almost every nation in Europe. I refused to grant them any rights of occupation to the soil, and told them distinctly that Her Majesty's government ignored their very existence in that part of the country, which was not open for the purposes of settlement, and [they] were permitted to remain there merely on sufferance; that no abuses would be tolerated; and that the laws would protect the rights of the Indian, no less than those of the white man."

Ever gregarious, the American miners gave Douglas a tour of their diggings. That very morning, the rocker that Edward Hill and two others had been working had produced six ounces of gold, a return of fifty dollars per man: very high wages indeed. The miners Douglas had already encountered, working bars farther down the river, were not making nearly as much.

"Other miners whom I questioned about their earnings, stated that they were making from $2.50 a day, the lowest, to $25.00, the highest usual returns to the man a day," Douglas wrote in his journal before reaching Hill's Bar.

The governor left the diggings a worried man. Much of his threat to the Americans was pure balderdash. He had no authority on the mainland at all except as chief factor of the HBC. But knowing he had to assert British sovereignty or face a repeat of the Oregon Territory disaster, Douglas stretched what little authority he had.

As the days passed, it became clear to Douglas that he'd created a monster he could not control. By July 1, more than ten thousand people were either headed for the Fraser River or already on the gold fields. Douglas had chosen his moment too well. The U.S. was wallowing in the economic doldrums following the collapse of twin booms in railway and western land speculation. California, where easily accessible gold was running out, was hit especially hard. The conditions were ripe for a mass exodus. In San Francisco, men quit their jobs and merchants liquidated their stock before crowding aboard steamers headed north.

In Puget Sound, saw mills lay abandoned by their workers. Even U.S. soldiers dispatched to protect the border surveyors deserted.

Instant towns sprang up at Fort Yale, Hill's Bar and other places throughout the Fraser River valley and canyon. Soon the canyon was crawling with a United Nations of fortune hunters from all over North America, Europe and the Pacific Rim. The newcomers were not, however, all miners. Only about a quarter of them would work the gold fields. The rest — merchants, businessmen, gamblers, prostitutes and various hangers-on who could supply goods and/or services of every description — were intent on getting as much gold from the miners as they could. The influx was mainly from California, but not everyone from that state was a U.S. citizen. Many were British or French subjects who had been drawn there by the great California gold rush a decade earlier. Douglas estimated the proportion of actual American citizens from the California contingent at less than one third. Still, they were numerous enough to present Douglas with enormous logistical problems and considerable political peril.

Douglas returned to Victoria to find his bucolic settlement utterly changed. The quiet village of five weeks earlier had been engulfed by new buildings, shanties and lean-tos. Tents of all shapes, sizes and colours were pitched along the water. The town was filthy and stank of raw sewage from open latrines. Mingled with the stench was the aroma of cigars and the odour of horses, cattle and other animals who added their waste to muddy streets. Water was so scarce that while rum was practically free, saloons charged twenty-five cents for a glass of aqua pura. The streets were rivers of mud when it rained, capable of swallowing wagons whole. On the hillsides above the town, fortune seekers lit great campfires and gathered around them to sing, reminisce and speculate on the richness of the Fraser mines. Coffee stands were everywhere, and Natives walked the streets selling buckets of clams, slabs of salmon and slices of venison. The harbour was alive with newcomers sawing lumber and hammering nails as they scrambled to build boats to get across the Strait of Georgia to the mouth of the Fraser River. These crafts often resembled coffins and all too often served their occupants as such. Rising above the ever-present beat of the hammer and scrape of the handsaw was the rattle of dice, the cry of the saloon keeper advertising his wares, the cacophony of ill-tuned fiddles and banjos and a chorus of bawdy ballads and other songs sung in a dozen different languages.

Gold coin, most of it minted in the U.S.A., became the currency of the colony. Wellington Delaney Moses and his advance guard of blacks had been joined by other entrepreneurs from their community, who had fulfilled Douglas's hopes and purchased land. In some cases they made a killing as prices rose and speculation ran rampant. Town lots (120 by 60 feet) started out selling for just over $10 an acre in 1858 and rose to $3,000 a lot within weeks of the *Commodore*'s arrival in April. Some 225 buildings had been thrown up in just six weeks. The first large non-HBC merchant house in Victoria was owned and operated by black merchants Peter Lester and Mifflin Gibbs, formerly of San Francisco. Hotels had also sprung up, as well as less-respectable businesses, like the brothels on Cormorant Street. These presented a moral and economic dilemma to Victoria. Prostitution was such an offence to the English settlers that the ineffective assembly was forced to do something about them. But, pragmatic as always, the elected members knew if they closed the Cormorant Street brothels, the miners would be tempted to find amusement — and spend their money — elsewhere. So they compromised and licensed the establishments as "dance halls."

Just Common Sense . . .

Douglas sought the security of the fort, and in the rare moments when he wasn't dealing with some new crisis, he pondered the situation he was now in. His two most serious problems were political and economic and both of them involved the United States.

Politically, Douglas's greatest fear was that the American government would use the massive immigration of Yankees as a pretext for seizing New Caledonia. Both Mexico and Britain had already been forced to give up vast chunks of territory after a flood of U.S. immigrants swarmed over the mountains and onto the Pacific Coast. With Britain and the U.S. embroiled in the boundary dispute over the 49th parallel, there were four hundred American troops sitting on what the Yankees proposed as their side of the line. Indeed, some of the Americans on the gold fields were U.S. army deserters. Two such culprits were pursued by none other than Captain George Pickett, who a year later was involved in the San Juan Islands' "Pig War"[15] and four years after that led the most famous charge of the Battle of Gettysburg, bent on breaking up the very country he had enlarged.

Another aspect of the political situation that concerned Douglas was the American attitude towards the aboriginal population. The Americans were at that time involved in yet another Indian War in the Washington Territory, and many of their countrymen on the gold fields were graduates of that famous school of inter-racial harmony whose core philosophy was summed up by the slogan "The Only Good Indian is a Dead Indian." There was bound to be a confrontation between the two forces, and something had to be done before the worst-case scenario — an attempted annexation from without coupled with an American-Indian War within — erupted.

Douglas also had pressing economic reasons to reassess his strategy. Already, hundreds of gold seekers were pressing up beyond the Fraser Canyon, looking for the mother lode that was presumed to be the source of the gold being panned from the gravel bars and flats of the lower river. The natural access to the Upper Fraser was not through the Fraser Canyon and its death-defying rapids and sheer cliffs, but via the old Hudson's Bay brigade trail through the Okanagan Valley and then along the Thompson River to the upper reaches of the Fraser. If this became the preferred route, all supplies and commerce would originate in the United States, diverting valuable revenues from Douglas's stretched coffers.

Douglas was nothing if not a realist. He saw quite clearly that this was no passing phenomenon. Things would never quiet down and return to normal. The world had finally discovered the HBC's private empire and wanted a piece of it. The Company would not be happy about this turn of events. Then again, Douglas was aware that there was a new government in London, one that was decidedly unfriendly to the HBC. How could he keep his two masters happy at the same time? And how, more importantly, could he prevent a repeat of the Oregon Territory fiasco? Douglas somehow needed to maintain the

HBC's rights and privileges on the mainland while at the same time enforcing British law and sovereignty over the territory. If he waited for instructions from London, he would almost certainly fail. He'd got himself and the Company into this mess. Now James Douglas would find a way to get out of it.

The solution he came up with was as cunning as it was practical and showed how canny a politician the old HBC war-horse was. On June 10, 1858, Douglas crafted a carefully worded despatch to Lord Stanley, the colonial secretary, technically requesting directions, but in fact informing the government what he was about to do.

To keep Victoria and the HBC as the main source of supplies for the miners, Douglas proposed making the Fraser River route to the gold fields more attractive and less dangerous than any overland trail from U.S. territory. He would sign a one-year contract with the Pacific Mail Steam Ship Company to transport goods upriver to the diggings. American steamboats, which had hitherto only been allowed to drop off passengers in Victoria, would now have permission to steam upstream as far as their boilers could take them. Instead of flotillas of tiny craft and canoes, paddle wheelers like the *Umatilla* and the *Enterprise* would make the perilous crossing of the Georgia Strait and push their way up against the Fraser's current, operating under a strictly controlled contract written by Douglas that ensured the HBC's role as the dominant commercial enterprise on the mainland. The steamers could ship only those goods supplied by the HBC and carry only those passengers who had purchased mining licences. The HBC received two dollars for every miner thus transported. Imposing import duties on goods delivered to Victoria, and forcing merchants there to take out trading licences, further supplemented Douglas's colonial income. To make his preferred route to the gold fields even more attractive, he had miners, driven from their gold seeking when the Fraser flooded, clear an alternate route to the Upper Fraser via a series of portage trails linking Lake Harrison to Lillooet.

As for the number of U.S. citizens in the territory, Douglas knew they could be controlled if they remained fractious and he gave them no single grievance around which to unite. Since he could not prevent the torrent of newcomers from settling the mainland, he would throw the territory open to settlement — but under the rule of British law. Towns would be surveyed, lots sold and the HBC would be compensated. In short, a whole new Crown colony, this one on the vast B.C. mainland, would have to be created overnight. For this plan to work, Douglas had to convince London to send him sufficient military force, officials and the entire apparatus of government. That would take time. Until the despatches could make their three-month round-trip to the colonial office and back, Douglas would do what he had always done best during his career: act on his own and make do with the resources he had at hand.

Despite the deluge of people washing over the territory, however, Douglas was faced with a paucity of human resources to form a bureaucracy. He had cast a recruiting eye on the inhabitants of the gold fields during his tour and found precious few qualified British subjects to fill key positions. While visiting Fort Yale, however, he met Richard Hicks, "a respectable Englishman engaged in mining pursuits there." Shortly after writing Stanley in June, Douglas appointed Hicks assistant commissioner for Crown lands and also district revenue commissioner. It was an appointment that Douglas would come to regret.

Born in Shropshire, Hicks had been a "49er," forsaking Old England for the California gold fields. Like many would-be argonauts, Hicks eventually gave up mining and was running the Howard House Hotel in San Francisco when news of the Fraser River rush reached him. He was one of the first adventurers to leave San Francisco, arriving in April aboard the *Commodore*. He and a party of five made it to the Fraser via Bellingham Bay and began mining in the vicinity of Fort Yale. After being appointed by Douglas, Hicks sent to San Francisco for his wife, Orinda. He was in Victoria in late June to pick her up when he gave a brief interview to a correspondent for the *Daily Alta California*, telling the reporter, "I never saw a stream as rich as the Fraser River." What Hicks failed to mention was that he was determined to get his share of those riches in any way he could, legally or otherwise.

Douglas made another ill-fated appointment on June 26, 1858, when he gave the post of justice of the peace for Hill's Bar to George Perrier, who he met during his tour of the diggings there. While Perrier wasn't the brightest man on the Fraser, he did have one redeeming quality: he was a British subject. Perrier was working away at his claim when the governor came calling and, according to Moore, asked the former sailor about his legal background.

"I remember when the Governor asked Perrier if he understood law, Perrier said he had read Blackstone. 'Tut-tut,' said the Governor, 'it is not Blackstone you want here but just common sense,'" wrote Moore.

Douglas had established a means to dispense law on the gold fields. He knew, however, that he needed police and troops to enforce it. His own resources were totally inadequate. The militia of Voltigeurs at his disposal numbered just thirty-five men: one officer, eight NCOs and twenty-six privates. The Royal Navy did have a substantial force based at Callao, Peru, and Douglas cut across official channels to take the distinctly improper step of directly contacting Rear-Admiral Robert Baynes, commander-in-chief of the Pacific Squadron.

"To prevent those people into the British territory is, perhaps, altogether impossible with any force that could be collected in a reasonable time; but what may be easily accomplished is — to maintain the authority of the government, to preserve the peace, to punish offenses, and to enforce obedience to the laws, until Her Majesty's Government are in a position to take more decided steps for administering the government of the country," Douglas said in his letter to Baynes on May 12. "I therefore take the liberty of making application to you for a sufficient force to aid and assist in maintaining the Queen's authority, until further instructions are received from England."

Baynes sent back a terse reply acknowledging receipt of Douglas's letter and baldly refusing to supply immediate help. He would send to London for orders.

Left to work with what he had, Douglas took extraordinary steps to recruit police officers both in the boomtowns of the mainland and in Victoria. In Fort Yale, the parsimonious Douglas opened up the purse strings and paid the extraordinary wage of $100 a month to those willing to serve and protect. Even more extraordinary, Douglas bent the rules and hired Yankee constables. The chief of police in Yale was an American named Dounellar, who took home $150 a month.

In Victoria, Douglas went even further, appointing several black constables. The black police force, though short-lived, had marvellous uniforms: blue coats, red sashes and high hats. Most members were Jamaicans and all were British subjects of some description. The very idea of black constables, let alone the colourful fact, must have been incredible to the Yankee miners, especially those from slave-holding states. The Americans refused to respect their authority. In one instance, a white thief caught red-handed in a tent by a black constable admitted his guilt, but refused to be arrested by a black man. His compatriots backed him up and it was impossible for the constable to bring the culprit in. Similar incidents followed and the blacks were retired from the force.[16]

In four short weeks Douglas had done everything he could to balance the interests of empire and Company while dealing with the massive influx of foreigners into British territory. He had done it on his own authority and without permission from London. But July brought the annual flooding of the Fraser River and a new problem. The high water covered the gold-laden gravel bars. Tens of thousands of would-be miners were forced to wait for it to subside. Supplies, money and patience grew short. Douglas and the HBC were blamed. Inevitably, this encouraged some of the Americans to wonder out loud if things might not be better if the United States were running the show instead of Douglas. In the Washington Territory, American hawks were already casting a predatory eye on the mainland. This charming little Manifest Destiny ditty was published in a Washington newspaper in 1858:

> *Soon our banner will be streaming*
> *Soon the eagle will be screaming*
> *And the lion — see it cowers*
> *Hurrah, boys, the river's ours!*

In the shanty-saloons of Victoria, meetings were held. Men with time on their hands and whiskey in their bellies spoke openly of fulfilling the American dream of "54 – 40 or Fight!" It was a tense time in Victoria. July 4, 1858, was an especially wild day. Douglas was on the alert, anxious about the prospects of a riot or worse. He was somewhat alarmed when an American vessel came steaming into the harbour that evening with guns blazing. The *Pacific* fired a hundred rounds from its two battered cannons to celebrate the Glorious Fourth of July. But the captain was blameless. The culprit, who had put the first mate up to the cannon volley, would soon carve himself a piece of B.C. history. Ned McGowan had arrived on the scene.

THREE

The Iniquitous Ubiquitous

There is no doubt that Judge Edward "Ned" McGowan has been given a bum rap in history, but it only continues the bad press he suffered from during his life. He was vilified by his enemies, and his enemies wrote most of the history books. He was supposed to be a murderer, a pimp who ran a brothel in a San Francisco hospital, the inventor of the false-bottomed ballot box, a shoulder-striking bullyboy, corrupt politician and magistrate, a disgraced police superintendent who masterminded a bank robbery, and an all-around cad. This is the McGowan we have had handed down to us by biased writers like Hubert Howe Bancroft and others. And it is the McGowan who has been superimposed on our own small piece of his extraordinary story — his exploits on the Fraser River gold fields.[1]

Separating truth from the libel has become difficult over the years, but McGowan was a difficult man. He was described by a friend as "you rusty old broken-down hack-horse, spavined, wind-galled politician — you infernal old schemer — you dreadful and to be dreaded shoulder-striker — you melter of wax candles — you stuffer of ballot boxes — you who reside at a French boarding house of equivocal character — you luxurious dog who lives on the fat of the land."[2] While his friend was making light of the lies being spread about Ned McGowan at the time, both the writer and the reader knew there was a fair amount of truth in the description.

Poet, politician, bon vivant, Ned McGowan's fearful temper — and his sense of mischief — got him into trouble at critical times during his career. If he'd had a longer fuse, he might have been a U.S. senator or, like his friend James Buchanan, even president. But after a knife fight on the floor of the Pennsylvania legislature, McGowan was ready for the rough-and-tumble politics of California. He survived his persecution at the hands of the Vigilance Committee of 1856, but Ned's sense of fun — firing a hundred-gun salute at a nervous Victoria upon his arrival on July 4, 1858 — did not endear him to James Douglas.

Early Years

In fact, Edward McGowan was an educated, articulate and witty man, a writer, poet and politician who might have been a statesman had it not been for a ferocious temper and plain bad luck. He was born in the Southwark district of Philadelphia on March 12, 1813, to an Irish-Catholic family. He was a man of his times — that is, a gentleman in that curious Anglo-American manner where duty and honour counted for everything, but duels were conducted with a Bowie knife as well as a pistol. He'd had his Grand Tour of Europe in his youth, and as he reached adulthood, became fond of fashionable clothes and fine wine.

McGowan apprenticed as a printer, but his ambition was to become a national politician. It was not such a long walk from Philadelphia to Washington, especially as a Democrat. McGowan also had very powerful political friends who saw great promise in the young man. Among them was fellow Philadelphian James Buchanan, president of the United States from 1856 to 1860.

McGowan's first steps were careful and prudent. Of medium height and weight, fair-skinned, dark-haired, with blue-grey eyes and a flowing mustache, McGowan was an appealing candidate on the hustings. He could be a fiery and absorbing public speaker. In 1838 when just twenty-five, he ran for the modest post of clerk of Moyamensing, Philadelphia County, on the Democratic ticket and won handily. He served faithfully and efficiently and was rewarded in 1842 with a seat in the lower House of the Pennsylvania state legislature. He was a Democrat in an assembly dominated by the Whigs, precursors to the Republicans. Armed with a letter of introduction to the party power brokers from Buchanan himself, McGowan arrived at the state capital of Harrisburg in January 1843, anxious to shine as a rookie assemblyman. Ned did make an impression, but hardly in the manner he'd wished.

McGowan, by dint of his early training, was placed on the Assembly's committee on printing. All would have been well had Pennsylvania not decided that year to create a state printer. It would be a lucrative contract for the businessman who got it, and competition was fierce and partisan. One of the bidders was John B. Bratton, editor of the *State Capital Gazette* and a Whig supporter. As it became apparent he was losing support within the printing committee, Bratton decided to use his newspaper to smear his opponents. On April 7, 1843, Bratton wrote an article suggesting McGowan and another Democrat on the committee had been bribed to support a competing printer's bid. Not content to sit back and let nature take its course, Bratton went to see McGowan's reaction up close. What followed was a scene that makes the goings-on in Victoria's legislative assembly look tame.[3]

Shortly after 10 a.m. on April 8, Bratton was allowed on the floor of the assembly (in clear violation of House rules) by the Whig leadership. He stood watching McGowan and the other Democrats from the fireplace to the left of the Speaker's chair. McGowan had just read Bratton's work, which had been thoughtfully placed on his desk. He was walking back and forth among the Democrat benches muttering, "The scoundrel! The scoundrel!" Then he spotted Bratton. McGowan headed straight for the editor. Words were exchanged. McGowan spat in Bratton's eye and kicked him. Bratton drew out a jackknife and struck McGowan with the butt. Staggered, McGowan grabbed a chair and smacked Bratton in the forehead. Bratton reversed his knife and pointed the blade at McGowan. Enraged, Ned drew out his own knife (standard debating equipment in the antebellum republic) and took a swipe at his opponent. Bratton fled. The House, now in an uproar, finally stirred itself to action. In the confusion, both McGowan's and Bratton's knives mysteriously disappeared.

The investigating committee was stacked with Whigs, and McGowan could see the writing on the wall. Rather than be expelled from the assembly, he resigned on April 12. He had hit a major speed bump on the road to Washington. The Democratic Party, knowing McGowan had been done over by its opponents, took care of Ned as best it could. In 1845 he secured the position of superintendent of police for Moyamensing. It should have been a quiet sinecure from which McGowan could emerge after a few years, once the infamy of the knife fight on the floor of the assembly had died down. But his ill star followed him.

In 1848 McGowan was implicated by a known felon as a participant in a robbery. Dr. William Darlington, president of the Bank of Chester County, was conveying over $50,000 cash to the bank by train. He had had a few Christmas drinks en route, and he *swore* he took his eye off the money for only a moment to speak to a small child. In the summer of 1848, one of the thieves, Robert Harper Lackey, was languishing in the Moyamensing jail, having been caught red-handed with some of the stolen cash. He arranged a plea-bargain with the district attorney by naming his two accomplices and the "Mr. Big" behind the robbery. Although they'd never met, Lackey had heard all about the fiery-tempered Ned McGowan.

Politics again played a role in the "trial." The presiding judge, William Kelly, was either a Whig or a personal enemy of McGowan, and did everything in his power to convict him. He ignored direct testimony from Lackey's guards, who stated that the prisoner had said he'd never met McGowan, yet accepted as evidence an anonymous letter implicating Ned. On October 5, 1848, McGowan was found guilty along with two others, while Lackey walked free. The verdict was so outrageous that it was quickly appealed to the Quarter Sessions Court, which unanimously found there was no case at all against McGowan. Ned was released after spending six weeks in his own jail.

In the spring of 1849, McGowan, who had won re-election as police superintendent, heard of the discovery of gold in California. He resisted the urge to pull up stakes until a fateful evening in September when he went for his daily drink at Harry Connelly's wine store in Philadelphia. Many Democratic stalwarts were present. So was a young man named Captain John Nagles, who was showing to all present a vial of gold dust from California. It had a profound effect on McGowan. He was at a crossroads. His political career, his ambition for high office in Washington, was as good as dead. He knew to what uses his enemies would put the fight with Bratton and his wrongful conviction (indeed, nearly forty years later, Bancroft would twist both tales to make McGowan out to be the villain). The lure of California was for him not just the promise of easy riches in the gold fields. It was also a fresh start in a new land.

Off to California

Within days, McGowan had decided to shake the dust of Philadelphia's streets off his boots and booked a passage to California via the Isthmus of Panama. He arrived in the City by the Bay on October 31, 1849. At the time, San Francisco resembled Victoria at the height of its gold rush, but on a much larger scale. A vast sprawl of tents and shanties choked by rotting rubbish and debris was serviced by roads that "were vile in dry weather and only for muskrats when it rained."[4] McGowan made a living at first by running a roulette wheel on the second floor of a whorehouse, which was considered a respectable profession at the time in a city that was overwhelmingly male.

Soon Ned gave up his career as a croupier and hung out his lawyer's shingle. He also plunged headlong into California's politics helping the founding Democratic Committee nominate a slate of four candidates for the inaugural state elections held that fall. In January 1850, McGowan met David Colbreth Broderick, a Democratic Party leader and soon to be a senator. Broderick, an Irish immigrant and Tammany Hall alumnus from New York, was the Democratic boss in California: few received office without his patronage. He led one wing of the bitterly divided party, which suffered from an urban-rural, slave-free labour split. Broderick was the chief of the city dwellers and drew much of his support from "The Boys" — Irish-Catholic immigrants, McGowan's countrymen. Broderick's rival, Senator William Gwin (formerly of Mississippi) ran the competing faction of mainly Southerners, known as the "Rosewater" wing or the "Chivalry."

The Democrats could, at times, unite and later that year acted in unison to help secure McGowan an appointment as a judge of the

Court of Quarter Session for San Francisco County. Now Judge McGowan, Ned could reasonably assume that he had made a fresh start on the road to Washington, D.C. But his own cursed luck and the nature of California politics once again put an end to his ambitions.

At the time, California's political culture was built on a Wild West base with European pretensions. The state's first legislature was known as "The Legislature of a Thousand Drinks." In San Francisco, politicians mixed the sense of honour of an Old World gentleman, who would duel to uphold his good name, with that of a cowboy gunslinger, whose murder defence was "He drew on me first, Sheriff."[5]

A popular method of duelling was "the affray," which dispensed with the rigmarole of a formal challenge, a date and place agreed to, and seconds. Instead, an aggrieved party, usually armed with a six-shooter, challenged his opponent on the street, shouting the required warning, "Defend yourself!" A few seconds were given the other party to compose himself; then the pair drew and fired. This cross between a formal duel and a good old-fashioned showdown was in vogue among San Francisco's elite and was the preferred means of settling affairs of honour.

"Honour" had to be satisfied, not just among feuding Democrats, but with members of opposing political parties. The Whigs, McGowan's old enemies in Philadelphia, were losing influence across the United States, but were still a power to be reckoned with in California. More vexing was the threat posed to the Democrats by politicians of the American Party, nicknamed the "Know-Nothings" for their peculiar habit of swearing members to absolute secrecy about their policies. Members asked to answer any questions about the party platform were told to say "I know nothing about it." Like a modern militia or a Masonic lodge, leaders swore party faithful into secret lodges called "Wigwams." Full members were called "Braves" — odd for a party whose members hated Native Indians almost as much as they hated the Pope. Popular among the merchant class of San Francisco, the Know-Nothings were anti-immigrant at a time when immigrants tended to be German or Irish Catholics. They were also anti-Chinese, partly because of garden-variety racism, but also because the Asian community was a powerful commercial force that competed with them. They used secret hand-signals and battle cries fit for a Masonic lodge or a Shriner's convention.

The American Party, like the merchant class of San Francisco, also wrapped itself in the cloak of respectable Protestantism. Many adherents were about as sincere as a modern-day televangelist, publicly attending church while secretly keeping mistresses, cheating their customers and creditors, and indulging in other vices. McGowan savaged them in a poem he penned entitled "The Age of Gas," which read in part:

> See how they doze, in well-dressed rows — broad
> cloth and velvet collar —
> In dreams they nod and mutter "God," but mean
> the Almighty dollar.[6]

In this macabre landscape, between 1850 and 1856, Ned's law practice thrived and his political career was a modest success. He presided over cases in a building whose ground floor featured a dance hall and casino. The defendants were often better armed than the sheriffs or the judges, but then, they had to be because, invariably, the jury and the courthouse spectators were also armed to the teeth.

The Committee of Vigilance

Vigilantism had long been a feature of the American political landscape. In Pennsylvania and South Carolina in the 1700s, ad hoc groups formed to maintain law and order in the absence of more formal authorities. In San Francisco, however, far from being a group of average citizens enforcing the law in a power vacuum, the Vigilantes were pillars of the business community, politically motivated men who laid careful plans to usurp the recognized authorities when they failed to get their way at the ballot box. San Francisco's Committee of Vigilance first made its shadowy appearance during 1851 in the courthouses of San Francisco.

The origins of the committee can be traced directly to warehouses full of unwanted goods that mysteriously caught fire in that year. With prices falling and a glut of supplies on the market, many of the city's richest businessmen were faced with ruin until all-too-convenient fires transformed useless goods into tidy insurance claims. Unfortunately, the hired arsonists did such a good job that huge areas of San Francisco were levelled and there was a general cry for vengeance from the populace.

Rather than face the wrath of the citizenry, the merchants took up their cry for retribution. They did so using slogans and tactics that have a familiar ring in this "get tough on crime" era of ours. Using their influence over most of the press (they owned it, after all), members of the business community convinced a large segment of the population that the fires had been set by thieves and criminals (without bothering to explain what possible gain a thief might realize by burning down a warehouse full of goods — this hole in their logic was not widely discussed among the Vigilante set). In fact, they took their argument a step further by saying the city was in the midst of a crime wave and those in authority were doing nothing about it. The courts were soft on criminals, there was a huge backlog of cases and murderers were roaming the streets with impunity.[7]

Once started, the momentum of the Vigilante movement was nearly unstoppable. Accused murderers (who later turned out to be innocent) were nearly lynched by a "People's Court." McGowan saw the results first hand. On one occasion he and his fellow judges — not to mention the governor — had to show their weapons to a mob that had packed a courthouse to demand the death sentence for a man who had slapped an opponent at a party.

The Vigilance Committee really took off when the merchants adopted the tactics that would later make the American Party so popular.[8] They understood the power of running the committee like a secret society, making a show of holding public meetings before the elite corps of decision-makers went behind closed doors for secret deliberations. The resulting decisions did not bear the names of the executive, only numbers they had assigned themselves. An order from the secretary, for instance, was not signed "Isaac Bluxome," but rather "Number 67." After this, there were no more People's Courts. Those who fell into the committee's hands were given a quick trial without the benefit of legal counsel, let alone the presumption of innocence.

These changes were the work of William Tell Coleman, a grocer who was originally from Kentucky and not a founder of the Vigilance Committee at all. Coleman said he only got involved with the committee shortly after its inception because of a chance encounter one evening after work. As he passed the office where the "Purest and Best," as they referred to themselves, were hopelessly divided, desperately trying to map out a strategy, Coleman "heard wrangling which told him that the club members didn't know how to go about doing what they wanted to do." It was Coleman who thought up the People's Court, the numbers-for-names and other effective committee tactics.

In June 1851 the committee finally hanged a criminal. John Jenkins was not a murderer, arsonist or even bank robber. He had been caught walking out of an unattended office in broad daylight with a small hand safe containing an almost negligible amount of cash. For this offence, to prove they were tough on crime, the committee hanged Jenkins in the plaza by Battery Street on June 11. "Hanged" is too gentle a word: the man was strung up, not dropped, and had the life painfully choked out of him. McGowan witnessed the extrajudicial execution. A large crowd had gathered to watch as Jenkins had the rope cinched around his neck and was hauled aloft by eager hands.

"After the man had been strangled to death and while the crowd was still holding on to the rope," wrote McGowan, "one of them, a Dutchman, turned to one of his fellows and said: 'Vell, vot did he do?' "[9]

Two other men accused of arson were similarly murdered in great haste and with absolutely no public explanation of their motives in setting the fires. This led many to wonder just how many nameless members of the Vigilance Committee had a personal interest in the poor men's deaths. The total number of victims was four, including Jenkins. The committee had, for political reasons, tried to take on McGowan as well and force him from the bench. It even passed a motion to have him investigated for his mythical role in the Chester County bank robbery. McGowan had his acquittal papers ready and the committee backed down. In late 1851, faced with a paucity of murderers or petty thieves to hang and, coincidentally, greatly improved business prosperity, the committee declared victory and disbanded.

McGowan and the rest of the Democrats who ran the city heaved a giant sigh of relief and got back to business: fighting among themselves and finding jobs for "the Boys." With a Broderick man in the governor's mansion, McGowan found himself appointed treasurer of the State Marine Hospital and state commissioner of immigration. He also rose to the position of chairman of the San Francisco Democratic Party. But the high point of his political career was as co-chairman of a Democratic Party convention that is the stuff of legend.

The "Two-Headed" convention of July 1854 (also known as the "Short and Long Hair Convention") was held to baptize Sacramento as the California state capital. It pitted the Boys against the Chivalry at a time when the two factions were growing especially bitter with each other and was, in a small way, a prelude to the Civil War. The party met at a Baptist church, a beautiful edifice with soaring stained-glass windows. The delegates were armed to the teeth with pistols, Bowie knives, derringers and other weapons. No one from Broderick's wing wanted to be chairman of such a tense and potentially bloody affair, so the nomination fell to the loyal McGowan. But the Chivalry nominated their own candidate, former governor John McDougall.

In the middle of the tense debate over which wing would control the convention chair, one of the Chivalry supporters had an accident. The pistol in his pocket went off, wounding him. As the report echoed in the church, the reaction was instantaneous. Assuming the debate had turned into a shootin' war, the delegates of both factions fled rather than return fire. Those who were too far from the doors dove through the stained-glass windows. In seconds, the church was a mess of shattered glass and nerves.

In the end, McGowan and McDougall co-chaired the proceedings. It was a long, thirsty day on the stage. Both men were too afraid to take a drink for fear their glasses had been spiked — until McGowan mixed two cocktails that had been passed up to the stage and gave one to McDougall. They drank and suffered no ill effects. The factions were unable to settle their differences and thereafter met in separate halls, even nominating two Democratic slates. Despite this, they did well in the congressional elections that fall.

But 1854 was the year of the Know-Nothings in San Francisco as they swept the city elections.

The American Party's life in California was brief, but spectacular. It flourished in the interregnum between the collapse of the Whigs in 1854 and the rise of the Republicans in 1860. The Know-Nothings on the West Coast were, sadly, behind the times in the rest of the United States. While the secret lodges were folding up all over the eastern seaboard, the American Party of California even elected a state governor, James Neely Johnson, in 1855. With the Democrats out of the governor's mansion, McGowan lost his patronage appointments, even though there was a petition to keep him on as immigration commissioner, signed by some of the very Vigilantes who had tried to force him off the bench in 1851 by reviving the Chester County bank robbery controversy. It appears while McGowan was hated by some in the business community as a damned Catholic Democrat organizer, he was at least respected for the honest, nonpartisan manner in which he handled immigration cases.

As 1856 rolled around, McGowan was not even an officer of the Democratic Party. He seemed content to add to his fortune, eat the best food and drink the best wine. He enjoyed the theatre and wrote articles for the city's newspapers under the pen name "Caliban." But the dark influence of McGowan's ill star was already working against him. That, and another drop in business.

The Purest and Best

The Vigilantes were getting restless. The business community was reeling from a series of bank failures, and creditors from the east would no longer accept the excuse of arson for nonpayment of bills. Their American Party had suffered some serious setbacks at the hands of the Democrats in the San Francisco city elections of 1856, and their hold on power was slipping. What they needed was a state of emergency. The organizing committee of the Vigilantes knew how to create one. And through a string of casual coincidences, McGowan was about to become their poster boy.

The complex series of events that eventually ruined McGowan's life would not be out of place in a Thomas Hardy novel. It involved the private lives and petty feuds of San Francisco society, the intricate conspiracy being planned and carried out by the Vigilantes and a large measure of bad luck.

The first character in the unfolding tragedy was James P. Casey, a San Francisco political organizer originally from New York. On his arrival in California, he looked up Broderick, but was rebuffed by the ill-tempered leader of the Boys. Casey went to work for the Know-Nothings and was instrumental in the American Party sweep of 1854. Some Democrats felt betrayed, and in September 1855 they ambushed him on the street in an "affray." Outnumbered five to one, Casey used his assailants' own weapons to drive his attackers off. In the process, he wounded John W. Bagley, a friend of McGowan, in the chest. Bagley wanted vengeance, and when his wound healed two months later he challenged Casey to a duel and asked Ned to be his second.

In the interim, Broderick had had a change of heart about Casey's abilities. Determined to recruit the talented organizer, he prevailed upon McGowan to talk Bagley out of his challenge. McGowan's silver-tongued blarney worked its magic, and the affair of honour was cancelled. Broderick, who was running for a seat in the Senate in 1856, welcomed Casey with open arms.

McGowan thought nothing of it at the time, but this piece of work was to change his life. Casey's departure stung the Know-Nothings, whose organization was close to collapse. Now a hated Democrat, Casey was fair game for the Vigilante press, whose chief standard-bearer was James King of William,[10] editor of the newly founded, merchant-backed *Bulletin*. Those who complain of media bias in newspapers ought to take particular note of King of William's tactics in fanning the flames of Vigilantism in early 1856 by sensationalizing the death of U.S. deputy marshal General William H. Richardson. Reputed to be a mean drunk, Richardson had gone hunting for the head of a gambler named Charles Cora on November 17, 1855. Earlier, Richardson's wife and Cora's common-law spouse, Belle Cora (the best-known, most charming madam in San Francisco), had been engaged in a public spat in a theatre. The drunker Richardson got, the more homicidal he became over the incident. He reeled along the city's sidewalks, stopping people he knew and demanding if they'd seen "Carter."

The drunken marshal found his man outside a gambling hall. Cora tried to talk sense to the intoxicated Richardson, but the marshal pulled out a pair of derringers and backed the gambler up against a wall. Seeing no other option, Cora shot Richardson in self-defence. He was immediately arrested, held without bail and waited for a court date.

Nothing was wrong with the legal system in this case, except that it was run by Democrats. King of William whipped the public into a frenzy by suggesting Cora would either be allowed to escape or let off scot-free. "Hang the Sheriff!" the *Bulletin* thundered. When in January 1856 a jury couldn't agree on whether Cora was guilty of murder or self-defence and was dismissed, the *Bulletin* portrayed it as proof the justice system had failed. "Will Cora be hung by the officers of the law? No!" screamed the newspaper, forgetting that the decision had, in fact, been in the hands of the jury of twelve honest and supposedly law-abiding citizens.

It was this kind of fair and even-handed journalistic treatment that was soon to be meted out to the unfortunate Casey, who was himself the publisher of the *Sunday Times*. It must be said, however, that Casey's own publication fired the first shot in the war that eventually led to his death. On May 11, a "card" (a sort of flyer expressing a private opinion) was inserted in the *Sunday Times* by its editor, John Cremony. This card attacked King of William's brother, Tom King, who worked for the competing *Bulletin*. It informed San Franciscans that Tom King had once been a bouncer in a Washington, D.C., brothel where his wife had worked. The card was signed, unfortunately for McGowan, "Caliban."

Tom King apparently had no self-deprecating sense of humour and immediately went to Casey to demand who the author of the card was. Casey refused to say, and Tom King was soon describing what he would do to the publisher and political operative when they next met. Casey believed he would be called out within days, so he visited a man he knew to have vast experience in affairs of honour: Judge Ned McGowan. Ned advised Casey to let things blow over, but knowing Tom King might not give the young man a chance, loaned him a knife and a pistol for the pending affray. The pistol was a very distinctive piece, a Texas five-shooter.

Had Tom King tracked down Casey, and had they fought their duel, things might have turned out differently. But the younger King let his brother James the editor do his dirty work for him. In the afternoon edition of the *Bulletin* on May 14, 1856, King of William ran a story that claimed Casey had served eighteen months in New York's Sing Sing Prison for stealing furniture for his prostitute mistress. The story was a complete fabrication, but King of William printed it as the gospel truth and said he had affidavits to back it up. Furious, Casey marched into the *Bulletin*'s office and demanded a retraction. King of William refused, words were exchanged, and as Casey left, he warned the editor he'd have to defend himself when next they met in the street.

When they did meet later that day, Casey followed the exacting rules of the affray. King had just left his office. Casey was about ninety feet away when he shouted a warning to King to defend himself. The two men advanced towards each other on the Montgomery Street sidewalk. Although armed with a five-barrelled pistol, King made no move to defend himself, merely staring belligerently as he walked towards Casey. Finally, at a range of about forty-five feet,

Casey drew and fired a single shot from the gun that McGowan had loaned him. It struck King just below the collarbone. Instead of returning fire, King (who talked in print very bravely about the guns he carried) dove into an express office.

As far as Casey was concerned, that ended the matter. By not defending himself and then running, King of William had proved himself "a dung hill." As the editor was not seriously wounded — no major blood vessel or artery had been severed and the wound was not life-threatening — most San Franciscans saw the whole thing as rather comic. McGowan himself did not hang around to watch the affray. Instead, he repaired to a nearby saloon, where he had a drink with John Nugent, editor of the *Herald*. Casey was immediately arrested and taken to jail, where he shared a cell with the unfortunate Cora. McGowan managed to joke about the affray at dinner with a friend that evening. But Cora, after hearing from Casey what had just transpired, shook his head and said: "You have put the noose around the neck of us both."

Cora was right. This was the moment the Committee of Vigilance had been waiting for. The secret society swung into action within hours, raising the cry of chaos, of murder in the streets, despite the fact that King of William was still alive. "Hang him!" was again the cry. This was no spontaneous expression of the people's will. The scale and scope of the Vigilantes' planning can be seen by the size of their operation. The forty-one-member executive committee, headed by the Vigilante hero of 1851, William Tell Coleman, had set up four departments — finance, police, military and medical — that superceded the city and state governments. Within two days they had an army of 2,500 men, many of them French and German soldiers who were camped around San Francisco awaiting the launch of various filibustering expeditions.[11] Many of these, especially the French, were from convict battalions and had been thieves or worse before being impressed into the army. At its peak, the Vigilante army numbered over 6,000, with several regiments of infantry, one of artillery and two cavalry battalions, many armed with weapons belonging to the state's National Guard, which had been turned over by National

Guardsmen sympathetic to the Vigilantes.[12] Another 2,000 members served as "police," clerks, thugs, jailers and fund collectors.

On May 16, the sheriff of the jail holding Casey became so alarmed at the committee's preparations that he called for a posse to defend the lock-up. Some of the leading citizens of the day turned out to defend due process, including William Tecumseh Sherman and McGowan himself. (They formed the nucleus of what was to become the Law and Order Party, an ad hoc group of mostly — but not exclusively — Democrats opposed to the Vigilance Committee.) That evening, however, their efforts were thwarted by the Know-Nothing governor of California, James Neely Johnson. With the threat of their 2,500-member army hanging over him, Johnson was forced to allow a detachment of Vigilantes into the jail to ensure Casey remained in custody. When McGowan saw the Vigilantes admitted to the jail, he threw down his arms in disgust and walked out along with several others.

The next day McGowan finally heard the rumours swirling around Vigilante circles regarding his role in King of William's shooting — that he'd written the card slagging Tom King and then given Casey the weapon he used to shoot James King. He also watched from a safe distance as a regiment of Vigilante militia marched to the jail (complete with a cannon, which they placed at the door) and dragged Casey away to the committee's headquarters on Sacramento Street. An hour later they were back for Cora, although they totally ignored a bona fide murderer, Rod Backus, who was languishing in the cells, for he was neither a Democrat nor a Catholic. Returning home, McGowan was greeted by several messages — some signed, some not — warning him he was next on the list of the committee's intended victims.

McGowan changed his residence and had his meals brought to him, refusing to go out in public. He considered the "evidence" against him. The card, signed with his own pen name "Caliban," tied him indirectly to Casey, as did the five-shooter. True, he'd given Casey the gun on the assumption he would be fighting Tom King and not his brother, James of William, but that hardly mattered. Given

the city's mood, the committee didn't need more evidence to condemn him to a gruesome death. The image of poor John Jenkins
being slowly strangled to death by the Vigilantes in 1851 must have
come back to him frequently.

When James King of William died on May 20 because of medical
bungling of his rather slight injury, Casey's fate was sealed and
McGowan went into hiding. Casey was tried and convicted of murder even before King of William breathed his last. Cora was, ironically, the subject of a hung jury, even in the Vigilante kangaroo
court. But having dispensed with the need for a unanimous verdict
for a conviction, the committee hanged him along with Casey from
the windows of their headquarters, a warehouse on Sacramento
Street known as "Fort Gunnybags" because of the wall of sandbags
protecting the building.[13]

On the Run

The next day, May 21, 1856, the Vigilance Committee issued a warrant for McGowan's arrest. McGowan holed up in a number of hiding places and was nearly caught several times. On the evening of
June 3 he disguised himself as a Mexican by blackening his hair,
mustache and face. He used a corset to push in his stomach and
donned an overcoat and slouch hat. Armed with a pair of derringers,
a six-shooter and a knife, he walked through the streets of San Francisco, unnoticed by sword-swinging cavalry patrols searching for
him and by people who he knew well.

McGowan met a friend with a waiting carriage on the Mission
Dolores Road and was smuggled to a house on the outskirts of the
city. The next morning he was alarmed to see a force of Vigilante
cavalry sweeping down on the neighbourhood until he discovered
the field next to the house was their training ground. For the next
four weeks he amused himself by watching the Vigilantes' horseman-
ship and writing poetry. Ned hoped that someone — the federal government, the state government, the army, anyone — would bring the
Vigilance Committee to heel. But as June slipped away it became

clear that no one wanted to tangle with "the purest and best citizens" of San Francisco.

With the help of Broderick and two other friends, McGowan was again smuggled away in his Mexican disguise and set out for Mexico on horseback, planning to take ship back to Philadelphia from there. The trip through the Coast Range would have been a challenging journey for an overweight, forty-three-year-old city slicker like McGowan at the best of times, but the pursuit of the relentless committee made it sheer hell. On July 6, having suffered from fever and an eye injury on the trail, McGowan and his companions rode into Santa Barbara, five hundred miles from San Francisco. They thought they were safe. They were wrong. The Vigilance Committee had spies even here, and a posse was raised to arrest Ned.

All seemed lost until McGowan was rescued by an unlikely saviour. Jack Power, a Robin Hood figure of early California, was a former soldier who had arrived in California with Colonel Jonathan Drake Stevenson's "Pioneer Regiment" from New York in 1847. Born in Ireland and well-educated, in 1853 Power ran afoul of the rather loose land registration system in Los Angeles County. He defied attempts to take his ranch away from him by stealing the county's only two cannons and parking them in front of his hacienda, though in the end the militia forced him to surrender. He moved to Santa Barbara County, where he became the legendary "Destroying Angel," a shadowy figure linked in lurid newspaper stories to a well-organized band of banditos, but never arrested. Now Power galloped up to Ned just as the mob was closing in. He led McGowan to a nearby house, rolled him up in a carpet, then raced back outside to lead the hunt for Ned astray.

Nearly suffocating with heat, tormented by the fleas infesting the fabric, McGowan listened as Power led over a hundred men on a wild goose chase. When one of McGowan's other friends in town swore he'd seen Ned flee into a nearby stretch of swampy grassland, the posse set fire to it. Power waited until darkness, then spirited McGowan to an adobe hut on the edge of town. He spent several days on the run on his own before Power returned to arrange a safe house for him at a ranch, Arroyo Honde, thirty-five miles from Santa Barbara. McGowan hid in the hills around the ranch for two weeks.

The Vigilance Committee stepped up its search, sending a force by steamer to Santa Barbara and posting a $500 reward for Ned's capture. Searchers came within a few yards of McGowan's hiding place in the hills and he was forced to flee again on July 28. The next day he made it to the hacienda of Dr. Nicholas Den, a wealthy rancher, originally from Ireland, who had no time for the Vigilance Committee. He hid McGowan in a field of tall corn, where a cot was set up for him. Temporarily safe, he found time on August 8 to write a letter to his friend, John Nugent, editor of the San Francisco *Herald*, thumbing his nose at his pursuers.

Nugent's was the only newspaper in San Francisco that dared to openly defy a Vigilance Committee that had already murdered five men and ruined the lives of dozens of others. While the hunt for McGowan was afoot, Nugent poured scorn on the committee's efforts and relished debunking every false report of Ned's arrest and capture published by his competitors, especially the *Bulletin*. They said that McGowan had been caught aboard a steamer in San Francisco Bay, was holed up at the State Marine Hospital or had been spotted near Carson Valley. He was reported captured, fled, or sighted "from Philadelphia to the Antipodes" so often that he earned the nickname "the Ubiquitous Ned," a cognomen that McGowan proudly adopted.

"Where is Ned McGowan?" Nugent taunted in an editorial on July 31, 1856.

McGowan was safe for the time being at Den's hacienda, but his fellow Irish Democrats, the Boys, were not so safe — not even Broderick. While Ned was fleeing for his life, the Know-Nothings running the Vigilance Committee, with one all-seeing eye firmly on the fall elections, set about destroying Broderick's San Francisco Democratic Party machinery. In the guise of ridding the city of thieves and criminals, the Vigilantes took dead aim at the party that had "stolen" so many elections from them. Over a dozen Democratic Party organizers and workers were arrested for disturbing the peace and being "destroyers of the purity of our elections, and active members and leaders of the organized gang who have invaded the sanctity of our ballot boxes."[14]

Unfortunates like McGowan's friend Martin Gallagher were forcibly deported, placed aboard steamers and shipped to Hawaii. They were forbidden to set foot back in California, let alone the city of San Francisco, on pain of death, and their families were left behind to fend for themselves. Others were shipped to New York, and at least one, Francis Murray "Yankee" Sullivan, the former U.S. heavyweight boxing champion, never made it out of Fort Gunnybags alive. He was stabbed to death in his cell by his guard, a former member of a French convict battalion, before he could be deported. Scores of other Broderick Democrats fled the city before the Vigilantes could arrest them. Popular support for Broderick bled away to the Vigilantes' "People's Party," the Know-Nothings by another name. As his machine hemorhaged, Broderick saw that San Francisco was a lost cause. Although he was personally untouchable, Broderick too left the city to try to rally support for the Democrats in the rest of California.

The Vigilantes eventually had problems of their own. Their army had become increasingly hard to control and expensive to maintain. And McGowan, who had been useful as a rallying cry in maintaining the ever-present threat to San Francisco, was nowhere to be found. The Committee of Vigilance did the only sensible thing it could: declared victory, held a party and on August 18, 1856, officially disbanded. But the People's Party/Know-Nothings, led by a handful of powerful businessmen, was still firmly in control of San Francisco. And the Vigilance Committee brain trust had designs on California as a whole, with fall elections fast approaching.

This presented McGowan with yet another problem. He couldn't return to San Francisco, but he had also given up on the idea of fleeing to Philadelphia. He felt certain that a fair trial would clear him of the trumped-up charges of accessory to murder, but for a fair trial he needed a change of venue. That could only be arranged by the state legislature, and it remained to be seen who would end up in control of that august body. Ned decided to wait at Den's hacienda until November and see which way the ballots fell.

November 1856 proved to be a sweet month for McGowan. Nationally, his old friend James Buchanan became president of the United States. David Broderick's campaigning outside San Francisco resulted in a landslide for the Democrats in every part of the state outside the City by the Bay. The People's Party was routed. Broderick realized his ambition to represent California in the Senate, and he and the Democrats were now in control of the legislature. They moved at once to help McGowan clear his name.

In early 1857 the Democrats moved a motion of privilege against the Vigilance Committee. Introduced by the esteemed General James Estell, it was a scathing attack on the purest and best, laying bare their real motives for usurping power and their acts of lawlessness. McGowan was shown to be the innocent victim of mob hysteria. The Sacramento papers ate it up. In late January, judging the political and public mood to be right, Broderick arranged for a special act to be rammed through the state legislature granting McGowan a change of venue for his trial. Then he sent word to Ned at Den's ranch outside Santa Barbara.

A Fair Trial

McGowan refused to take the easy road to Sacramento. The hard life on the run had whipped him into physical shape. He'd lost weight and gained muscle. The effect of the change in fortune, both personal and physical, filled him with new strength. He set out for the state capital in the dead of winter on horseback with two attendants, choosing to come out of the wilderness on his own terms.

Arriving in Sacramento in early March, McGowan put up at the Magnolia Hotel. He was on hand when the bill granting him a fair trial was introduced in the state legislature on March 3, 1857. It was swiftly passed by the Democrat majority and signed by Governor Johnson, who had no love of the Vigilance Committee. The State District Court chose Napa County, northeast of San Francisco, as the neutral site. In the minds of the state's judiciary, Napa was far enough away from San Francisco to guarantee an impartial jury, and neither McGowan nor the Vigilantes had any sort of organization in place there to influence the outcome. McGowan was duly conveyed to Napa City and housed in the local jail to await his trial.

The proceedings were a feast for California's newspapers. The top legal guns of the day assembled, not for the defence, but the prosecution, desperate to convict McGowan and justify the actions of the Vigilance Committee. To assist the district attorney, the committee executive hired Henry Stuart Foote, a respected lawyer, orator and politician who would one day become governor. McGowan's lead counsel was James Cofforth, a local lawyer who became a good friend in a tight corner. Both sides gave fulsome interviews to newspaper reporters, not only stating their own case, but also trying to sway prospective jurors. The Vigilance supporters used newspapers like the *Bulletin* to dredge up earlier incidents from McGowan's years in Philadelphia, including the knife fight with Bratton and, of course, the Chester County robbery. McGowan's side shot back in friendly papers like the Napa *Reporter* with testimonials of Ned's good character from President James Buchanan and Vice-President George Dallas. McGowan himself wrote a card that was inserted in the *Reporter* to "prove to you that I am not the fiend and outlaw that the Vigilante press of San Francisco have for the past twelve months endeavored to prove me."[15]

Things did not go well for the prosecution from the start. The trial had to be postponed for a week because one of the witnesses was discovered to be a member of a chain gang and needed a court order to be released to testify. When proceedings started on May 29, 1857, the prosecution witnesses contradicted each other. Worse, a doctor who had been at King of William's bedside testified that there was no actual murder to prosecute, even if McGowan had anything to do with the affray. Dr. Beverly Cole told the jury that King died as a result of attending physicians inserting sponges into his wound. The sponges prevented the wound from healing and caused the infection from which King ultimately died. Most providential of all, the gun McGowan had loaned Casey — the supposed "murder weapon" — was never produced in court. The Texas five-shooter had been spirited away by a helpful San Francisco jailer before the Vigilante mob descended on Casey a year earlier.

Throughout the trial, an anxious McGowan whispered advice and legal points to Cofforth, who at one point lost his patience.

"Judge, I am your counsel in this case!" he snapped.

"Oh yes, Colonel, I know that; but if this jury convicts me, I am to be hanged," replied McGowan.[16]

On June 1, 1857, the jury retired to consider the evidence. It took the members just ten minutes to emerge and declare McGowan not guilty. The Napa *Reporter* remarked, "The prosecution scarcely made out a case against the defendant. Indeed, there was not enough evidence against him to hang a cat."

McGowan was free, but at a terrible price. He'd lost his law practice, his property and fortune. The city he loved was still in the hands of the Vigilance Committee brass, now elected to public office. The newspapers, led by the *Bulletin*, still vilified him and called his acquittal "a farce." His second chance at a happy life had been blasted.

The Phoenix

Many men would have been content to fly the state and try their luck elsewhere, but McGowan wanted vengeance. He tried to get it by exposing the Vigilantes for the hypocrites and criminals they were. In July 1857 he published the story of his persecution and flight in a book entitled *The Narrative of Edward McGowan, Including a Full Account of the Author's Adventures and Perils While Persecuted by the San Francisco Vigilance Committee of 1856*. But it was as a newspaperman that McGowan became a scourge to the "Stranglers" who had ruined his and dozens of other lives.

The *Phoenix* commenced publication in Sacramento on August 30, 1857. It was a single-issue paper, dedicated solely to exposing the Vigilance membership's vices. In poetry and prose, McGowan chronicled the failings of San Francisco's purest and best. Its flagship series was "McGowan's Lives of the Stranglers," which gave readers intimate details of Tom King's former vocation as whorehouse bouncer, Vigilance Committee executive Charles Gillespie's flight from China after embezzling funds, and the fall from grace of top committee member Gabriel Post, who went from being a wealthy merchant to a bankrupt prison guard in less than a year. The committee's membership included thieves, rapists, murderers, wife-beaters, armed robbers and even body-snatchers, and this fact, along with the petty infighting among the upper echelon of the business and political leaders of San Francisco, meant that Ned was never short of material.

The *Phoenix* so enraged committee members that on at least one occasion they had police arrest the paperboys hawking the sheets and impound the offending issue. No one was safe from McGowan's acid pen, from the chief Vigilante, William T. Coleman, down to the lowliest foot soldiers.

The Vigilance faction tried to shut McGowan up, launching a series of unsuccessful libel suits against his paper. Despite these difficulties, McGowan used the *Phoenix* and his own connections not just to pillory his opponents, but also to work tirelessly on behalf of those who had been exiled by the Vigilantes. A combination of diplomacy and public pressure born of McGowan's exposés resulted in an amnesty being granted in October 1857 to those who had been deported or run out of town. Pointedly excluded from the amnesty was McGowan himself.

After twenty-five issues, McGowan folded the *Phoenix* to avoid further legal trouble — a trick used by other satirical publications to this day. But out of its ashes rose another McGowan news sheet: the *Ubiquitous*. It lasted for eighteen editions before McGowan closed it down on June 20, 1858.

Although he had managed to help some of his friends, McGowan was dismayed that the Democratic governor who succeeded Johnson in 1858, John Weller, would take no action against the former Vigilantes. He also lost his close friend and political patron when Broderick, scenting the wind in Washington, switched sides from the doomed Democrats to the rising Republicans. In June 1858, Judge Ned McGowan decided to try his hand at prospecting for a second time.

A Narrow Escape

McGowan's trip to the gold fields of the Fraser was almost as eventful as his year on the run from the Vigilance Committee. He turned down an offer to travel by horseback up through the Oregon Territory and into "the British Possessions" because, as he told the friend who made the offer, his flight over the mountains in 1856 had given him "a dread of horseback riding." Instead, McGowan made arrangements to take ship to Victoria via San Francisco. He was reasonably sure that, if the arrangements were handled with care, he could sneak into the city and board the ship before the business cabal that still wanted his blood was the wiser.

Shortly before he left Sacramento, he received a tip from an informant that a group of San Francisco policemen had formed a pact to murder him if he dared set foot in the city again. McGowan had not spared some of the members of San Francisco's finest from the lash of the *Ubiquitous* and the *Phoenix*. He would have to tread warily.

McGowan planned to stay at the house of an old friend, General Joseph Palmer. Ned's lawyer, James Cofforth, would accompany him on the steamer down the Sacramento River. On June 25, 1858, Cofforth sent a telegram to Palmer: "Your friend will be down tonight." McGowan was smuggled into a private cabin aboard the steamer before any of the other passengers boarded. It made for a dull and dreary trip, but McGowan thought he was tolerably safe.

He wasn't. Two things tipped McGowan's hand. One was Cofforth's telegram to Palmer giving the date of McGowan's arrival in San Francisco. It was sent via a company owned by John Middleton, who was a member of the Vigilance Committee. McGowan's missive was intercepted and never reached Palmer. The second gaffe had been made earlier by Palmer himself. The well-meaning general decided to smooth McGowan's way through the city, and without Ned's consent or knowledge he had met with two Vigilance Committee executives: Thomas Smiley and Richard Jessup. Palmer received assurances from them that McGowan would be given safe passage when he arrived. Satisfied, the general then went to call on a friend in San Jose, even as Middleton was informing his confederates that the fugitive who had long eluded them was walking right into their trap.

McGowan knew something was wrong when the steamer tied up in San Francisco Harbour and Palmer was not there to greet him. He and Cofforth were just about to leave the ship when two San Francisco policemen arrived, armed with a warrant for McGowan's arrest. One was Officer Jim Boyce, the brother of a policeman who had received a thorough going-over in McGowan's news sheets. The other was Jake Chappell, who had personally been pilloried by McGowan for robbing a prisoner in the county jail and causing a disturbance in a brothel. ("He there destroyed furniture and abused the inmates thinking that, as they were women, he need apprehend no fear of chastisement," Ned had written. "In this he counted without his cost, for the girls went in and gave him a severe thrashing.") McGowan was arrested on charges of libel, placed in a closed carriage with Cofforth and driven with speed to city hall.

Hauled up before a hostile judge, McGowan had to promise to appear the next morning. Bail was set at the then-outrageous price of $1,000. McGowan was fortunate to have two friends on hand to post the bond. Everyone in the court, including Officer Boyce, knew that McGowan, once out of the building, had no intention of appearing for trial, so when Ned stepped out of the courtroom and into a darkened corridor, Boyce and Chappell were waiting on either side of the hall. Boyce held a derringer in one hand and a blackjack in the other. He calmly walked up to McGowan, said he had a score to settle with him and took deliberate aim. No one raised a finger to stop Boyce as he pulled the trigger. Although the policeman was just three feet away, somehow the bullet missed its mark, travelling through McGowan's clothes and burying itself in the doorway behind him. Boyce, convinced he'd shot McGowan fatally, hightailed it down the rear stairs of the building.[17]

Amazed he was still alive, McGowan turned back into the courtroom and threw himself on the rather passive mercy of the judge, who had witnessed the whole affair. He received a less-than-enthusiastic police escort (which didn't include Boyce) out of the building. A crowd largely made up of Vigilantes began to gather around Ned as he, Cofforth, several friends and his hostile escort made their way to Palmer's house. Discovering the general was in San Jose, McGowan and his friends lured the ever-growing crowd to the International Hotel. McGowan then made a run for it and managed to escape in the darkness. Making his way to the harbour, he found refuge aboard the revenue cutter USS *Polk*, which had once been skippered by his brother, Captain John McGowan.

McGowan was the guest of the U.S. Navy for several days until arrangements were made for him to meet a steamer bound for Victoria at Horseshoe Bend, an isolated point near the Golden Gate Bridge. The *Pacific* was commanded by Captain John Haley, an old associate of McGowan, who had once won the Democratic Party nomination for San Francisco harbour master with Ned's help. The steamer itself was owned by another friend, George Wright, who paid for McGowan's passage. It was dinnertime when McGowan boarded. Haley ushered him into the crowded cabin and to a seat beside his own. McGowan received champagne treatment on the *Pacific*, which was crowded with gold seekers of all stripes and nationalities, including many Vigilance Committee members and supporters.

Also on the voyage were a number of filibusters from William Walker's attempt to take over Nicaragua, including a friend of McGowan's, Major Tom Dolan. A "real" major, as Colonel Richard Moody would point out a few months later, Dolan was a veteran of the Mexican-American War as well as the 1856 expedition to civil-war-torn Nicaragua (where Walker had had himself declared president).

Bearding the British Lion

It was to Dolan that McGowan turned the day after the *Pacific* dropped anchor in Victoria Harbour on the evening of July 3, 1858. It was a hot, sunny morning, and one of the Royal Navy's vessels was in sight when McGowan decided to celebrate the Fourth of July in style. With Captain Haley on shore, Ned convinced the *Pacific*'s mate to fire a hundred gun salute to the United States and pressed Dolan and his fellow mercenaries into service as gun crews. All hands were piped on deck as the *Pacific*'s two battered cannons opened fire.

"As volley after volley pealed out, down on the beach came hundreds of Indians and others, subjects of Great Britain, as well as our own inquisitive 'Yankees,' not knowing what was up," wrote McGowan in his reminiscences. "No one for a moment but imagined we were bombarding the town or bearding the lion in his den."[18]

Having made his point, McGowan and the rest of the *Pacific*'s passengers went ashore. Ned found lodgings with his friends Pat and Peter Owen, two American businessmen cashing in on the rush by staying in Victoria. He frequented the Fashion Hotel, a well-known gambling house and dance hall on Yates Street run by yet another California friend, John Keenan. But even here, McGowan's troubles followed him. Just after arriving in the city, he ran into Vigilance Committee executive member Miers Truett outside the Fashion Hotel. Truett recognized McGowan and tried to shoot him there in the street. He might have succeeded had he not been quite so drunk. Truett had to be restrained by fellow San Franciscan, Theodore Shillaber. The incident was at once relayed to the Vigilance-controlled press of San Francisco, which of course made McGowan out to be the aggressor. But McGowan didn't have to go all the way to San Francisco to get bad press.

In mid June 1858, James Towne, Henry Williston and Columbus Bartlett arrived in Victoria with a complete printing office. The trio had been deeply involved in the Vigilante press of San Francisco. Towne founded the San Francisco *Christian Recorder* in 1854 and the *Weekly Intelligencer* in May 1856. Williston had been editor and co-publisher of the *Weekly Sunday News*. Bartlett was a partner in the *Daily News* between 1853 and 1856 and was part-owner of the *Daily True Californian* in 1856. In Victoria, the trio started the bi-weekly papers the *Gazette* and the *Anglo-American* (within a month, the *Gazette* went daily). McGowan's bad press had preceded him, and now that he was in Victoria it would only get worse.

Nor had the manner of McGowan's arrival been appreciated by Douglas, who was near the height of his paranoia that the Yankees would try to snatch his mainland possessions from the Crown. Furious, Old Square Toes issued a proclamation that, in future, no such salvos could be fired without his permission. He also summoned an unrepentant McGowan to his house for a little chat. McGowan was greeted by one of Douglas's daughters (likely Agnes, who McGowan described as "a very pretty half-breed girl, who was quite accomplished"). It was not a happy meeting. Douglas kept his talk brief and to the point. He expected the notorious Ned to behave himself and observe Her Majesty's laws. Douglas's formal and imperious bearing rubbed the Democratic McGowan the wrong way.

"He patronizingly called me 'my man,' and had a chair brought for me to sit down," wrote McGowan. "It did not take me very long to find out that his Excellency looked on the Americans as an inferior race to his own countrymen."[19]

For his part, Douglas categorized the newcomer as a troublemaker. But right now, he had more important things to worry about than Ned McGowan.

FOUR

The Canyon War

July and August 1858 were two of the most trying months of Douglas's life. The Fraser's waters remained high and Victoria was full of grumbling miners who felt they'd been "humbugged" by exaggerated claims of the river's riches. Those who were American held public meetings where every man could speak his mind. Most speakers denounced Douglas and the Hudson's Bay Company as the source of all their troubles.

One evening while one of these spleen-venting sessions was in full swing at the Fashion Hotel, McGowan was recognized and called upon to give a speech. With Douglas's warning still fresh in his mind, McGowan respectfully declined. Others were not so diplomatic, and on July 31 the tension erupted in a full-fledged riot. Douglas called on the contingent of troops that had been sent to protect the Boundary Commission to come ashore from HMS *Plumper* to help put the disturbance down. Although order was restored, Victoria seethed with frustration and resentment.

Bloodshed on the Fraser

The miners weren't the only ones feeling frustrated and angry. The shovel-breaking incident between Con Mooney and White Cap at Hill's Bar set a precedent for white-Native relations all along the Fraser. The wave of miners was flooding a Fraser Canyon that was divided between the Sto:Lo in the south and the Nlaka'pamux to the north, with the boundary between the two around Spuzzum, upriver from Fort Yale. Nlaka'pamux territory reached up the canyon almost as far as Lillooet, and along the Thompson River to Ashcroft. To the east, their territory bordered on that of the Okanagan. They had long-standing relations with their neighbours, including the Similkameen, the Skagit and the Nooksack in northwest Washington state. Economic and marriage ties eased these boundaries and wove a rich tapestry of interconnectedness prior to the gold rush.

The Nlaka'pamux were also known as the Thompson or Couteau ("Knife") Indians and had a reputation for cutting the heads off those they killed. The whites they encountered viewed them as much fiercer than the Sto:Lo. Their chief, CexpentlEm (known to non-aboriginals as David Spintlum), was no great friend to the whites. Shortly after Fort Yale had been established in 1848, CexpentlEm — who objected to this station on the border of his territory — had briefly taken the post's chief, Ovid Allard, hostage.

At first the Sto:Lo and the Nlaka'pamux of the canyon entered into a wary economic relationship with the newcomers. The Natives supplied guides, canoes, food and women in return for trade goods and, occasionally, men.[1] But as the non-Native miners began to vastly outnumber the aboriginal people of the canyon, tensions rose and disputes became more frequent. The miners put pressure on the Nlaka'pamux and Sto:Lo to provide camping space, firewood and fodder for their animals. The Nlaka'pamux and the Sto:Lo watched as the miners literally destroyed their land. Huge swaths of gravel bars disappeared as the miners washed them away in their search for particles of fine gold. Salmon-bearing streams were dammed and diverted. Potato terraces and houses vanished as the land beneath them was shovelled into sluices and rocker boxes. Fishing camps were obliterated. As the rush continued and the ranks of the white miners swelled, Native miners, like Kowpelst's people on Hill's Bar, were pushed off the gold fields.

The Sto:Lo and Nlaka'pamux retaliated by charging what the whites considered outrageous sums for transporting them in their canoes. Some miners who objected to the fees had all their possessions taken. Relations were not helped by hungry and ill-provisioned miners who stole the Natives' salmon and other food (the Sto:Lo name for Europeans is Xwelitem, meaning "hungry people").[2]

There were also numerous sexual assaults on Native women, and it appears the rape of a Nlaka'pamux girl by two French miners just above Fort Yale in July ignited a general assault on all whites. The girl's family hunted the rapists down, killed them, cut their heads off and threw the decapitated bodies into the river as a warning. The corpses found their way to an eddy known as Deadman's Bend, just opposite Fort Yale. The two dead Frenchmen soon had company and the Canyon War was on.

Douglas had foreseen the hostilities that followed and had warned the colonial office of the likelihood of armed clashes between miners and First Nations months before. His appeal for troops had been ignored. He was left with the two weapons he'd used successfully to this point — bluff and diplomacy — but even the capable Douglas was aware of just how delicate the balance was on the gold fields. In June he had written to Lord Stanley about the situation, stating: "It will require, I fear, the nicest tact to avoid a disastrous Indian war."[3]

Douglas had only to look south of that theoretical border to find an example of "a disastrous Indian war" being waged. The Yakima Indian War had erupted in 1854 in the eastern Washington and Oregon Territories. The Yakima Indians had forged an alliance of First Nations to stop white settlers from taking their lands. Because the concept of a border between the United States and British Territory was meaningless to the aboriginal people of the Northwest, the alliance included some First Nations, like the Okanagan, whose territory sat on the other side of the invisible 49th parallel.

The hostilities south of the line had placed Douglas in a sensitive position. He didn't want to be seen helping the U.S. authorities, fearing that would incite the First Nations in British territory. But it certainly wasn't in the interests of the tiny colony of Vancouver Island (with its white population vastly outnumbered by Natives on the Island, let alone the mainland) to see white settlers driven out of Washington. In the end, Douglas opted to remain officially neutral, but quietly sent arms, ammunition and money to Governor Isaac Stevens of Washington Territory to help him fight the Yakima.[4]

Despite help from Douglas, the war was going badly for the U.S. Army. On May 17, 1858, the army had suffered a humiliating defeat at the Battle of To-hots-nim-me, near modern-day Rosalia, south of Spokane. A force of about six hundred Yakima and allied mounted troops had attacked a cavalry column led by Colonel Edward Jenner Steptoe. The 150-strong American force was soon trapped on a hill-top with its ammunition running dangerously low. The Yakima leader, Kamiakin, was not interested in giving quarter. Steptoe held out until nightfall, then fled with his surviving troopers back to Fort Walla Walla, having lost twenty-five men.[5]

In the midst of these hostilities, parties of American miners still tried to make their way to the gold fields via the old HBC brigade trail along the Columbia River and up into the Okanagan. Groups as large as three hundred men passed through the war zone by force of arms, and there were casualties on both sides as the Yakima and the Okanagan tried to stop the miners' progress. The struggle of one such group was recorded by Herman Reinhart, a gold seeker from California.

The Okanagan Lake Massacre

Reinhart's party crossed into British territory at the southern tip of Lake Okanagan in early July 1858. They travelled in ordered, para-military companies under the command of a Major Robinson. Rein-hart states that the majority of the gold seekers were moderate and didn't want to trouble the Natives. But some, mainly those from California, took delight in shooting Indians, destroying their property and food and killing their dogs.

> In a few days, we got to O [Okanagan] Lake. Our advance guards saw some Indians just leaving their camp and cross the lake in canoes for fear of us. The boys saw a couple of their dogs at their old camp ground, and shot them down, and they saw some old huts where the Indians had stored a lot of berries for the winter, black

berries and nuts, fifty or a hundred bushels. They helped themselves to the berries and nuts, filling several sacks to take along, and the balance they just emptied into the lake, destroying them so that the Indians should not have them for provision for the winter. I, and a great many others, expressed their opinion that it was very imprudent and uncalled for, and no doubt the Indians would retaliate. But they only laughed and thought it great fun to kill their dogs and destroy and rob them of their provisions. Most everyone but those who had done it disapproved of the whole affair.[6]

The miners moved up along the lake, shadowed by the Okanagan. After a few days of this, the advance guard of Reinhart's formation decided to ambush the Natives. They waited until the miners broke camp and started marching, then hid in the bushes by the shore. The Okanagan walked right into trap.

As soon as the Indians saw the whites, they were so frightened that some turned back and ran towards their boat, some fell down on their knees and begged for [them] not to shoot, as they had no arms at all, and they threw up their hands and arms to show that they had nothing. But the whites all commenced to fire and shoot at them, and ran out to the lake after those who were getting in their canoes, and kept on shooting till the few that got into the [canoes] got out of reach of their guns and rifles. And lots jumped into the lake and was shot in the water before they could swim out of reach of their murderers — for they were nothing else, for it was a great slaughter or massacre of what was killed, for they never made an effort to resist or fired a shot, either gun, pistol, or bow and arrows, and the men were not touched, no more than if they had shot at birds or fish. It was a brutal affair, but the perpetrators of the outrage thought they were heroes, and were victors in some well-fought battle . . . the Indians knelt down and begged for life, saying they were friends. There must have been 10 or 12 killed and that many wounded, for very few got away unhurt. Some must have got drowned, and as I said before, it was like killing chickens or dogs or hogs, and a deed Californians should ever be ashamed of, without counting the after consequence.[7]

After the massacre, the column pushed on north, watching smoke signals and other signs of Natives scouting their movements. The whites captured two Shuswap men who were on their way to Washington Territory and forced them to accompany the miners, using them to interpret the signs. The Okanagan fought back by trying to ambush stragglers. They succeeded in killing one member of the company who strayed from the column. By the time Reinhart reached Fort Kamloops, several contingents, including a French company, had abandoned "the blood-thirsty Americans." At Kamloops they met one of the most powerful and influential First Nations leaders of his time. Hwistesmexe'qEn, chief of the Okanagan, known to the whites as Nicola, ruled an area half the size of Scotland. A venerable old warrior in his seventies in 1858, Nicola (called "old Nicholas" by Reinhart) fearlessly confronted the leaders of the white company to denounce their brutal treatment of his people.

> Old Nicholas, the head chief of the Indians around that country, came to see us about the two prisoners we had brought back from Lake O [Okanagan]. He was an old man, about 65 or 70 years old wore a stovepipe hat and citizen's clothes, and had a lot of medals of good character and official vouchers of good conduct for many years. He was quite angry and said he was surprised to see 300 men take two Indian prisoners and bring them back two or three hundred miles because we thought they were spies, and it was mighty little in us, and did not show great bravery. And about the O [Okanagan] Lake massacre, that it was brutal, and he could not think much of the Bostons, or Americans, that would do the like. Some of our boys were awful ashamed and some were angry to hear an old man tell them so many truths, and some were mad enough to kill him for his boldness in his expressions to us all. But it was a fact that none could deny, and Major Robertson [Robinson] let the two prisoners go.[8]

Nicola was the grand old man of the Interior, a great leader in war and peace who had favoured a mutually beneficial policy of trade with the "King George" men (the British) of the HBC. But dealing with "Bostons" (Americans) was something else, and he was under pressure from his own people to declare an all-out war against the intruders.

He blamed us for butchering the O [Okanagan] Indians in cold blood and the O [Okanagan] Indians had sent some messengers to him to avenge the death of his people, but he said he had better teachings from good men and priests, and good advice from Capt. [Donald] McL[ea]n [HBC trader at Fort Kamloops], . . . and they advised him and his people to overlook the great crime. But . . . he had great trouble to quiet and calm down his young warriors, of which, with the Lake O [Okanagan] tribe, he could have raised from 1,800 to 2,000 warriors, and could have surprised our command and cut them off to a man, utterly annihilating the whole of us, and taking all our animals and all our plunder. But he could not have told how it would have gone after, for he would have lost all control of his people, and the war chiefs would have usurped his power and carried on a general war against the whites, Americans and English. Being the massacre had taken place in British Columbia, it would be the duty of the English Queen Victoria to see justice done to her subjects.[9]

Nicola was also being urged to wage war against the whites by the other Interior First Nations to which he was bound by blood and tradition. He had over fifteen wives from nations like the Colville, Spokane, Secwepemc (Shuswap) and Nlaka'pamux. The latter two were begging Nicola to help them in the Canyon War. In early July 1858, Nicola was still sticking to his old policy of peace, but it was not clear how long he could hold out against the wishes of his people.

Douglas, the man to whom Nicola looked to avenge the killings, didn't want incidents like the Okanagan Lake massacre or a flood of American miners taking Reinhart's route to spread the Yakima War north along the curving arch of B.C.'s major rivers and into British Territory. Nor did he want the fighting in the canyon to be the first shot in a larger conflict. If it came to a general war with the First Nations of the Northwest coast, he could enforce the law and prevent bloodshed using the scant naval force at his disposal. But he was totally powerless to do anything inland, and as the fighting erupted in the canyon, Douglas was forced to sit in his office in the fort at Victoria, trying to make sense out of the reports sent to him by his officials, especially those working for the HBC, and reading sensational accounts of the conflict in the newly established newspapers of Victoria.

It's hard to say with any certainty just how many whites and how many Natives died in the Canyon War. Douglas was as uncertain as anyone else. The scale of the battles and the casualties on both sides were exaggerated. Allegedly dozens of white miners were murdered, and their bodies washed up in various eddies of the Fraser. There were reports of nineteen more corpses washing into Deadman's Bend, of ten headless whites being taken out of the water in front of Fort Yale, of another thirty-two found in an eddy in front of Fort Hope, and speculation as to how mortal remains had made it unseen all the way to the sea.

Finally, at the end of August, definitive news reached Douglas and the rest of Victoria. The *Victoria Daily Gazette* reported that the war was over, for the moment at least, and an American soldier had won it. Capt. H.M. Snyder, commander of a company calling itself the Pike Guards, had written a letter to the paper detailing a ten-day campaign that took his militia from Fort Yale to Lytton, where, he said, his show of force had convinced the First Nations to agree to a series of peace treaties. Soon after, Douglas received a full report from Snyder.

Snyder's simply stated (but ill-spelled) account is a remarkable document that paints a picture of war, intrigue, treachery and surprising common sense in a shadowy chapter of B.C.'s past. It is dated August 28, 1858 and was written in Fort Yale in the first flush of victory.

Captain Snyder's Campaign

Early in August, conflicting rumours and speculations swirled around Fort Yale where, driven from the diggings, hundreds of miners had congregated. When some Native chiefs and elders appeared to negotiate peace, they were set upon by a mob. One of them, Suseechus, was nearly lynched and had to be rescued by George Perrier of Hill's Bar and Ovid Allard of the HBC.

On August 16, 1858, the miners held a meeting to decide on their strategy. They split into two camps: one faction wanted to wage a war of extermination; another, larger contingent wanted a show of force that would persuade the Natives to sign peace treaties. Armed companies were formed on the spot.

In his report, Captain Snyder describes the meeting at Fort Yale, where the crowd was divided between those who wanted to fight and others who wanted to flee. "It had become so alarming that the miners had been Driven from their claims from with in fourteen miles of the forks [Lytton] as far down as the Indian Rancherie twelve miles above this place [likely Spuzzum]. In fact so alarming was the news from above that hundreds ware leaving this place to return to their homes," Snyder wrote.[10]

The Pike Guards formed, and Snyder was elected unanimously as their captain, immediately after the meeting. They left Fort Yale on the morning of August 17, 1858, a ragtag company of fifty-two men, poorly provisioned and equipped, but well armed. Attached to the company as interpreters were William Yates, an HBC employee from Fort Yale, and a Mr. Battiece. After marching two miles, Snyder ordered a halt and called the roll. He reminded his company its mission was to "make pease with the Indians, by peasible meanes if we could, And by force if we must."[11] The company then elected the rest of its officers: John Gordon, first lieutenant; J. McWarrier, second lieutenant; orderly sergeant, D. McEachern; and quartermaster, J. Gascoigne.

Snyder's company marched upriver towards Sailors Bar, eight miles above Fort Yale. There they met up with another roaming militia, an eighty-man "Austrian company," commanded by Captain John Centras, who was of the same mind as Snyder, preferring negotiations to extermination. With the help of one of the interpreters, the two captains made peace with some Natives in the area.

The two companies carried on to Spuzzum, where they were treated to the spectacle of five to six hundred miners, driven from their claims, crammed into the narrow space. There were throngs of men from a dozen countries camped out by the river, as well as two other armed companies, headed by Captains Golloway and Graham, but precious few Indians with whom to "make pease."

The Nlaka'pamux who lived around Spuzzum kept a healthy distance from so many agitated white miners. Snyder, Centras and an interpreter finally found a chief on the outskirts of Spuzzum who was willing to talk to them. They were led two miles down the river for their parlay and then, "giving a whoop, some 290 Indians made their appearance from amongst the rocks and out of the ravines" and surrounded the two captains. The scene was described in the *Victoria Daily Gazette*.

> *Capt. Snyder explained to them that he had come up to make peace with them — to punish those who had shot and robbed the whites, and as this trail [tribe?] had not been engaged in the troubles, to merely give them notice that the white men were in arms, and determined not to be further molested; that whilst they would punish those who did wrong; in return, he would guarantee that on the White man's molesting them, he should likewise be punished on their informing him or any of the miners. The Indians were well-pleased at this.*[12]

Later that day, at Spuzzum, Snyder and Centras held "a counsil of war with some Sixty indians, and pease was made with them."[13]

But peace was the furthest thing from the mind of Captain Graham, leader of the Whatcom Company. He wanted to use the Californian solution to Indian trouble, which was to wage a war of extermination.[14] It was not to Snyder's taste.

"I had a consultation with the 2 captains that we found at this place," he wrote, "as their views ware different from mine and the Captain of the Austrian company [Centras]. They wished to procede and kill every man, wooman, & Child they saw that had Indian blood in them. To such an arrangement I could not consent to. My heart revolted as the idea of killing a helpless wooman or an inocent child was to horrible to think of."[15]

Hundreds of miners had gathered around to watch the confrontation between the captains. Graham challenged Snyder to lay out his plan in front of the entire assembly. Given the atmosphere and the emotions running through the crowd of frightened and angry men, it was a risky thing to do, but Snyder spoke convincingly. "They requested me to state my views to the crowd, which consisted from six to seven hundred. I consented to do so and after I was through and on taking the vote, I found they ware almost unanimous in supporting my course."[16]

Snyder had won for the moment, and his speech convinced thirty-one more men to join his company, bringing its strength up to eighty-two. The next morning, August 18, 1858, Snyder and Centras ferried their companies in canoes across to the east side of the river, to the foot of the Big Canyon, which stretches from Spuzzum to Boston Bar. They followed the brigade trail along the east side to the Anderson River, which flowed into the Fraser at the Nlaka'pamux village of Quayome, near Boston Bar.

Just above Spuzzum, Snyder and Centras overtook Graham, his lieutenant, Carmack, and the rest of the Whatcom Company. Defying the will of the majority of miners, Graham had left early to hunt Natives in the canyon and had driven them into the mountains. Snyder again conferred with Graham by the river. An angry and adamant Graham refused to listen to reason and stated his intention to press on until Snyder finally threatened to leave him and his men to fight the Natives alone. This elicited a reluctant promise of good conduct from Graham.

"I then stated to him that if he was still determined to persue his course that I would returne with my men as I did not feel disposed to make so long & tedious a journey for nothing," Snyder wrote. "He finally consented to remaine where he was until I had went to the head of the canion and if I could make pease with the indians & send a white flag through the canion that he would returne to this place [Yale], on those conditions and understanding. We took up our line of march, taking the old brigade trail."[17]

Graham agreed to stay camped where he was and await word

from Snyder. If all was well, Snyder would send a white flag and Graham would stand his men down. If things went badly, Graham would be in a position to relieve Snyder. Clearly, Snyder didn't trust Graham, and to hedge his bets he sent a messenger ahead of his company up the canyon with orders to find CexpentlEm on the Thompson River and ask for a meeting with the great chief.

Thinking he had finally dealt with Graham, Snyder and his companies marched the next morning, August 19, 1858, along the HBC brigade trail on the east side of the Fraser to China Bar, where he signed peace treaties with three more chiefs. Accordingly, Snyder sent a white flag down to Graham at Spuzzum, entrusting the message to the HBC's William Yates, five of his own men and the son of a local chief.

Warring Natives were not the white miners' only concern. The next morning, Snyder and his force turned their attention to the Chinese miners, who they suspected of being in league with the Indians.[18]

"On the morning of the 20th we took up our Line of March after having notafyed the chinees that they must leave their claims for four weeks or until such times as pease was restored. As they ware suspected of being partly the means of the difficulties with the Indians, at the same time there was an unanimous vote given that their claims should be protected to them."[19]

Snyder continued up the canyon, holding his councils and making treaties with the chiefs of the villages along his route. He and his men pressed on through a landscape of burned villages, ruined fishing camps and spoiled food caches created by other American militias and groups of miners who had preceded them. This was a new kind of war for the Nlaka'pamux, who were accustomed to raids, retaliation, and ambush. It was becoming clear that the "confrontation between the Nlaka'pamux and the miners could not be won through the combination of armed raids and guile that characterized the previous Nlaka'pamux experience of war. In those conflicts there might be some loss of life, but influence over territory of a neighboring people was more commonly gained through intermarriage than through war, which was generally a matter of raid and reprisal."[20]

Finally, on August 21, Snyder bivouacked just seven miles from the forks of the Fraser and Thompson rivers. Behind him he had a loose cannon in Graham, who might undo all his work at any moment. Ahead of him lay the great village of Camchin (Lytton), ruled by CexpentlEm. Snyder had no idea how many Nlaka'pamux warriors and their allies were waiting there. His men were well armed, but they were pitifully supplied. Many were wearing rags; some were barefoot. The outcome of a protracted campaign was uncertain. Everything now depended on what the First Nations themselves had decided: was it war or peace?

It was at this spot above The Forks, at night, that a meeting took place which sealed the fate of both parties in the Canyon War. CexpentlEm had finally received Snyder's message, and he came to talk.

> *Here we was met by Spintlum [CexpentlEm], The war chief of all the tribes for some distance up & Down Frazer River and for an hundred miles up Thompson River they had heard of our coming. I had sent a runner after him Seventy five miles above the forks on Thompson & he had got the news and met us at the latter place. We held at this place a counsil of war with a large boddy of Indians they ware well pleased with what we told them. Then the War Chief made a Speech to the Indians that had collected together, he is a very cool calculating man and spoke to them for at least half hour. At ten oclock he left us, to meet us next Morning at the forks.* [21]

Snyder and CexpentlEm had worked out the framework for a general peace. The next morning, both parties made it official. At 9 a.m., Snyder and his company marched through the rain into Lytton, where CexpentlEm and hundreds of chiefs and warriors waited for him. The Nlaka'pamux considered their world, bounded by the Fraser and Thompson canyons, to be like a house, and The Forks were the centre of that world. "Lytton is my centre-post," CexpentlEm said. "It is the middle of my house and I sit there." [22] Now an American soldier of fortune was sitting in the centre of the Nlaka'pamux world, and nothing would be the same again.

In the same spot, just fifty years earlier, CexpintlEm's uncle, Pa-hal-ak, and 1,200 Nlaka'pamux had met Simon Fraser during his descent of the river. On that occasion, Fraser had been greeted as the "Son of the Sun" and been obliged to shake every single person's hand. On this day, all Snyder wanted was the signatures of CexpentlEm and his fellow chiefs on his peace treaty.

"Our grand counsil," wrote Snyder, "... consisted of Eleven Chiefs And a very large number of other indians that had gathered from above and below. We stated to them that this time we came for pease, but if we had to come again, that we would not come by hundreds, but by thousands and drive them from the river forever. They ware much supprised and frightened to see so many men with guns & revolvers."[23]

Snyder's threat may have been true enough in the long term, but his position at Camchin was tenuous. Heavily armed he may have been, with three companies in arms in the canyon totalling perhaps 250 men. But his ragtag unit was desperately short of supplies and exhausted from forced marches over extreme terrain. It was in Snyder's interest to make peace as much as it was in the Natives' interest. The problems of supply and terrain figured heavily in his strategy for the campaign, and as Snyder later explained, his decision to go the way of treaty-making was dictated by an assessment as sound as it was utilitarian, based on present need, not sentiment. The Nlaka'pamux controlled the Upper Canyon and could stop all traffic through their part of the river unless a settlement was reached. "True, they could be driven out — but it would take time and money to effect it. The mining season was just commencing, and the object to be gained *now* was, to enable the men to go up the river as soon as possible."[24]

With the salmon ready to run in the river, the Nlaka'pamux had supply problems of their own. The war was denying them access to their fishing sites. Winter stores had already been destroyed and it was getting late in the season. CexpentlEm signed the treaty (which Snyder believed would be "held Sacred by the Indians") and the formalities were over. Now Snyder faced the problem of getting his tired company back to Fort Yale.

We remained at this place [Lytton] but five hours, as we ware scant of provisions & had but little money. All we could get here was beef, and that was worth fifty cents [a pound]. And but few had money to buy any. We then took up our line of march at 2. P.M. To return we marched some fifteen miles and camped for the night. At Day break we ware on the march on the morning of the 23rd and camped at Boston Bar at the mouth of the Anderson River the same time having made thirty miles this day as most of our men ware out of provisions. At this place all we could get was twenty pounds of flour. The next morning at sunrise, the 24th, we ware on our line of march for the head of the big canion. We arrived there at 9 oclock at this place. I sent part of my men over the mountain trail in charge of my orderly Sargent to see if they could meet any one packing provissions for my men. With the rest of my men I proceded though the canions, taking with me the Chief from the head of the canion For the purpose of bringing him to Fort Yale.[25]

Snyder had chiefs escort him all the way down the canyon, partly to ensure a safe passage and partly to spread the news of the peace that he and CexpentlEm had agreed to.

"We came through the canions safe And camped at the Indian village twelve miles from Fort Yale, after having performed one of the hardest days labour that it ever fell to the lot of men to perform, half starved waren [worn] down with fatigue and some of them barefooted . . . Here we camped for the night and among all of my men there was not enough provisions for to make a meal for three men."[26]

It was also here, near Spuzzum, that Snyder received word of the contrary Captain Graham.

At this place I saw one of the men that came through the canion with the white flag. From him I learnt the following particulars of the fate of Capt. Grayham & his Lieutenant. He stated to me that on the evening of the 19th instant when within 4 miles of the foot of the canion he met with Capt Grayham & a part of his men just at dusk. The first thing Grayham done was to order his men to take the white flag that I had sent to him and throw it a way, which was done. One of my men went and picked it up and slept on it the balance of the night.

> *They then layed down, My Men Some two or three rods from the*
> *rest, he says If Grayham had any guard posted that they must have*
> *been a sleep. About twelve o clock they ware arroused from their*
> *sleep by the firing of some guns. Grayham was shot through the*
> *back at the first fier. And died some two hours afterwards. He thinks*
> *that the Indians had watched him. if It was Indians, and had scene*
> *the treatment he gave the white flag. His firs Lieutenant [Carmack]*
> *was also killed in the first firing. Had he of Done as he promised to*
> *do he would now be a live.*[27]

It is significant that Snyder, who thought Graham and Carmack died during a night attack by the Nlaka'pamux, didn't blame the Natives at all. Rather, Snyder implied Graham's death was his own damn fault for treating a flag of truce with disrespect.

The next day, the morning of August 25, Snyder and his men walked into Fort Yale around 11 a.m. They were "Woren Down and many of them Bare footed & their clothes allmos torn off. We had traveled at least two hundred & ten miles in nine days by forced Marching on the account of being short of provissions." Snyder gave an account of his exploits, then sat down to pen his report to Douglas. He wrapped up his despatch to the governor by praising his men and "Mr Yates, our Interpreter, for assisting in Laying the foundation of our good work." As for the Pike Guards:

> *To Those noble generous hearted men that volunteered and was*
> *under my command to much praise can not be awarded to them.*
> *they packed their own blanketts provissions & guns, and was at all*
> *times willing to obey my orders & to Execute my orders &*
> *commands. It is true we are all of us strangers & in a fareign land*
> *Seperated from all the fond ties that bind the loving heart to Their*
> *native homes, But from this you will see that they ware ever ready*
> *and willing to take up armes to have redress of which we had so*
> *much to complain of, and hoping at the same time it will meet with*
> *your approval. I have the honour of subscribing my humble name to*
> *this, H.M. Snyder.*[28]

Snyder added a postscript, asking if Douglas might be able to pay his men for their time and effort, which must have left the parsimonious governor cold. The whole episode did not meet with Douglas's approval at all. Peace had been restored in the canyon under the auspices of American militia units. Treaties had been forced onto the First Nations of the mainland without the consent of the Crown or the Company. It was time to see for himself what had really happened.

The Fact-Finding Mission

Douglas raised a meagre force of twenty marines and fifteen Royal Engineers and set out for the Fraser by steamboat on August 30, 1858, on a fact-finding mission. At Fort Langley the steamer stopped to pick up passengers, and Douglas received a detailed account of American depredations by long-time HBC chief trader James Murray Yale, who was aggrieved as any of the Natives. According to Donald Fraser, correspondent for *The Times* of London, who chronicled Douglas's journey, "The gentleman in charge [Yale] complained of the Yankees having been very intrusive, impertinent, and lawless when they first came up the river in force, and when they fancied they were beyond control of the authorities. They invaded his cornfields, ate the green peas, stole the oats, tore down the fences for firewood, and misconducted themselves in other ways."[29]

It was also at Fort Langley that Douglas had his second encounter with Ned McGowan. The Ubiquitous had left Victoria for Whatcom in Washington Territory a couple of days after avoiding the impromptu public-speaking engagement at the Fashion Hotel. McGowan, Dolan and several others braved a hellish passage of the Georgia Strait during a gale and then tried to find a way to the gold fields through the Interior, but were frustrated, like many other gold seekers, by the ongoing Yakima War. McGowan was wondering what to do when he received a letter from Martin Gallagher, who had escaped exile in Hawaii and made his way to Hill's Bar, urging Ned to come without delay to join him. McGowan decided to take Gallagher up on his offer.

Ned settled on the tried and true route to the gold fields and travelled with his party by canoe to the mouth of the Fraser River. There they were met by the *Satellite*, still patrolling the gateway to the gold fields. On the shore opposite the vessel were hundreds of canoes, boats, skiffs and other craft strung along the beach. Hundreds of would-be miners were camped at the water's edge, unable to pay the five-dollar mining licence fee. When McGowan grudgingly went aboard to pay for his licence, he chanced upon a Californian acquaintance named Parker, who was being held on the *Satellite*. McGowan demanded to know what the man had done to warrant imprisonment and was informed by a ship's officer that when paying for his licence, Parker had asked, rather impertinently, what the British were going to do with his money. Parker suspected the ship's officers would keep it. When informed the revenues collected from Americans were to be "used as pin money for Her Majesty the Queen," Parker snapped: "Oh, BLANK the Queen!" He had been seized and forced under the hatches.

"You can't *do* that, you know," added the officer earnestly.[30]

McGowan and his companions fought the Fraser's current as far as Fort Langley. There, McGowan decided to go ahead of his party and gratefully booked passage on the steamer carrying Douglas and his entourage. He was less grateful for Douglas's display of the perks of imperial office. As darkness closed in, the steamer was run up onto the shore by the mouth of the Harrison River for the night. McGowan watched the governor and his retinue troop down onto the shore to set up camp.

"He was traveling with all the comforts and luxuries of life," wrote McGowan. "He had a fine and capacious hamper and cooks and servants. After dining, I observed that one of his suite got him his pipe, and another filled it with tobacco. They watched his every movement, and never laughed until he laughed first. It was the greatest piece of toadyism I ever witnessed. I felt proud of being an American."[31]

McGowan, a shrewd judge of character himself, was not repelled by Douglas personally, but rather by the British imperial system that he served. McGowan observed in the same breath that "Douglas was a gentlemen . . . he was prejudiced against us, it is true, but he had seen very little of America and her people." The next morning, when word reached the steamer that Douglas was considering having his breakfast on shore rather than onboard the vessel, many of the passengers were upset, since this would delay their journey by two hours and perhaps prevent them from reaching Fort Hope by nightfall. Time was money on the gold fields, and several miners asked McGowan to petition the governor on their behalf. The second meeting between McGowan and Douglas was much more pleasant than the first — at least according to Ned. McGowan was conducted into Douglas's tent on shore, where he politely laid the concerns of his fellow passengers before the governor. Douglas himself was in a hurry to reach Fort Yale and consented immediately to the suggestion.

"Certainly, my man," said Douglas. "I don't want to keep the men out another night."[32]

This incident was reported to the *Daily Alta California*, a staunchly Vigilante newspaper, which put a different spin on things. Instead of a polite, formal chat, the newspaper reported that McGowan had stormed ashore with a gang of bullies, personally burst into Douglas's tent and roused the governor out of bed, crying: "Hallo, Gov! Steam's up, and the boiler's a'humming old fel."

Whatever the truth of that encounter, the steamer made it to Fort Hope that day. McGowan disembarked, waiting for the rest of his party to arrive with the canoes before proceeding to Fort Yale. Douglas pressed on, stopping at every mining bar along the way, asking miners and Natives alike what had happened during the hostilities in the canyon.

Many of the miners were more interested in other problems, like how far back their claims reached from the riverbank, and which legal system applied in New Caledonia: Californian, Australian or "the law of all creation," which was invoked by at least one miner to justify the extent of his claim.

Natives also flocked to the governor, stating their grievances and asking for relief. Just below Yale, a delegation of Natives pleaded with Douglas "for a small spot to draw up their canoes, and to dry their fish upon, to be exempted from mining. The request was granted by the Governor, and the boundaries marked by the subcommissioner."[33]

It took Douglas until September 13 to reach Fort Yale. The remote HBC post had become a typical gold rush town, with a collection of tents and shacks sprawled around the Company post. David W. Higgins, pioneer journalist, was a young man when he arrived at the settlement that year. He reported that "every other store was a gambling den with liquor attachments" and "ruffians of the blackest dye, fugitives from justice, deserters from the United States troops who strutted about in army overcoats which they had stolen when they deserted for the British Columbia gold mines, Vigilance Committee refugees who had been driven from San Francisco under sentences of life banishment, ex-convicts, pugilists, highwaymen, petty thieves, murderers and painted women all were jumbled together in that town and were free to follow their sinful purposes so far as any restraint from the officers of the law were concerned."[34]

A bit of an exaggeration, perhaps, but not so far from the truth. Yale was the Wild West at the mouth of the Little Canyon. Donald Fraser of *The Times* described it as "a modern Sodom." Here, Douglas put up his pavilion and started his weeklong investigation, hearing from miner and Native alike. As he listened, it became apparent how little influence his few government officials had had during the Canyon War without military force to back them up.

This was illustrated by the tale of Captain Charles Rouse, a former Texas Ranger, who led the first of the five militia units to roam the canyon during the conflict. Rouse's force of forty miners (which became known as the "Rifle Company") left Fort Yale on August 9, 1858, marching to Boston Bar to protect miners there. On August 14 they fought the "Battle of Boston Bar." A correspondent for the San Francisco *Bulletin* who witnessed the hostilities described a three-hour fight in which nine Nlaka'pamux were killed and three wounded before the Natives withdrew into the hills. Rouse took three prisoners. Two of his own men were wounded, and one of them later died.

Rouse fell back to Fort Yale, leaving scorched earth behind him. He burned three villages just upriver from Spuzzum, destroying winter stores of salmon and berries. The Rifle Company reached Yale around noon on August 17, dragging a special prisoner with them:

Kowpelst. It may be that Kowpelst was trying to act as a hostage, ensuring his people's safety, but as he was dragged through the streets, a sizable mob of miners gathered, and the Spuzzum chief was almost lynched. Rouse finally delivered Kowpelst to Ovid Allard at the HBC post.[35]

Kowpelst was Douglas's own magistrate, appointed at Hill's Bar back in March, and his treatment was another affront to Britain's tenuous hold over the mainland. Kowpelst himself gave Douglas his version of events in person at Fort Yale. From other First Nations leaders (such as CexpentlEm, who met with the governor on September 5, 1858[36]), Douglas learned how close the territory had come to that disastrous Native war he had foretold.

As Snyder marched up the canyon giving out white flags,[37] hundreds of First Nations warriors from all over the Thompson and Fraser rivers had gathered at Lytton, determined to make a stand there to stop Snyder's progress, then drive him and the rest of the miners down the river. The war chief of Lytton, CuxcuxesqEt, "a large, active man of great courage," led the faction in favour of driving the whites from the gold fields.[38] The Nlaka'pamux had been promised help by the neighbouring Shuswap, Kamloops, Savona, Bonaparte and Spokane Nations. The war party had also sent word to Nicola of the Okanagan, begging him to join the war. That would have linked the conflict in the canyon with the war being waged farther south by the Yakima and their allies.

CuxcuxesqEt, dressed in his full regalia of eagle feather headdress, painted and armed for battle, argued ceaselessly that the people must drive the whites out of their lands. When he finished a speech, he danced a war dance or imitated his guardian animal, the grizzly bear. Dancing around the fire in front of the people and the council of chiefs and elders, the young warriors behind him, flanked by Cuna-mitsa, the chief of Spences Bridge, and several other prominent leaders, it must have been an impressive show.

But CexpentlEm, "with his great powers of oratory, talked continually for peace, and showed strongly its advantages."[39] The people were divided, but eventually CexpentlEm prevailed. He assisted Snyder's peace-making by sending the sons of chiefs along with the Pike

Guards on their way down the canyon. These chiefs' sons handed Snyder off from village to village and carried more weight than white flags. It was said that CuxcuxesqEt never forgave CexpentlEm.

Douglas did not entirely trust CexpentlEm, perhaps because of the 1848 hostage-taking incident at Fort Yale involving the post's chief, Ovid Allard. However, he needed CexpentlEm to be a good host to prevent a repeat of the American militia roaming freely in the canyon. The governor tried his best to keep CexpentlEm onside by giving "him a present and . . . a charge concerning the treatment of miners visiting his country. Reported to be a treacherous Indian, but it is prudent to pursue a conciliatory policy at present."[40]

Douglas also had the opportunity to hear from William Yates, lately interpreter for H.M. Snyder. Yates had a somewhat different version of the "Indian night attack" that had resulted in Captain Graham's death. Yates described how he and Snyder's advance party intercepted Graham just before he could attack the Nlaka'pamux in the steep hills of the canyon beyond Spuzzum. Graham was firm in his resolve to "wipe the Indians out, if he could,"[41] but Snyder arrived at dusk and got the overexcited Graham calmed down. Graham had his men stack their arms and bivouac for the night.

According to Yates, things did not go as smoothly the next morning as Snyder let on in his report to Douglas. Graham tried to give Snyder the slip, leading his party across the river at Spuzzum in the grey light of dawn. Snyder spotted him and sent Yates and twenty-five men in pursuit. When they caught up with him and gave him yet another warning, Graham replied: "Tell your Captain Snyder, sir, that he is on the way to hell and I hope you will be joining him."[42] Five men, including Yates, were dispatched to carry the reply to Snyder.

The two competing columns stayed on opposite sides of the river. Snyder was content to leave Yates and his party to shadow Graham as he took his main force over the mountain to Boston Bar, hoping to get ahead of Graham and cut him off. Graham spent the day looking for Natives, but they had withdrawn. After a day of pointless manoeuvring, Graham ordered his men to bivouac on a large shelf of rock near the river's edge. On the far bank, Yates and the rest of his observer group did the same. Darkness fell, the black night of the canyon occasionally relieved by the moon's light. Sentries were posted as the rest of the men rolled up in their bedding. Yates describes what happened next. "About 2 o'clock we heard parties rushing down and singing out that they were murdered — that they were murdered by Indians. We got up and made inquiry about it. Some of Captain Graham's men rushed right through us and said that the indians had been shooting at them and that a great many of their men had got balls in them and were lying up there."[43]

A sentry in Graham's camp had fallen asleep and been startled awake by the sound of a twig snapping or some other noise in the night. He decided to shoot first and ask questions later. The entire camp was instantly in an uproar as the Americans blazed away into the dark. The company's second-in-command, Lieutenant Carmack, was accidentally shot by his own men. Captain Graham was also killed.[44] In the morning, Yates and Snyder's men conducted a thorough search.

"We found one or two dead bodies in the morning," Yates remembered. "We thought it was not indians but that it was their own party that got in a panic some way and started shooting in the night. Some of the men were drowned in the river and some were shot and killed or wounded by dragoon pistols and five-shooters — not by indian guns at all. The indians had nothing but old fashioned Hudson's Bay guns in those days."[45]

What Douglas learned about the Canyon War worried him on two scores. He was appalled by the killings of Natives and the destruction of their land and resources. But more alarming was the fact that the conflict had proved the Americans were capable of quickly raising large, well-armed and well-organized militia on British soil. Such a force could presumably be counted on during any attempt by the U.S. Army or a filibustering expedition to annex the territory. Douglas had been quite helpless to prevent the conflict or to stop Snyder. He would be equally helpless if the U.S. troops just south of the line used the bitter wrangling over the border survey or the need to protect American citizens from Indian attacks as an excuse to invade. The reluctant Admiral Baynes was not set to sail with his flagship, HMS *Ganges*, and its eight hundred marines and sailors until late August and would take weeks to get to Victoria.[46]

Douglas had spent a week at Fort Yale looking for answers and finding some ugly truths. By September 20, 1858, he was ready to go home. But the miners wanted some answers of their own from the governor. Many wanted to buy land, build homes and open businesses. What were the plans of the British government for New Caledonia? Under pressure from the democratically minded Yankees, Douglas finally bowed to the masses. In an extraordinary scene, Old Square Toes climbed a stump in front of the Hudson's Bay post to address the miners.[47] As he stood on that stump, he finally had some answers to give his audience — and a very big personal decision to make because of them.

A New Colony

Between June, when he had written Stanley about his plans, and the end of August, Douglas tried to protect the HBC's trade monopoly on the mainland as well as exert British sovereignty over the territory in the face of fierce opposition. As usual, Douglas was trying to please both his masters. But one of his masters had changed. Early in 1858, just as the rush was starting in New Caledonia, the HBC-friendly government of Palmerston had been replaced by the Earl of Derby's administration, and the amiable colonial secretary Henry Labouchere had initially been replaced by Lord Stanley.

The timing for the Hudson's Bay Company couldn't have been worse. Its licence for exclusive trade west of the Rockies (in the area known as New Caledonia) expired in 1859, and the Company was having a tough time in front of the parliamentary committee that would recommend whether it should be renewed or not.

Labouchere, now in opposition, defended the HBC both on the committee and in the House of Commons. But the committee hearings also provided a forum for one of the most bitter critics of James Douglas and the HBC: Richard Blanshard. The former governor of

Vancouver Island delighted in describing for the committee how the Company of Adventurers had deliberately discouraged settlement of a huge area of British North America, leaving it vulnerable to U.S. expansion. He was paying Douglas back for the shabby way he'd been treated during his brief tenure as governor.

However, Blanshard was not the biggest headache faced by the committeemen of the Company. That honour went to the new colonial secretary, Sir Edward Bulwer Lytton.

Lytton had replaced Stanley as colonial secretary in the first week of June. Stanley was busy shepherding the Government of India Act through Parliament, ending the great trading monopoly of the British East India Company. It would be Lytton's mission to end that other great trading monopoly, the Hudson's Bay Company. Lytton is best known today for such overwritten Victorian melodramas as *The Last Days of Pompeii*. His writing style is parodied every year in the annual E.B. Lytton Contest for the worst opening sentence of a fictitious novel. But the committeemen of the HBC found nothing funny about Lytton during his short tenure as colonial secretary. An implacable foe of the HBC, Lytton placed the question of the legality of the Company's charter before the government's lawyers. That move gave him a strong hand in the ongoing war over the future of the Company's vast empire in North America, for Lytton had big plans for New Caledonia in general and James Douglas in particular.

In his very first official despatch, Lytton told Douglas in no uncertain terms who his real master was. He blasted Douglas for his attempts to protect the HBC trade monopoly on the mainland (as reported by the British minister to America, Lord Napier) and ordered the governor to throw the doors open to free enterprise from Victoria to the Forks.

"The Hudson's Bay Company have hitherto had an exclusive right to trade with Indians in the Fraser River territory, but they have had no other right whatever," Lytton tersely informed Douglas in a letter dated August 14, 1858, but which didn't reach Victoria until September. "They have had no right to exclude strangers. They have had no rights of Government, or of occupation of the soil. They have had no right to prevent or interfere with any kind of trading, except with indians alone."

It was an official rebuke. In an earlier, private letter to Douglas dated July 1, Lytton had warned the governor not to overstep his bounds: "The importance of avoiding any act which directly or indirectly might be construed into an application of Imperial resources to the objects of the Hudson's Bay Company, in whose service you have so long been engaged. Even the suspicion of this, however unfounded, would be prejudicial to the establishment of civil government . . . and would multiply existing difficulties and dangers." In order to avoid further confusion and conflict of interest, Lytton offered Douglas the governorship of a new colony on the mainland. The appointment would be for six years and pay £1,500 annually, but there was a catch: Douglas would have to sever his ties with the Hudson's Bay Company to receive the post.

Lytton made Douglas's decision somewhat easier by informing him that the HBC licence for New Caledonia was about to be revoked. Lytton had introduced a bill to create a Crown colony of the territory in the House of Commons on July 1, 1858. It sped through the House and on August 2, 1858, was given Royal Assent. Lytton, who was concerned that his new colony would be confused with that *other* New Caledonia, a French possession in the Pacific, had written to Queen Victoria, asking Her Majesty if she had any suggestions for a different name. Victoria went off and consulted her maps, then wrote her response in the third person.

If the name of New Caledonia is objected to as being already borne by another colony or island claimed by the French, it may be better to give the new colony west of the Rockie Mountains another name. New Hanover, New Cornwall, and New Georgia appear from the maps to be the names of the subdivisions of that country, but do not appear on all maps. The only name which is given to the whole territory in every map the Queen has consulted is "Columbia," but as a Columbia [Colombia] in South America, and the citizens of the

United States call their country also Columbia, at least in poetry,
"British Columbia" might be, in the Queen's opinion, the best
name.[48]

By the time Douglas stood up on the stump to speak to the miners at
Yale, he had already decided to accept Lytton's offer, though he
would wait till October before making it official by resigning from
the Hudson's Bay Company service. Now, as the crowd of miners
gathered around, Richard Hicks stood beside Douglas, gazing up at
his boss and listening with pride as the governor outlined the government's plans for the future and his part in it. Imperious to the last,
Douglas started off by letting his audience know just how lucky they
were.

"It is not the custom of Governors of British Provinces to address
the public, but as this is a particular occasion, and the circumstances
are peculiar, and as you have expressed a wish to learn the truth, I
will depart from the custom and explain to you in a few words what
are the views of the Government in relation to this country," he
said.[49]

Douglas went on to say he was commanded (by Lytton and the
Queen — certainly not by his own inclination) to welcome the Americans and other nationalities (especially the French, Britain's late
allies in the Crimean War) to the territory. In a complete about-face
from his speech to the miners at Hill's Bar just four months previously, Douglas announced the territory was open for settlement. He
would have town lots laid out at Yale. Those who wished to settle
could lease the lots, then buy them once the colony was officially pro-
claimed. As to the difficulties of navigation, roads and other general
concerns, Douglas proudly produced the grey-haired, respectable-
looking Hicks.

I have given orders to Mr. Hicks, the Commissioner for Crown
Lands, to have a town site surveyed here, and to dispose of the
building lots to any person wishing to hold them under lease, with a

pre-emption right when the land is sold by the Crown. This will give confidence and security to everyone.

In the same manner, I have given Mr. Hicks instructions to lay out the farming lands near the town in convenient lots of 20 acres and to make grants of them under the same tenure.

I have also given him instructions to permit the building of sawmills, to establish ferries, to open roads, and generally to carry out the views of Government in the manner best calculated to give development to the resources of this glorious country.

Every wise man and every good man knows the value of good laws, and every man who expects to receive their protection when he himself gets into trouble must be ready at all times to come out manfully in support of those laws.

Let all do so, and there will not be a better or more quiet community in any part of Her Majesty's dominions than will be found at Yale . . .

Gentlemen, I have now done and I have only further to wish you all well.

It was more like a Speech from the Throne than from the stump, but it had its effect. The miners cheered. Hicks must have smiled. He was in the dining car of the gravy train. He would make Yale a British town fit for the purest and best.

FIVE

Putting the Pieces in Place

Yale was, however, already full of the purest and best from San Francisco, as McGowan had already discovered. In early September, after being joined by Dolan and the others at Fort Hope, Ned's company made for Yale. They arrived the next day in the late afternoon, dead broke and without a place to stay. Yet again, another friend from San Francisco appeared on the scene to give McGowan a hand. Alec MacCrellish had fifteen dollars to his name and he gave McGowan eight of them. With money in their pockets, McGowan's company took in the sights of Yale, which brought back fond memories of a decade earlier.

San Francisco on the Fraser

"I went strolling around sight-seeing; met a number of old Californians, and saw 'history repeating itself,' in reenacting the scenes of the city of San Francisco in 1849, but on a much smaller basis," wrote McGowan.[1]

McGowan's next feeling of *déjà vu* was less pleasant. On Front Street, Yale's main thoroughfare, he discovered the offices of yet another member of the Vigilance Committee. He was not one of the executive committee members, but in Yale he was a civic leader and a force to be reckoned with.

Dr. Max William Fifer had come to California in 1847 with Colonel Stevenson's regiment of New York volunteers.[2] Stricken by typhoid fever, Fifer became a hospital orderly. He either received training at an unknown medical school or, more likely, apprenticed under another doctor (a fast-track method of training physicians in a state desperately short of medics: rather like the hastily trained doctors immortalized in *M*A*S*H*). By 1856, he had established his practice on Washington Street in San Francisco. There was pressure for all merchants and professionals to support the Vigilance Committee, so Fifer took his number with the all-seeing cabal, but it is questionable how active a role he played. He certainly didn't partake in any of the judicial proceedings (although to McGowan, that wouldn't have made any difference).

His reasons for heading north are much clearer. Fifer received the same insider tip that sent James Moore and his crew to the Fraser River. A San Francisco mint employee — quite possibly the same superintendent / volunteer fireman — told him about the *Otter's* golden cargo on April 1, 1858. At age thirty-six, Fifer was ready to make a fresh start in what promised to be the new San Francisco: Yale.

Fifer left his personal goods in the hands of fellow Vigilance Committee member Jules David and struck out for the Fraser. He and his Chinese assistant, Ah Chung, sailed from San Francisco aboard the *Sierra Nevada*, which was grossly overloaded with 1,900 passengers, well above its legal 900-person capacity. The ship fought heavy winds and high seas, but made it to Esquimalt in nine days. Fifer and Chung boarded the *Enterprise* for Fort Hope, then made their way to Yale by canoe, landing there in July 1858. They slept in their blankets on the beach and, in the morning, headed for the Hudson's Bay post to learn the medical lay of the land from the chief trader, Ovid Allard.

Born in Montreal in 1817, Allard had in his time fought Indians with Kit Carson before joining the Hudson's Bay Company at Fort Vancouver. He was transferred from the Columbia River to Fort Langley in New Caledonia. In 1848, Fort Langley's chief trader, James Murray Yale, sent Allard at the head of a party of twenty men to construct a new store and rest house for the Company's brigades at the mouth of the Little Canyon. Allard named the place after his boss and survived being taken hostage by the unwelcoming CexpentlEm. Married after the custom of the country, he was described by one European observer as having become "half savage by living so long in the far West."[3] He was, much to his subordinate Yates's consternation, a heavy drinker. But he knew everything about the town springing up outside his post.

It was from Allard that Fifer learned there was just one other sawbones working in the district. Dr. Silas E. Crane was by all accounts a quack, whose breath always reeked of liquor and who refused to see a patient unless first served a large gin. No one would ask for Crane's help unless they couldn't afford to travel to Fort Hope to see a more reputable physician, Dr. Edenshaw. Seeing that there was no real competition for medical services, the well-heeled Fifer bought a house on Front Street from a fellow San Franciscan, paying with gold coin, and set up his practice. His business was flourishing by the time McGowan arrived two months later.

Finding Yale crawling with and controlled by Vigilance Committee members and their supporters, McGowan and his party decided to look farther upstream for their riches. Dolan ran into a fellow filibuster, described by McGowan as "a Nicaraguan Colonel," who gave them his claim on New York Bar. They wangled $50 worth of supplies on credit, bought tools from a discouraged miner for $10 and set off into the Little Canyon. Now, at last, McGowan, ex-49er who never actually panned for gold in his life, was about to get his share of the riches of the northern El Dorado. The mining process was aided by liberal swigs from a bottle of schnapps of dubious quality. While McGowan and Tom Dolan shovelled sand and coarse, heavy gravel, their associate Rube Raines worked a rocker. At noon, hot and sweaty, they peered into the box to see the fruits of their labour. A thin patina of gold flecks stared back at them. They had realized about ten cents for their morning's work and consumed a bottle of bad schnapps worth $2.50. Both schnapps and their patience for hard work were exhausted. McGowan was resolved.

"I pitched the rocker, pick and shovel etc. into a deep canyon running past the claim and that finished the first days work we ever did in the mines," he wrote. "I saw there was money in the country and I wanted to get some of it before I left."[4]

The party returned to Yale the same evening. McGowan was in time to catch part of Douglas's inquiry into the Canyon War. But he had no intention of lingering in the town of the Vigilantes. He had decided to take Martin Gallagher up on his invitation.

McGowan Arrives at Hill's Bar

A ferry service consisting of two rowboats supplemented by Native canoes ran between Yale and Hill's Bar, connecting the two communities. It was in one of these small craft that McGowan arrived at Hill's Bar in September 1858. He found it quite changed from the boulder-strewn gravel bar Moore and his company had stumbled upon in March. McGowan saw miners working the bar in a long line stretching for over a mile along the shore. Some dug in the sand, some worked with rockers and still others were using sluices on their claims. Over seven hundred miners toiled in the confined space, earning between $10 and $50 a day on the richest bar in the Fraser River.

Stepping ashore, McGowan walked into the town proper. Hill's Bar was smaller than Yale, with a single road that was even muddier than Front Street. Its buildings were less permanent, mostly tents or hurriedly constructed log cabins. There were a few ramshackle hotels with fine, square fronts that belied the barnlike structures behind, which leaked and creaked. There was a single saloon. Hill's Bar, the original single-industry resource town, was not the centre of commerce Yale was — the real estate was too valuable to build on. Its residents tended to come and go more frequently, and they depended on Yale for supplies. The division between the mercantile class and the workers of British Columbia was established here. Just like San Francisco, Yale, under the rule of the purest and best, was the Sodom and Gomorrah of the gold fields, with gambling, prostitution and murder rampant. Hill's Bar, ruled by so-called lawless men, was quiet and orderly.

The transient nature of Hill's Bar helped McGowan and Dolan get in on the action of the gold fields. Gallagher and a number of the Boys from San Francisco were selling their shares in a claim. A new company was being formed, and Gallagher wanted McGowan to be part of it. Gallagher himself was returning to San Francisco to press a suit against the owners of the ship that had forcibly shipped him to Hawaii.[5] McGowan and Dolan bought in and became members of the Boatmen of San Francisco claim. They set to work and in three days made nearly $1,600. They continued to extract gold at this rate until winter set in.

Meanwhile, McGowan started making contacts with the main players in Yale: partly to protect his own interests and partly to keep an eye on Fifer. This naturally led him to the house of Ovid Allard. Soon Allard and McGowan were friends.

"I made myself agreeable to him [Allard] and his family," wrote McGowan. "He kept good, dark brandy, and had a pretty half-breed daughter. I made her a present of a new dress, and had taken her and her mother to a ball."[6]

McGowan became a confidante to Allard's daughter and discovered she was being courted by no less than three suitors: justice of the peace George Perrier, Fifer and "a young, good-looking Englishman — a captain of the police," likely William Kirby. McGowan, determined to frustrate Fifer, used his influence over Allard to lobby for his man, Perrier. Fifer responded by visiting the Allards frequently and regaling them with tales of McGowan's wickedness. His invective was reported back to McGowan, who swore he would get even one day.

"I saw him [Fifer] often at their house, but I bided my time," wrote McGowan. "I had made up my mind, however, to square accounts with my dapper little hospital steward who was playing the role of doctor."

It was perhaps fortunate for all concerned that Ms. Allard settled on her English policeman, for McGowan and Fifer would surely have come to blows had she chosen Perrier or the "dapper little hospital steward."[7] The two men would eventually end up engaged in fisticuffs, but not over Allard's daughter.

For the present, McGowan had plenty of money and was ensconced in a nice cabin on a bar full of friends and supporters from the Law and Order Party. But it was not like McGowan to stay out of the politics of any community in which he was living. In any case, controversy soon came knocking at Ned's door in the person of Richard Hicks, who was about to do his damnedest to put an end to McGowan's good times.

Richard Hicks

Richard Hicks, like McGowan, saw there was money to be made in the country and was determined to get some. The difference between the two men was that Hicks was willing to do anything to get his share — or anyone else's share, for that matter. Hicks was corrupt from the very start and went into public office with the sole intention of abusing it. This much was candidly admitted by his wife, Orinda, to no less a confessor than Bishop George Hills, the Anglican priest appointed as the Church of England's chief representative in British Columbia. On June 25, 1860, Hills spent the night at a roadside hut, the way station for the ferry at Spuzzum. There among the express-men, packers and miners he found a single female: "a seemingly worthy woman, a Mrs. Hicks, the wife of a man who held office under our government at Yale and was dismissed. [She] also resided in the house, or near, and did the housekeeping department."[8]

By this time, Orinda Hicks had been abandoned by her husband, who took out an ad in a San Francisco newspaper disavowing all her debts. She confessed all her husband's manifold sins to Bishop Hills, who was moved enough to note: "She alluded to her husband's defalcations and informed us [that] during his term of office he had made $5,000 dollars [or] 1,000 lbs, and that had he known all he knew afterwards, he could have made very much more."[9]

It is hard not to be impressed by the sheer scope of Hicks's malfeasance. Taking advantage of his position as revenue officer and assistant commissioner for Crown lands, he extorted "fees" and created an empire of bootleg liquor to pad his wallet. Using his power to license saloons and regulate the sale of liquor, Hicks granted a Mr. Kingham a monopoly on wholesale liquor dispensing. No one else in Yale could supply the numerous saloons and gaming houses. In return, Hicks received between a third and a quarter of the profits. Given the rate at which the miners drank, Hicks's share must have been prodigious. This was likely the principal source of Hick's income, but he had others.

The ferry at Spuzzum was one of his lesser scams. He had been publicly charged by Douglas to help open up the country and improve the road and transportation system. Hicks duly granted the ferry licence on December 4, 1858, to Mr. Franklin Way, on the condition that he, Hicks, would get half the proceeds.

When he wasn't whooping it up in one of Yale's many saloons, Hicks initially had his headquarters in a tent, temporary digs pending the construction of a government building. It was an arrangement that Hicks was at pains to remind Douglas of in every letter to the governor.

"I am, I assure Your Excellency, very uncomfortably located and all my books and papers are getting damp and mouldy . . . perhaps you will be pleased to order me a small stove," wrote Hicks, Bob Cratchit-like, to his master in Victoria.[10]

Despite his humble office, anyone who wanted to do business in and around Yale had to go through Hicks. When Land, Fleming and Co. approached him about building a sawmill to supply lumber for sluices and rocker boxes (not to mention all those new houses and government buildings), Hicks readily agreed to give them a licence and access to timber — as long as he was granted an interest in the venture.

Even the survey of the township of Yale, which had been entrusted to him, was not safe. Hicks altered the terms of the Crown leases without any authority from Douglas and started handing out pieces of the town to further his own interests. He stopped mining activities on two choice parcels of waterfront land that he had his eye on. To cover his tracks, he even had new official forms printed up.

"I have herewith forwarded copys [*sic*] of receipts for trading licences and receipts for Building lots which will be very much cheaper to have printed. It will also save much paper," Hicks wrote to Douglas in the fall of 1858.[11]

Claims in the new township overlapped and conflicted. In short order, the townsite was a mess. But Richard Hicks was getting richer.

Hicks's one failure was a scheme placed before him by none other than Dr. Max Fifer. The good doctor was rather liberal in his attitude towards the sick. He never turned anyone away because they could not afford to pay him. He had also been called upon by some government officials, including Hicks, to tend to prisoners in jail and conduct post-mortems on murder victims. Fifer gave his time freely, but he felt it only fair that the government should pay for the medical supplies used, which cost outrageous amounts on the gold fields. Laudanum was a dollar a drop, quinine $64 an ounce. Fifer approached Hicks about being compensated. Hicks agreed it was a just case. Fifer promptly wrote up his bill and gave it to the assistant commissioner to submit to Douglas.

Time passed and no word came from Victoria. Fifer got his opportunity to get the inside dope, literally, when, in late October, Hicks came to him complaining of feeling "quite bound up." Fifer must have enjoyed the sensation of coating his finger with lard and inserting it in the biggest rectum on the gold fields. It may have crossed his mind to raise the matter of his money right then and there, but he was polite enough to finish his exam, diagnose constipation and prescribe calomel while Hicks hitched up his britches before raising the thorny question of his expenses. Hicks, as usual, proposed a solution that would ultimately benefit himself. Fifer should draw up a proposal for Douglas, a contract with the colonial government, which he, Hicks, would present to the governor himself. Hicks would, of course, charge a modest fee in return — a cut of Fifer's salary.[12]

Fifer agreed and drew up his proposal on October 26, 1858. It was a very formal proposal to bill the colonial government for the care of the "indigent sick," furnish them with necessary drugs and medicines and, further, to carry out all post-mortems for the Yale district for the monthly fee of $100. Hicks sent off the proposal for B.C.'s first doctor's fee schedule on October 28, 1858. It was duly received by Douglas, who instructed his secretary, William Alexander George Young,[13] to write back and inform the doctor the proposal would be given "due consideration." Unfortunately for Fifer (and Hicks), this turned out to be the beginning of the first doctors' dispute with the B.C. government. Ultimately, in the spring of 1859, Douglas said no to this scheme.

Hicks had much more luck skimming funds using powers that were already in his command. As the official in charge of granting water rights, Hicks wielded an enormous amount of power and was open to an enormous amount of graft. Water was a vital resource on the Fraser, which may sound strange, but to work the sluices and engage in hydraulic mining it was crucial for miners to have access to the streams and creeks draining into the big river. The cost of building flumes to carry water to the various bars was an astronomical four to five thousand dollars, depending on the size of each project. Hicks reasoned that people with that kind of capital could afford to pay a little extra, so in October 1858 he granted several large companies water rights to build flumes to supply "more than one thousand claims." Taxes were to be $5 per flume and Hicks, naturally, would get his share of that revenue. Hicks estimated there would be over two thousand flumes and sluices in service in the next year, and that meant thousands of dollars in his pockets.

Hand in hand with water rights went the power to register mining claims. Hicks took money to record dubious claims, though often he didn't bother to register them officially — unless, of course, he was given a share of the profits. In such cases, Hicks would go to extraordinary lengths to make sure a claim was properly registered and approved. It was here that Hicks overreached his abilities and ran headlong into a formidable foe: Ned McGowan.

As early as September 1858, Hicks had figured out that coupling water rights with the registration of questionable claims was extremely lucrative. On September 21, 1858, Hicks granted a thirteen-member consortium thirteen claims on either side of one they already held on a bar called Prince Albert's Flat, south of Hill's Bar. The consortium had discovered "remunerative diggings" two hundred yards from the river. Even though claims were supposed to extend from the river only as far as the high water mark, Hicks personally measured off these claims to five hundred feet from the river.

For good measure, he also granted the consortium exclusive water rights. Hicks knew the large size of the claims was unprecedented, but told Douglas the gold deposit on the flat was eight feet down and otherwise, "it will not pay." He implied that it was the miners' idea: "It was to open these mines and encourage these men on that induced me to comply with their wishes," he wrote.[14]

Whatever the kickback Hicks received on this venture, it wasn't worth the trouble he was about to get into. He had set a very important precedent for all those other miners who were anxious to push their claims' boundaries as far as they could. Among them were the Boatmen of San Francisco, led by McGowan. There was a dispute on Hill's Bar as to just where the high water mark was. Many miners were eyeing the flat behind the hamlet with covetous eyes, for preliminary digging there had proved it very rich. If a claim could be stretched to extend five hundred feet from the river's edge on Prince Albert's Flat, why not on Hill's Bar?

On October 12, 1858, Hicks, Ovid Allard and two Native elders arrived on the bar to officially mark the high water line. They were joined by, among others, Henry Hickson, the constable for Hill's Bar (answerable to Perrier, the justice of the peace), and McGowan. The party spent an entire day going over the ground, Hicks relying on the expertise of the elders, who, he said "ought to know best the bounds of the river." McGowan, being a Philadelphia lawyer, disputed the proposed boundary. Whether Hicks tried to solicit a bribe or not is unclear, but what is certain is he and McGowan quarrelled. According to Hicks, the judge pulled a revolver and threatened him, which seems rather unlikely, given Hickson's presence.

That evening the Boatmen of San Francisco held a meeting on Hill's Bar and voted to send a "memorial" to Douglas protesting Hicks's actions and demanding his immediate removal. They also proposed they be empowered to write up their own mining regulations governing claims.

Meanwhile, in Yale, Hicks repaired to his damp, mouldy tent and dashed off a frantic, pre-emptive missive to Douglas. "Some of the miners have taken great offence, expecting they could dig up to the very mountain on this flat and indeed the mountain or side hill would soon be worked out," wrote Hicks, adding the miners had mistreated the Native elders. "The miners swore and insulted them to the disgrace of the white man as they call themselves. The fact is, there are a set of men on the river who are doing their utmost to treat the Authority with contempt and establish the same system as in California."[15]

But the memorial from Hill's Bar had its effect. Letters of complaint from other aggrieved parties were also starting to come across Douglas's desk. When asked by the governor to explain his conduct, Hicks fell back on an oft-played card: he blamed that notorious Yankee bad man, Ned McGowan, for all the trouble.

> *I am under the necessity of informing your excellency that the notorious Ned McGowan who is on Hill's Bar has been trying the last two days to excite the miners to revolt and I can prove that he asserted that your excellency "had better mind your own business in Victoria, for that he was the ruler of Hill's Bar and that if the miners would only stand by him he would put all Englishmen to defiance" and with oaths not fit to name openly declares he will be master of Hill's Bar — such men as these are the first to ask for protection, the last to obey.*[16]

Hicks was already in trouble with the governor and didn't need any attention drawn to him at the time. Douglas was, if nothing else, a devil about details, especially when it came to money, and though Richard Hicks was nothing if not energetic in accumulating wealth for himself, he had a deficiency when it came to collecting money for the Crown. For a man employed by Old Square Toes, this was a fatal flaw.

One of Hicks's most important tasks, in Douglas's eyes, was to collect the $5 monthly mining licence. Real cash was often scarce on the bars, and many miners paid in gold dust. But the money had to be accounted for, down to the cent. What with the money pouring in from his other ventures, Hicks could scarcely be bothered collecting the fees, let alone recording those funds he did manage to bring in. His books were rudimentary at best and misleading at worst. Hicks did send $3,525 in cash and gold dust for mining licences to Victoria in August 1858, in the middle of the Canyon War when mining was at a low ebb. After that he almost ceased to bother with such trifles. In October he told Douglas he had excused some 876 miners from paying their fees as "they are ... hardly making $1 a day." Others simply refused to pay, unconvinced their fees would ever make it into government coffers. Two weeks later, Hicks suggested collecting the mining licence fees quarterly as opposed to monthly. This would save him the bother of the monthly journey up and down the river.

If Douglas was annoyed by Hicks's inability to collect every last penny of the miners' fees, he was alarmed when he learned of another deal Hicks had scribbled down on a stray bit of paper. On October 1, 1858, in a handwritten note,[17] Hicks granted Joseph M. Williams and two other partners a claim for a silver mine eight miles up a creek east of French Bar, just above Emory's Bar. Hicks gave them a half mile along the vein and fifty yards on either side. Pressed on the point by Douglas, Hicks admitted he had obtained a share in the venture. "Mr. Williams gave me one fourth interest in the mine. I trust I shall not be overstepping my duty in accepting it. This is my first speculation. I hope it will turn out rich. I will forward your excellency some of the ore."[18]

By today's standard, this was a pretty obvious conflict of interest. But Douglas was too busy at the moment to attend to it. He was preparing for the official proclamation of the Crown colony of British Columbia and his new duties as governor, dealing with Lytton's unending stream of directives, under attack by a hostile press in Victoria (led by Amor De Cosmos's *Colonist*) and in one of the most curious quirks of fate, at his wits' end with none other than John Nugent. The newspaper editor and McGowan's stout friend had pulled a few strings to get an appointment from fellow Democrat, President James Buchanan, that July. He presented his credentials to Douglas as special agent of the United States government on September 20, 1858. Officially, Nugent was supposed to look out for the interests of U.S. citizens on the gold fields. Unofficially, he was an anti-British agent whose views on Manifest Destiny were well known. His appointment had been marked by rejoicing and meetings featuring congratulatory messages to Washington, D.C., in Fort Yale and on Hill's, Texas and New York bars.

Douglas was well aware that another U.S. special agent, Thomas Larkin, had arrived in the Mexican state of California a decade earlier and promptly started conniving with the American populace there to have the U.S. annex the territory. A week after Nugent's arrival, his newspaper, the San Francisco *Herald*, had observed that since there were far more Americans in New Caledonia than British subjects, "the presence of an American war vessel of suitable force, such as the Frigate *Merrimac*, would, therefore, be a desirable feature in the neighborhood of Victoria." Nugent himself immediately set about giving Douglas a diplomatic struggle by demanding American lawyers be empowered to represent U.S. citizens before British courts in the colony. Douglas saw this as an infringement of British sovereignty and refused. After holding meetings of American citizens at his hotel in Victoria, whipping them into a fine frenzy, Nugent set off for the gold fields in an attempt to exploit this "injustice." He managed to stir some embers of discontent, caused in most cases by empty gold pans rather than any patriotic fervour, but his efforts met with little overall success. Upon returning to Victoria, Nugent found a furious Douglas would only communicate with him by letters via his secretary, Young.[19]

In the end, however, the steady stream of complaints about Hicks pouring into Victoria could not be ignored. Nor could Douglas accept Hicks's increasingly desperate excuses for not providing an accounting of revenues. Hicks tried to explain the lack of revenue from fees never collected by pleading the poverty of many miners. He was unable to give further details about the silver mine because he suddenly realized he didn't know its exact location (even though he'd written up the claim himself). But surely the bureaucratic keeper of them all came on November 1, 1858, when Hicks tried to convince Douglas that he couldn't give an exact accounting of his office expenses because "the furniture hasn't arrived yet."

"My office will be ready as soon as I get the fixtures from Victoria.

I must therefore ask your indulgence until that is completed," Hicks wrote. "I beg to assure your excellency kept the expenses down all in my power. I have not spent one penny wastefully."

Things came to a head on November 12, 1858, the day before Hicks was due to at long last move out of his tent and into the new government building on Front Street. It had been raining for a solid week. Hicks was already suffering from a vicious cold and was depressed under his canvas. But he was appalled to learn that McGowan, seeking to nudge Douglas into action, had organized a petition against him and had published it in Victoria. McGowan followed this up by taking out an advertisement in the Victoria newspapers denouncing Hicks as unfit for office. Hicks at once dashed off a letter in his spidery handwriting to Douglas, claiming the case made against him by McGowan was a fabrication.

"I feel assured your excellency will treat it with the contempt it deserves," Hicks wrote. "I am, sir, ashamed to be so constantly brought to notice by my public conduct . . . [Americans] are a disgrace to civilized society and I defy any officer in power to satisfy their grasping propensities."[20]

But even as Hicks finally moved into his office (a modest, four-room affair, which also served as his residence), Douglas had already decided to act. He needed someone to keep an eye on Hicks. Unfortunately, the governor could not have picked a worse watchdog.

Peter Brunton Whannell

Douglas had met Peter Brunton Whannell on August 28, 1858, just before he set out on his Canyon War fact-finding mission. It was Sunday and the governor was smoking his forbidden pipe in the garden. It was an island of peace amidst the chaos that had engulfed Victoria. Bounded by a shrubbery of spreading willows, it was full of daisies and other bright flowers. Douglas was sitting by two large arbours covered in green grape vines that he had brought from Fort Vancouver, a reminder of his lost empire in Oregon, when his moment of tranquillity was interrupted by the arrival of an insistent petitioner.

A tall, slender man appeared under the arbour wearing a deep green uniform, dripping with gold braid and with red facings on the collar and cuffs. The helmet, carried respectfully under the man's arm, was of black leather, surmounted by a black plume of Prince of Wales feathers and with a corps badge fitted on front. The badge showed a crowned garter with the initials "VYC" in the centre. A magnificent sash, a silver belt buckle fashioned like a snake, and a gold-hilted sword completed the impression of an officer and a gentleman. That was just the impression that Peter Brunton Whannell wanted to convey — an impression that was as far from the truth as Whannell was from his birthplace.

Douglas conducted his interview with Whannell as they walked in the garden. The governor needed British subjects to fill official positions. But pressed as he was, Douglas could not immediately offer Whannell a post as they ambled about under the willows. He promised he would keep the dashing-looking Whannell in mind if anything came up. It would be two months before Douglas made good on his promise. It would be a further two months before he regretted it.

Whannell was born on July 23, 1816, in Madras, India, and baptized at St. Mary's Church. He was the son of Colonel Peter Thomas Whannell, deputy military auditor-general for Madras. His mother was Eliza, nee Bulow. Raised in India, Whannell was in England in his twenties, serving as an ensign in the Argyleshire Militia. His father attempted to get him a job with the Nizam of Madras. The request was not granted and Whannell remained in Britain, landing a job with the Bank of England on December 15, 1840.

A few months earlier, on April 21, 1840, Whannell had married Maria Jane Blake, the daughter of a well-connected colonial administration family from Madras, whom he had met in London. Maria Jane, eighteen at the time, was the youngest daughter of the late Thomas Blake and grandniece to Sir Edmund Stanley, formerly the lord chief justice of Madras. The blessed event took place in St. Pancras Old Church in London. Their first daughter, Maria Lily Whannell, was born in London the following year.

The newlyweds had to move three times within two years as Whannell knocked about the branches of the Bank of England. He started in the London cash booking office, then moved to the Birm-

The officers of Whannell's former outfit show off the splendid uniforms that helped Peter Brunton land a government job in British Columbia. It's easy to see how Douglas could mistake Whannell for an officer. The Yeomanry Cavalry formed in 1855 to defend Australia from attack by Russian forces.

ingham branch in June 1842. Just two months later he was off to Plymouth. Whannell realized that his career prospects with the bank were limited. When his father wrote to him and asked him to come back to India, Whannell quit and set sail for Madras in December 1842. En route, the Whannells' second daughter, Catherine Margaret, was born at sea off the Cape of Good Hope in April 1843.

Back on the subcontinent, Whannell got a job as a postmaster in Trichinpoly at the salary of 1,200 rupees a year. Maria Jane continued to produce children — four in India, three of whom died as infants. Whannell's return to India was frustrating for the ambitious young man. Despite his wife's connections, he was not advancing in the colonial administration, so in 1851, Whannell decided to try his luck in Australia.

Whannell tried to forge a new life for himself and his wife and children in Melbourne, the gateway to the New South Wales gold fields, but the best he could do was a job at the port customs house. Whannell started as a landing waiter, at a salary of £500 annually, on September 19, 1853. It was one of the lowest jobs on the customs totem pole. A glorified clerk, Whannell checked goods landed on the Melbourne wharves against the ship's manifest.

Despite his lowly position, Whannell considered himself a gentleman. A horse lover, he eagerly joined up when the Victoria Volunteer Yeomanry Corps was formed in 1855 to protect Australia from invasion by the Russians during the Crimean War. He spent £60 he didn't have to do so, and, like the other gentlemen of the corps, he provided his own equipment, including that lavish uniform. Whannell boasted that he had been a member of his father's regiment, the Nigaria Brigade, back in Madras. Whether it was because they suspected this was a falsehood or because Whannell couldn't afford to purchase a commission, the officers of the regiment were content for Whannell to remain a trooper. Nor did he get along with the corps' commander, Lt.-Col. James H. Ross. An able and experienced cavalryman, Ross watched Whannell's performance on the exercise ground and concluded that the man had never been in an Indian cavalry regiment.

For three years Whannell toiled on Melbourne's rough and wild waterfront, trying to support his lifestyle and his ever-expanding family. Maria Jane had produced two more children since their arrival in New South Wales.[21] She was pregnant again when, on February 1, 1856, Whannell was demoted from landing waiter to locker. A locker supervised a bonded warehouse and was in charge of its keys. Little better than a security guard, the position paid just £350 a year. Whannell now had real problems. His income had been substantially cut just when he'd taken a mistress. Georgina Henrietta Alford was young (by a strange coincidence, just eighteen, the same age Maria Jane had been when she and Whannell were married), already married and quite beautiful. Faced with a choice between his wife and his mistress, Whannell chose the latter and left the pregnant Maria Jane and the children that month.

For the next nine months, Whannell and his mistress lived the high life in the port's rowdy bars and gaming houses. Soon, he was desperately short of money. Maria Jane had gone to court and sued him for child support.[22] He may have resorted to thievery — certainly that was hinted at when Whannell was fired from his job with customs on November 1, 1856. Drinking away his sorrows in one of the dark, seedy gaming houses of the Melbourne port, Whannell considered fleeing the country with Georgina, but he was nearly penniless. Where was he going to raise enough money? It was then, through the smoke and blue haze of the saloon, that Whannell saw his ticket out of town.

He must have seemed an easy mark, the thin-featured, nervous young English clerk, wearing a high white collar to hide the "port-wine stain" that spread from ear to ear, discolouring his neck. But William Holdman Branson suffered from more than *Nevus Flammeus*, the reddish discolouration of his skin. Branson, thirty-two, had arrived from London five years earlier aboard the *City of Manchester*, hoping to make his fortune in the colonies. All he had managed to attain was a position as a clerk at businessman John Dight's firm. Disappointed, self-conscious, Branson's ego suffered a further serious blow after his wife left him. He was utterly alone and wretched. It was all too easy for Whannell to befriend him, and in the gaming halls of Melbourne, Branson let his thin, greasy brown hair down enough for Whannell to notice a certain desperation in his dark eyes and his play around the tables.

When Whannell sidled up to Branson on that November evening, the clerk had just started his brief career as an embezzler. His first theft was all of £70 and 16 shillings. Branson had cooked the books, making it look like a banking error. He was now trying to win enough money at the gaming tables to pay back his ill-gotten gains, but without success. It was small-time stuff and could have easily been repaid before Dight was the wiser. But Whannell played his mark well, hooking him solidly before reeling him in. Over the next few days Whannell encouraged Branson to gamble, to whore and to drink.

"With my own wickedness of heart in his [Whannell's] society, I gambled and lost, and indulged in late hours and much vice, and alas! my embarrassments increased!" wrote Branson in a public letter of apology to Dight.[23]

Branson took more and more from his employer to cover his new debts. Finally, Branson unburdened himself, telling Whannell they had been spending Dight's money. Whannell scoffed at the youngster's concerns. In for a penny, mate, in for a pound, was his attitude. If Branson had been skimming, then why not make it worthwhile? Steal a really large amount and ship out with Whannell and his "wife" to Callao, Peru.

Absolutely desperate, Branson agreed. He stole over £200 and turned it over to Whannell, who promptly bought some new clothes for himself and Georgina, as well as three passages to Callao. Whannell and his mistress went under the name of "Mister and Mrs. Stanley," borrowing the name of his wife's uncle (Whannell listed his "wife's" age as twenty-four). They were set to sail aboard the *Zaboah* on November 7, 1856. Whannell had the money and Branson's luggage. But on the way to the docks, Branson got cold feet. He had too little stomach and too much conscience to be a real criminal. He also mistrusted Whannell and suspected a double cross. Branson told Whannell he could not leave, and Whannell simply abandoned his partner in crime, leaving the panic-stricken clerk to face the music alone. Whannell and Georgina were the only two passengers aboard as the ship pulled away from the quay and headed north with Branson's money and belongings.

After a few days, Branson changed his mind yet again. Terrified of being caught and sent to one of Australia's infamous penal settlements, he resolved to follow Whannell. He booked passage for Callao the following week on the steamer *Echo*, but as he sat in his berth, waiting for the ship to set sail, no fewer than five officers of Dight's company came aboard to confront the would-be absconder. Realizing he'd been found out, Branson bolted before he could be arrested and went into hiding around Melbourne. A warrant was issued for his arrest on November 22, 1856, on charges of embezzlement of £500 from his employer. Dight put up a reward of £50 for his capture. Branson stayed at large for a short time before turning himself in. He threw himself on the mercy of the court, pleading guilty in February 1857. Although he confessed his wrongdoing thoroughly, he made it clear that Whannell had put him up to it.

"I fell in with a man whose society I had previously shunned, and of whom my poor wife and others warned me, but in vain. This man was Whannell of the Customs," wrote Branson. "I do humbly hope and pray that you will, Sir, deal mercifully with me. On my own account I ask nothing. I can only confess that I am exceedingly guilty. The agony of a self-accusing conscience and the bitterness of remorse, constitutes a severer punishment than any other that could be inflicted."[24]

Mr. Justice Molesworth was sufficiently moved by Branson's sincere remorse and mitigated his sentence. In May of that year, Branson received two years in a penal colony. He was paroled in June 1858, just over a year later and just before Whannell started mischief anew in another Victoria.

Whannell and Georgina arrived safely in Callao, then, using Branson's money, took ship to San Francisco. Perhaps because he'd told Branson he intended to sail to San Francisco and was worried about pursuit, or maybe because high office still eluded him, Whannell ended up in Shaw's Flat, a small mining town in Tuolumne County, California — James Moore's old stomping grounds. One of the original centres of the rush of 1849, it was a tough town. Whannell was reduced to running one of its many saloons.

In August 1858, Whannell succumbed to gold fever once again and joined the hordes flocking to the Fraser River. He and Georgina arrived in Victoria on August 27. The next day, Whannell donned his fancy uniform and called upon Douglas in his garden. Sword clanking, he dropped just enough offhand hints and remarks to lead the governor to believe he was a Crimean War veteran, a captain of the Victoria Volunteer Yeomanry Corps and before that, a trooper in the Nigaria Cavalry in the East Indies.

On October 28, 1858, Douglas appointed Whannell justice of the peace for Yale. He was also expected to act as the postmaster for no extra pay. Douglas told Whannell that if he performed his duties well and faithfully, he could expect promotion to bigger and better positions. Delighted, Whannell immediately made arrangements to travel to Yale. After that initial meeting, however, it cannot be said he started off on the right foot with Douglas. No sooner had he boarded the *Otter* than Whannell filed a travel expense claim. Enraged that he, his wife and his luggage were not given free passage, he wrote an indignant letter to the penny-pinching Douglas on November 13, 1858, informing the governor he had already spent his $100 advance and demanding more cash. He received no further expense money.

Whannell and Georgina arrived at Yale on November 17, 1858, at five o'clock in the afternoon. Hicks was on hand to greet them. Hicks liked Mrs. Whannell "very much," telling Douglas she "appears like a fine young English woman," but he loathed Peter Whannell on sight. Hicks was an Englishman, born and bred, and considered Whannell, who had been born in India and lived in Australia, little better than a convict. The feeling was mutual. Whannell would later tell Douglas that he didn't consider Hicks beneath him, just "contemptible." But at first, the two men maintained a facade of civility.

"The Captain is busy making his house arrangements. I have afforded him every assistance," Hicks assured Douglas in his November 17, 1858, missive. If Hicks really did have any hand at all in arranging the Whannells' accommodation in a small cottage, it was the last help Richard Hicks would offer Peter Brunton Whannell.

By all accounts, Whannell no sooner arrived in Yale than he went mad with power. In the morning he would dress in his uniform and walk to work down Front Street, past the hotels, saloons, gaming houses and restaurants, until he reached a bar that caught his eye. He'd walk into the saloon, have two or three stiff drinks, then continue down the sidewalk. Often he'd draw his sword and slash the air, cutting back and forth, clearing a path before him, shouting: "I am the law and this sword is my voice!"[25] Bystanders had to leap aside to avoid being hacked. Then Whannell would enter his log-cabin courtroom and dispense an unequal justice. It was quite a transformation for the former saloon keeper and locker.

Whannell cut a swath through Yale society in the same manner. He once broke up a party attended by the town's business and social elite by swinging his sword around wildly. The guests abandoned their galoshes and topcoats and scrambled over snow banks to escape the judge's slashes. If he was a bit wild in polite company, Whannell was absolutely contemptuous of the average worker. William Yates got a dose of the judge's arrogance when he dropped by to check on the mail.

"Judge Ounell [*sic*] was a tall, spare man," Yates remembered. "He was very overbearing. I went one time to the post office to ask for letters. The judge turned around and said 'No — no letters for you or your firm. Why don't you take your hat off when you come in here?' I said I did not know it was necessary to take my hat off when I came to ask for letters. 'Yes,' he said. 'And I want you to wipe your feet too.'"[26]

This kind of behaviour cut no ice with the small Anglo-American elite, nor with the many Californian miners who recognized the judge from his days in Shaw's Flat. They could only shake their heads and wonder what Douglas had been thinking in appointing such a man. Hicks they knew was corrupt, but Whannell was crazy and in charge of the justice system. In Yale, the law truly was an ass.

The Colony of British Columbia

Certainly the lack of English manpower had something to do with the dubious appointments of Hicks and Whannell. Yet Douglas was sometimes reluctant to make use of capable men if he took a dislike to them or, worse still, thought their services were being foisted upon him. Such was the case on November 8, 1858, when a ship arrived in Victoria with reinforcements for the beleaguered governor. Captain John Marshall Grant's detachment of twelve Royal Engineers (bolstering the advance guard of twenty, led by Captain Robert Parsons, which had reached Victoria on October 29, 1858) were welcome.

But on the same ship was a man Douglas wanted nothing to do with: Chartres Brew.

Brew was a veteran of the Royal Irish Constabulary and had served with that force during the Crimean War. He almost didn't get to the new colony at all. Brew was one of the 528 passengers and crew aboard the German steamer *Austria* when it caught fire in the mid Atlantic. Brew was praised afterwards for trying to save the ship by taking the wheel after the officer steering the *Austria* fainted. Brew turned the steamer into the wind, but the fire spread quickly and the ship was doomed. He helped as many passengers as possible escape before the ship went down, still burning. Brew himself survived by clinging to a half-burned lifeboat. He was one of only sixty-seven survivors who were rescued and taken to Halifax. Penniless and with nothing but the clothes on his back, Brew managed to convince the authorities in Halifax to loan him £100 so he could continue his journey, which he did immediately, arriving just a week behind schedule.

Brew was supposed to be B.C.'s first inspector of police, but Douglas did not want Brew or his police force, which was to consist of 150 officers recruited from the Royal Irish Constabulary. This would cost the new colony a fortune. Relying on the Royal Navy and the Royal Engineers was more cost-efficient because the home government (i.e., London) paid for the expense. The penurious Douglas gave Brew the cold shoulder, ignoring his letters and reports and finding other, more pressing, duties for him to attend to that had nothing to do with policing.[27]

Two days before Whannell reached Yale, a somewhat more welcome official arrived from England. The remarkable Matthew Baillie Begbie, B.C.'s first chief justice, had, like Douglas, been born in the colonies, in South Africa, at the Cape of Good Hope, in 1819. Educated at Cambridge, Begbie definitely had an eccentric side. A striking six foot, four inches in height, straight as a flagpole and possessed of tremendous energy, when not holding court on horseback, "Dear Matthew" was a dandy of sorts. He often walked to official functions in Victoria dressed like an Elizabethan courtier,

Begbie swearing Douglas in as governor of British Columbia on November 19, 1858. A cold, wet, dismal day forced the ceremonies inside the fort. The governorship was a mixed victory for Douglas, who was forced to sever his ties with the Hudson's Bay Company and give up his Company pension in exchange for viceregal status.

complete with velvet breeches, flowing cape and big-buckled boots, leading a pack of spaniels. He sang in the church choir and had a surprisingly high voice for such an imposing figure.[28] Begbie specialized in contract law, and while he knew the ins and outs of wills and trusts, he'd never argued a criminal case before his appointment as chief justice. But he was bright and witty and well-loved. He was an instant hit with the ladies of Victoria, for he was a bachelor of forty when he arrived, and he remained single to the end of his days.

Begbie officiated at the ceremonies in Fort Langley marking the birth of British Columbia as a Crown colony. It was November 19, 1858, and typically for B.C., it was pouring rain and freezing cold. The grey, gloomy clouds hung low overhead as Douglas disembarked from the HBC steamer *Beaver* with his entourage, which included Admiral Baynes, Begbie, David Cameron (chief justice of Vancouver Island[29]), and others. They walked carefully up the slick, slippery clay slope that led from the Fraser River to the palisades, accompanied by an honour guard of Royal Engineers commanded by Captain Grant. An eighteen-gun salute boomed out from the *Beaver*. Douglas entered the fort, passing under a Union Jack, which, according to the *Victoria Gazette*'s correspondent, "was floating, or to speak the truth, dripping over the principal entrance."

Because of the weather, Douglas, his entourage and a small crowd of a hundred or so witnesses had to cram into the fort's main building for the solemnities. Douglas and Begbie stood by a stone fireplace, next to a small desk. Douglas swore Begbie in as chief justice of British Columbia. Having had his commission officially laid upon him, Begbie then installed Douglas as governor of the new colony. Douglas went through all the legal formalities: proclaiming the Act Establishing British Columbia; declaring that English law would be the law of the colony; and, finally, officially revoking the Hudson's Bay Company's exclusive trade privileges on the mainland. For Douglas, it must have been a bittersweet moment. On one hand, it was his hour of triumph. He had almost single-handedly preserved the territory for the British Crown. But the cost was the forced severing of all ties with the company that had been his life for thirty-seven years.

It was a full day's work. The ceremonies were over. The task of governing had officially begun. But the unofficial government apparatus Douglas had already put in place was about to precipitate McGowan's War.

SIX

To Rule a Fierce Democracy

As soon as Brunton Whannell arrived in Yale, complaints about Richard Hicks reached his ear. A steady parade of people let the new justice of the peace know just what sort of man his brother civil servant was. Given Whannell's fondness for saloons, one of the first things he learned of was Hicks's liquor licensing racket. Whannell saw a chance to advance his career at Hicks's expense, but he needed proof before he could approach Douglas. Whatever verbal exchanges he had with Hicks proved unsatisfactory, for on December 1, 1858, he followed the time-honoured rule of the mandarin — Always put your version of the truth down in writing — and penned a memo to his fellow bureaucrat. Whannell stated that he, as magistrate of the district, had power over licensing and demanded he immediately be provided with a list of all retail and wholesale liquor licences, as well as all merchant licences.

Hicks must have been aghast. This threatened one of his most lucrative sources of income. He fired back a memo of his own the same day, refusing to comply. Not to be outdone, Whannell sent another missive — still on the same day — threatening to visit each and every business in Yale, demand to see their licence and fine those who did not have the proper documentation. In the face of this threat, Hicks backed down and completed the battle of the duelling memos of December 1, 1858, by stating the whole thing had been "a misunderstanding."

When Hicks finally submitted his rather sketchy records on

December 3, he sent along an apologia as well. The prose is tortured as Hicks tries to emulate Douglas's style and is not up to it.

> *Sir: I have the honour of enclosing herewith a list of licenses Traders in the Town of Fort Yale for your guidance. Wessy, Yorke, Kingman and Burnett have paid their annual license. The others have paid a quarter's license only.*
>
> *1. – With respect to the collection of the licenses, my instructions from His Excellency the Governor were not to oppress the miner or trader but encourage them all in my power. I have carried out those instructions and I regret very much that at this season of the year the means about to be resorted to will drive what few inhabitants are now here entirely out of the territory.*
>
> *2. – In a Country like this, it must not be expected that laws and regulations can be so strictly enforced were [sic] there are so many conflicting elements to contend against and the facilities very limited and with but a small protecting force at command.*
>
> *3. – In granting quarterly licenses to retail liquor dealers, I was compelled to resort to that course to conciliate all parties and to raise a revenue to carry on the Government of my district — and all the acts of Her Majesty's servants are approved and indemnified by the recent Proclamation.*
>
> *4. – With regard to the legality of my having the power to issue liquor licenses, which I understand you question — I have to state that that power was conferred on me by my instructions from His Excellency the Governor. In England, I am perfectly aware that no one Justice of the Peace can license any house, it must be done by a bench of Magistrate's in quarter Sessions — therefore by the strict letter of the law, the same will apply here — I however do not believe that it was or is the intention of His Excellency to disturb the present arrangement until the whole Government machinery came into operation.*
>
> *5. – You will find it very difficult to please a mixed people that we have here. I have found it so and altho' I have displeased a few aspirants to office, yet I have had the confidence and support of the intelligent portion of the community.*

6. – With these remarks, I beg most respectfully to solicit your advice and co-operation and that by our mutual exertions we shall be able to gain the good will of the inhabitants of Fort Yale without compromising ourselves.

I have the honour to remain your most ob. hble. serv., Richard Hicks, Assistant Commissioner of the District of Fort Yale.[1]

Hicks's appeal for understanding of what he considered the unique circumstances in Yale fell on deaf ears. Whannell felt he had the proof he needed to nail Hicks and sent a long letter to Douglas, informing the governor he had "discovered a system of partiality has been in existence in the granting of wholesale and retail liquor licenses." Whannell informed Douglas of the monopoly granted Kingham and described how saloons that played ball with Hicks were allowed easy payment plans for their licences, while three merchants who refused to cooperate had been forced to shell out $600 in cash on the spot in order to continue operating.[2] Whannell went further: he sent summonses to all those merchants and saloon operators he deemed "delinquent," ordering them to show up at his office and pay their fees by December 9, 1858, or face closure. Hicks, not to be outdone, wrote to Douglas himself, countering with allegations that Whannell's fines and sentences were "cruel."

Whannell's interference in Hicks's affairs couldn't have come at a worse time for the crooked commissioner. He was at that moment facing more charges against his character and conduct. Douglas was upset over reports that Hicks had been drunk and disorderly in public and was fond of doing his business in gaming houses. Worse, a certain I.G. Hawley had made allegations of wrongdoing against Hicks that were so serious the commissioner was compelled to send documents to Crown Solicitor George Pearkes to rebut the accusations. In fact, he was headed to Victoria on December 6, 1858, to defend himself. Wary of what Whannell would do in his absence, Hicks locked his office / house and gave the key to his assistant (a Native referred to only as "Tom"), ordering the man to guard it. Then he boarded a steamer for the capital.

Hicks's fears were well-founded. No sooner had he gone than

Whannell tried to get into the office. When he learned Hicks had entrusted Tom with the only key, he roughly dismissed the assistant and broke into the building. He then tore Hicks's office apart, looking for evidence. Finding none, Whannell went into Hicks's bedroom and threw all his bedding and personal possessions onto the pile of papers heaped up in the office. By nightfall, Whannell and Georgina were comfortably ensconced in Hicks's house.

When Hicks returned, Whannell forbade him to sleep in the building. Hicks still had his office there, though, so by day the two feuding officials spent much of their time cheek by jowl. Despite this proximity, they had ceased to communicate in anything but official memos. The only words they exchanged after this came when Hicks arrived at the office one morning after a night of drinking and became abusive, using what Whannell delicately called "epithets" in despatches to Douglas. Whannell was no stranger to invective, but he was offended that Hicks used such language in front of his wife.

"This aged man ... blaspheming and using indecent epithets," Whannell complained to Douglas in a letter. "I have only wondered how it was possible for so grey-headed a man to make use of such foul language."[3]

Battle Lines Are Drawn

The power struggle between Whannell and Hicks was the subject of much amusement on the gold fields at a time when a little light entertainment was desperately needed. Winter had set in and mining had stopped. The steep mountain walls of the Cascades, clad in thick forests, made Yale a dark, gloomy place when the days got shorter and the sun lower. Everything was soaked with rain or coated with frost. The sluice boxes and flumes dripped sullenly. As the temperature plunged, ice formed in the river, mining equipment became half frozen, and gravel that was barely thawed enough to run down the riffled sluices first slowed, then stopped work. The miners were crowded into cabins choked blue by tobacco smoke as kerosene lamps burned yellow. Red-hot stoves filled with green wood gave off their indifferent heat, and steam from wet clothing mingled with the stench of the unwashed miners. It was enough to drive many to drink. But the war between Hicks and Whannell would soon deprive them of even this consolation.

On December 24, 1858, the thirteen saloons that lined Front Street in Fort Yale were doing a booming Christmas Eve business. The rules for payment in these establishments were simple: if you were broke, you could charge it. If you had money, you paid up, in cash or in gold dust. In a saloon owned by Americans Billy Foster and John Anderson, a young Irish miner, Bernard Rice, was having a few drinks. Rice, who worked a claim just above Yale, was known to be flush with money, unlike many of his fellow miners. But when Foster demanded he pay up, Rice refused. An argument ensued and ended with Foster showing Rice the door. Shortly afterwards, Rice reappeared in the doorway of the saloon with a gun in his hand aimed at Foster. Without hesitation, Foster drew and fired his own gun, killing Rice instantly. The dead man was examined on the floor of the saloon. Someone opened Rice's pistol and discovered it hadn't been loaded.

In the normal American way of justice just south of the border (wherever that was), the shooting would have caused little excitement. Foster could claim self-defence. The fact that Rice's gun was empty didn't signify — the threat of a brandished pistol would have been enough in any Californian courtroom. But this wasn't San Francisco. An American barkeeper had murdered a British subject in what Whannell considered an unlicensed establishment. Foster must have had a pretty good idea of the pains Whannell would take to bring him to what he would consider unequal justice. He wisely fled.

Whannell descended on the Foster-Anderson saloon and demanded the murderer be surrendered to him. Anderson told Whannell that he had not seen Foster for an hour. Whannell, frustrated, arrested Anderson and his servant, Allmeyer, and dragged them both into court. Determined to set an example, Whannell set bail for Anderson at the absurd level of $10,000 and for Allmeyer, $1,500. Anderson paid some in cash and used his assets as security for the balance of the bond. Whannell took the opportunity to seize the rest of the saloon's assets, even though he had no legal right to do so. When Allmeyer — who had nothing to do with the murder — couldn't make bail, Whannell threw him in jail.

Whannell also held an inquest. According to McGowan, Whannell discovered a money belt containing $600 on Rice's body and kept it for himself.[4] There's no proof the story was true, but tales like this about Whannell spread quickly in Yale and were believed at once, further fanning the flames of discontent among the miners.

Whannell's next actions raised the temperature even further. He determined to use the murder to shut down all the establishments licensed by Hicks. Yale's six-man police force was obviously too small, so he appointed three more men to the detachment and swore in several "special constables" for good measure, spending a considerable sum of Douglas's money to raise a squad of about a dozen. Not everyone cooperated. William Kirby, a former policeman who had resigned after the American William Dounellar was appointed chief of police, refused to be sworn in as a special constable. A puffed-up Whannell noted as much in his report to Douglas a week later. But Whannell still had sufficient manpower to shut down Front Street the day before Christmas. The American saloon keepers were furious and so were their customers. So too was Hicks. But with a British subject lying dead, murdered by an American citizen, he could not oppose his colleague. Whannell posted a $100 reward for Foster's capture, hoping the size of the bounty would be enough for some desperate miner to turn him in.

Whannell soon learned that Foster had fled to Hill's Bar, where he found protection under McGowan's wing. Learning of Whannell's saloon closures, McGowan took aside Justice of the Peace Perrier (who he considered "a devilish good fellow") and convinced him to write a letter to his counterpart in Yale, requesting the bars be allowed to reopen. The letter sent Whannell into paroxysms of rage. He demanded Foster be handed over to him. But Perrier held firm. There would be no search of Hill's Bar by a Fort Yale magistrate.

Dr. Fifer seized upon this moment in the same manner that the Vigilance Committee of 1856 had used the death of James King of William. After all, was not history repeating itself? There was a murderer at large, harboured by "lawless" men who had defied those trying to bring him to justice. Fifer and others convened a meeting in Yale to discuss the possibility of organizing a Vigilance Committee on British soil. McGowan and the Boys heard the news and were determined, at all costs, to prevent any such committee from becoming organized.

So, on a sullen Christmas Eve, the battle lines were drawn. Americans were set against British subjects. The Vigilantes were gearing up for battle in Yale. On Hill's Bar, McGowan, Dolan and the Boatmen of San Francisco pondered their next move. The only thing on which almost all parties could agree was that Whannell was a pompous fool for closing the bars and saloons on Christmas Eve.

The Christmas Dance

Christmas 1858 would see no peace or goodwill between men in Yale. For many of the miners celebrating in their tents and shacks along the banks of the Fraser, there was little to be thankful for. They were in a foreign land, it was cold and snowy, and there wasn't a legal drink to be had. The diggings hadn't been as rich as they had heard and it was anyone's guess how long it would be before the weather improved so they could return to work and try their luck again.

Given the events of the preceding twenty-four hours, the Christmas dance held in Yale was a rather tense affair as Law and Order supporters rubbed shoulders with their Vigilance Committee counterparts. The festive atmosphere was further spoiled by Hicks, who went to the dance with two constables in tow, hoping to catch Foster.

The dance was attended by every race and nationality on the gold fields, including a number of blacks and Natives, free to party under the protection of British law. Some of the white American miners took exception to this.[5] Many of the white American miners were from slave-owning states and could not accept the freedoms granted non-whites. The spectacle of black policemen and Nlaka'pamux magistrates under the rule of a mulatto governor married to a half-breed woman must have been hard for some of the Americans to swallow, and the sight of black miners dancing with Native women may have been the last straw.

Whether it was personal or purely a matter of race, two men from Hill's Bar, Farrell and Burns, picked a fight with Isaac Dixon. One of the first arrivals in the wave of black immigrants, Dixon was Yale's barber and was known as "Ikey."[6] Although small in stature, Ikey was, as D.W. Higgins describes him, "a saucy and presumptuous creature with a mischief-making tongue in his head." Dixon had met all sorts of ruffians in the boomtown. One day, California bad man Tom O'Neill entered his shop, laid his revolver on his lap and threatened to shoot Dixon if he drew a single drop of blood. O'Neill didn't know it, but he was fortunate Dixon managed to shave him without cutting him.

"If I'd a cut that man ever so little I made up my mind I'd cut his throat from ear to ear," Dixon said. "It would ha' been my life or his'n, and I was shore it wouldn't a be mine."[7]

Dixon was not a man to back down, especially to the likes of Burns and Farrell. As an oblivious Hicks and his men searched for Foster among the crowd, a small race riot broke out on the dance floor. Dixon was beaten and pistol-whipped, likely by Farrell, who was the more aggressive of the two white assailants. While this was going on in Yale, Foster fled downriver from Hill's Bar in a canoe. Did the Hill's Bar men start the fight as a diversion to help Foster's escape? If that was their purpose, they succeeded. But the scuffle had other, unforeseen, consequences.

The feisty Dixon went to Whannell a few days later, and on Wednesday, December 29, 1858, he swore out a formal complaint of assault against Burns and Farrell. Whannell, still smarting over Foster's escape, must have seen this as an opportunity to get back at McGowan and the Hill's Bar gang that had sheltered the murderer and secreted him away during the fisticuffs. Whannell dispatched one of his constables to Hill's Bar with arrest warrants for the two culprits. In the meantime, he took the unusual step of taking Dixon into "protective custody," locking him up in the Yale jail. Dixon languished in the cells, waiting for the wheels of justice to turn, but his "imprisonment" appears to have been a rather lax affair, as he was spotted wandering around town two days later.

The warrants for the arrest of Burns and Farrell were duly presented to George Perrier at Hill's Bar. The affable JP was at a loss as to what to do until McGowan intervened. Ned knew of Whannell's harsh sentences and had a pretty good idea what the Yale justice of the peace would do to his friends. The Ubiquitous had once avoided conviction on accessory to murder charges by a change of venue to a friendly jurisdiction. There was no reason why Burns and Farrell should not do the same. McGowan told Perrier the two suspects need not travel all the way to Yale. He could haul the two culprits before his own court, thus ensuring a fair trial. Perrier thought this a capital idea and passed the warrants on to his own constable, Henry Hickson.

Hickson took his time rounding up the men, and it was the next day before Farrell and Burns appeared before Perrier. They pleaded provocation. With McGowan's assistance, Perrier came to the conclusion he would have to interview Dixon if there was to be due process. He set bail for the two miners and ordered them to appear in court at noon the next day. In the meantime, Perrier sent Hickson to Yale with an order to have Dixon appear at Hill's Bar to testify.

Again, Hickson took his own sweet time. It was Friday morning, New Year's Eve, before he made his way to Yale. Hickson was walking towards Whannell's courthouse when he bumped into Dixon on the street. Hickson told Dixon he had a warrant for his appearance in Hill's Bar and read him Perrier's letter. The barber refused to go with the constable, saying he had to check with Whannell first. Hickson reluctantly agreed and set out for Whannell's house. They found the JP at home, and after Hickson explained his errand, Whannell told the constable and the barber to meet him in a few minutes at the courthouse, where he would write a formal reply to Perrier's request.

Hickson waited for some time in the log-cabin justice building. There were about a dozen men in the courthouse, for watching Whannell in session was one of the premier forms of entertainment in Yale. Among the spectators was Thomas Piesley, who lived in Hole in the Wall, north of Yale. Also present was Fifer. When Whannell finally showed up, the audience members took their hats off (obviously wishing to avoid being found in contempt). Hickson handed Whannell the letter from Perrier. The Yale magistrate read the missive by the grey light filtering through the front window and was thrown into a rage. He went behind his bench and sat down. According to both Hickson and Piesley, Whannell was "very much excited" as he called Hickson up to the bench. Whannell flatly refused to surrender Dixon and demanded Burns and Farrell be brought before him immediately.[8]

"You'll go back to Hill's Bar and bring this man Farrell before me," he ordered Hickson.

Hickson, however, refused. "Not without an order from Judge Perrier," he replied. "Farrell is coming up before him."

This wounded Whannell's immense sense of pride. "I am your superior and I desire this man brought before me!" he cried. "Don't you acknowledge me as your superior?"

The courtroom was, by now, crowded. There were plenty of witnesses to what Hickson said next. It was exactly the wrong response to give a man who fined those who failed to take their hat off in his presence.

"No, not as a superior," said Hickson.

Whannell's immense legal majesty was outraged. He wasn't about to let some Hill's Bar constable speak to him like that.

"I shall commit him to jail!" shouted Whannell.

Without bothering to write out a formal commitment, Whannell found the constable guilty of contempt of court right then and there and ordered his jailer, Mr. Wright, to throw Hickson into the cells with a newly reincarcerated Dixon, the unfortunate Allmeyer and several other inmates. As Begbie wryly noted in his report to Douglas, "the gaol at Yale, which, being circumscribed in its limits, must, when thus containing prosecutor, witnesses, and constable — everybody but the accused persons — have been rather inconveniently crowded."

Legal Vengeance

Piesley hurried downriver with the news. Hill's Bar was soon in an uproar. Such an insult had to be answered. Calmly, McGowan told Perrier he would look after things. It had been a week since Rice's death, and Ned hoped he could not only prevail upon Whannell to let Farrell off and release Hickson, but also convince him to reopen Yale's saloons. To McGowan, who'd had many similar quiet chats in political and legal circles over the years, it did not seem such a daunting task. With a bag of gold dust in his hand, McGowan set out for Yale.

He found Whannell in his courtroom, for Whannell was always holding court, seven days a week. A small crowd, including Fifer, was present as McGowan approached the bench. He offered to pay any fine Whannell wished to impose on Burns and Farrell. Then Hickson could be set free. Further, McGowan proposed to settle things so Anderson and others could reopen their saloons in Yale.

"I was about to say something in regard to the law in such cases, but he cut me off," wrote McGowan.[9]

"Do you know that lawyers are not permitted to appear in Her Majesty's courts except by courtesy of the judge?" asked Whannell sharply.

McGowan replied rather smoothly that he was not appearing as a lawyer for Burns, Farrell or Anderson; he was in Whannell's courtroom as "a friend." Whannell, bent on having his way, brushed this aside.

"He declined to accept the fines and costs, and wanted to know where the accused parties were," wrote McGowan. "I further informed him that his proceedings were illegal, and not in accordance with the common law or written statutes of his country; that it was an axiom of the English law that everyone accused had a right to a hearing, and to meet his accuser face to face. He turned on me with a look of supreme contempt and said: 'Ah, my fine fellow, that may be good law in California, but Jack is not as good as his master here.'"

McGowan told Whannell he would take Burns and Farrell up before Perrier for trial, where they would plead guilty and pay a fine and court costs. By now, Whannell's blood pressure must have been alarming.

"Are you a constable?" he demanded.

McGowan, aware that Whannell had already jailed one constable that day, said he was not and, bowing, backed out of the courtroom.

His own mercurial temper rising, he stalked off to the ferry landing by the river's edge. But Whannell's question "Are you a constable?" had planted the seed of an idea in McGowan's brain.

After a few minutes, Fifer followed McGowan down to the ferry with a message from Whannell. The judge had reconsidered, he said, and would be pleased to settle the case on McGowan's terms. But McGowan had had enough of Whannell and his puffed-up pride. And he had no time for Fifer either.

"I told Fifer to go back and tell his friend, the judge, that I would not give him as much gold-dust as would turn the nicest balanced gold-scales in the dominion," McGowan wrote.

Having spurned Fifer's last-minute deal, McGowan returned to Hill's Bar with a plan for a little legal vengeance. He persuaded Perrier that as justice of the peace for Hill's Bar, he alone had jurisdiction over the case and advised the judge to have Burns and Farrell appear before him without Dixon being present. The two men pleaded guilty and paid fines of $25 each, plus court costs. The entire proceedings were recorded, and McGowan made sure he had copies of the transcript. Burns and Farrell were, technically, in the clear.

But McGowan went further, formulating a legal sleight-of-hand that would exact a measure of revenge on both Whannell and Fifer. He suggested to Perrier that Whannell had insulted his legal majesty and was guilty of contempt of court. After all, he'd locked up Hickson without trial or charge. Surely the man should be arrested and brought down to Hill's Bar for trial.

Perrier's only objection to such an extraordinary course of action was that he did not now have a constable to serve the arrest warrant, as Hickson was still languishing with Dixon et al. in the Yale jail. McGowan naturally had a solution. He made the proposal that must have been burning in his brain since his conversation with Fifer on the riverbank.

"I suggested to him that he had a right to deputize an officer, and that I would serve him in that capacity. He fell into the trap. I knew he had no power to arrest for contempt of court outside his own court-room," wrote McGowan.

McGowan and his friend Terence Kelly (another Law and Order

Democrat who had been illegally expelled from San Francisco by the Vigilance Committee) were solemnly sworn in as special constables, along with nine others. McGowan made sure it was all legal: Piesley swore out his affidavit, giving Perrier the evidence he needed to act. A commission giving McGowan and his party status as constables was drawn up. The posse was also well-equipped with firearms in the event of trouble. They were, McGowan observed, "armed to the teeth as well as with the majesty of the law."

The operation was carried out with military precision. In charge was Major Tom Dolan, who in addition to his Nicaraguan experience was also a veteran of the Mexican-American War and a sometime faro dealer. Dolan lined the west bank of the river with armed men, who used the cover of trees and logs to command the approach to the river. When they reached the other side at Yale, Dolan sent out skirmishers to guard the route to and from the courthouse. Packing legal papers and pistols, McGowan's party made its way back to Whannell's courthouse.

Whannell was standing by the stove, having a laugh with a few of the boys and the officers of his court, when McGowan and party entered and, without ceremony, arrested him for contempt. Stunned, Whannell turned to his cronies.

"My men, do you hear that?" he cried.

With McGowan and his armed posse staring them down, not a single one of Whannell's employees stirred or came to the JP's defence. Whannell saw his number was up this time. But he put a brave face on things.

"I will go, but you take me at your peril," he said.

Whannell surrendered his pistol, gave his clerk, G. Tennent, a bag of gold dust he had on him and asked to see his wife. McGowan agreed and committed Whannell to the tender mercies of two of his men, telling them to take Whannell to the riverbank after the visit. A crowd began to mill around the courthouse. When Whannell was led out, a cheer went up.

Inside the jail, McGowan and his "special aids" — Con Mooney (who had broken the shovel over White Cap's head), Sam Banta (a fellow Democrat) and Kelly — made for the cells. There, Wright the jailer challenged McGowan, drawing his pistol. McGowan was unflappable. He drew himself up haughtily and said to the guard: "How dare you, sir, resist one of Her Majesty's officers in the discharge of a sworn duty?"

Much to even McGowan's astonishment, Wright at once surrendered both his revolver and his keys. McGowan threw open the jail cell and liberated Hickson, Allmeyer, "an Englishman and all the Americans illegally held," as well as Isaac Dixon. McGowan took Wright with him, and the entire posse trooped down towards the ferry.

Whannell was ahead of them. The whole of Yale turned out to watch as he was marched to the river by hooting captors firing their pistols into the air. Men emerged from the gaming houses and hotels to watch the impromptu New Year's Eve parade down muddy Front Street. Dixon followed behind, shouting and making acerbic comments. Delighted that Whannell was getting a dose of his own medicine, some onlookers sang, others fired a salute with their revolvers into the ether. Whannell made the humiliating journey along the same sidewalk where he had been wont to slash his sabre back and forth. But on this occasion, his voice — both literal and figurative — was muted.

At the river, McGowan's boats were hauled up on the banks. Whannell glared at an American flag on the stern of one of the vessels. He clearly saw this as a case of the Yankees trying to usurp British authority. He turned to McGowan. "Ah! I see you are going to make a national affair of this!" he said.

"Not much," shrugged McGowan.

Fifer hurried to the front of the mob and demanded to be allowed to accompany Whannell and Wright. McGowan had no love for Fifer, but he probably thought someone who could pay Whannell's fines should come along, so he agreed. The party crossed the river and landed at Hill's Bar, where Whannell and Wright were hauled up before Perrier.

McGowan presented his prisoner and carefully filled out the back of the warrant, legally discharging himself of the office of special constable. He was then invited to sit beside Perrier on the bench and give advice. It must have been an ordeal for Whannell to be charged and listen as Hickson and others took the stand to prove the case for contempt.

Fifer, acting on behalf of Whannell, came up with a novel defence: If McGowan and Kelly had arrested Whannell while court was in session, were they not too guilty of contempt? After each witness testified, Fifer cross-examined them, hoping to prove this point. McGowan was firm, as were the others. A judge standing next to a stove, warming himself and cracking jokes, did not amount to a court being in session.

As if there had ever been any doubt as to the outcome, Whannell was quickly found guilty, for, as McGowan put it, "he made no defence, which was the only sane act I ever knew him to be guilty of." Perrier then gave Whannell a stern lecture about "his tyrannous and illegal acts." In the report of the proceedings he sent to Douglas, Perrier states he told his fellow magistrate he "showed heinous contempt of this court." On McGowan's advice, Perrier fined his fellow magistrate and made him pay the court's cost. The total came to $50. Fifer had the cash on hand and Whannell was released. So was Wright, who was discharged without being fined because Perrier ruled he was only following Whannell's order in refusing to release Hickson.

While Wright, the humiliated Whannell and his friend Fifer made their way back to Yale, McGowan, Perrier and company took the $50 fine and adjourned to Patrick "Paddy" Martin's saloon — the only one on Hill's Bar — "for drinks all around." They celebrated far into the night. Unfortunately for them, Whannell did not.

A Show of Force

Upon his return to Yale, Whannell hurried back to his post office / home. By his own admission, he was "vexed and mortified" when he wrote a letter to Captain John Marshall Grant, commander of the detachment of Royal Engineers at Fort Langley, requesting immediate military aid. He also penned a hysterical note to Douglas about the actions of "that notorious villain, Edward McGowan." He described how McGowan, "at the head of a lawless band of ruffians," had arrested him and busted Hickson out of jail. He denounced Perrier as "unfit to serve in any capacity." Then he "set the heather on fire," as Judge Fredric Howay put it, with his description of imminent insurrection.

> *This town and district are in a state bordering on anarchy. My own and the lives of the citizens are in imminent peril. I beg your Excellency will afford us prompt aid. I have applied to Captain Grant for assistance already, as troops can easily be billeted in this town . . . An effective blow must at once be struck on the operations of these outlaws, else I tremble for the welfare of the colony.*[10]

Whannell took the opportunity to add that Hicks was to blame for the disturbances and denounced him as "unprincipled and corrupt." After threatening to resign his post if aid was not sent at once, Whannell finished his letter by rather spitefully pointing out that William Kirby had refused to be sworn in as a special constable during the saloon-closing operation. He entrusted both letters to his clerk, G. Tennent, who immediately went downriver and gave the first missive to Grant at Fort Langley. Tennent then crossed the Strait to Victoria, where Douglas was not very happy to see him.

Douglas had received similar notes from Hicks that fall demanding soldiers and had ignored them. But this was different. McGowan, whom he had already marked as a troublemaker, was once again twisting the tail of the British Lion. The Ubiquitous had also harboured Bernard Rice's murderer. Perhaps Douglas was still regretting he hadn't had a chance to do more to stop the Canyon War before it erupted. This time, he would do something before it was too late. And as it happened, Douglas finally had the troops he needed for a real show of force. He also had someone other than himself to lead them.

London had sent Douglas two very able officials. They were of the type thrown up in the Victorian age: larger than life, moral, Christian with a capital CHRIST, extraordinarily confident of their abilities and steadfast in their duty to the greatest empire on earth. In short, they were a pair of officials who would in time become royal pains in the ass for Douglas. One was Begbie. The other was Colonel Richard Clement Moody.

Moody, the newly arrived lieutenant governor of B.C., had much in common with Douglas. He'd been born on Barbados in the West Indies in 1813. He entered the military service at fourteen, attending the Military Academy at Woolrich until 1829, then serving in Ireland and St. Vincent in the West Indies until he was invalided home in 1837 because of yellow fever. After a tour of the United States, Moody rose steadily up the ranks as an exceptionally gifted young man. By age twenty-five he was a professor of fortification at Woolrich and was appointed Britain's first governor of the Falkland Islands when just thirty. He served there for eight years before returning to England. By 1858 he'd been posted to Malta, survived Malta fever, returned home to become Commanding Royal Engineer of North Britain and finally reached the rank of full colonel.

Colonial Secretary Lytton had handpicked Moody for yet another difficult assignment: to lead the Royal Engineer detachment to British Columbia. This was no banishment to the farthest edges of empire. The Royal Engineers were an elite force, and the melodramatic Lytton saw their task as vitally important. They were to make British Columbia nothing less than "a second England on the shores of the Pacific," the empire's bulwark in the farthest west. The Engineers were to be "pioneers in the work of civilization, in opening up the resources of the country, by the construction of roads and bridges, in laying the foundations of a future city or seaport, and in carrying out the numerous engineering works which in the earlier stages of colonization are so essential to the welfare and progress of the community."[11]

Moody and his family left England with a detachment of Royal Engineers on October 30, 1858. It took them until December 21 to reach San Francisco, where they boarded the steamer *Panama*. They finally arrived at Esquimalt on Christmas Day. Moody was looking forward to a brief respite. He had no idea how brief it would be. Douglas swore Moody in on January 4, 1859, just three days after he received Whannell's letter. The governor had quite a task in mind for his new lieutenant: putting down the Yankee insurrection on the gold fields.

Used to dealing with crises by himself, Douglas was sure two seasoned officials like Begbie and Moody would need only a small detachment to settle affairs on the gold fields. Besides, a small force was cheaper. Believing that speed was critically important, Moody and Begbie started for the Fraser River on January 5, 1859, aboard the HBC steamer *Beaver*, accompanied by a few Royal Engineers. The military expedition to show the Yankees the might and majesty of British law and the empire got as far as the outer Gulf Islands before dropping anchor for the night. The next day they sailed across the Strait of Georgia and up "Frazer's River," as Moody called it. It was winter, and cold lay heavily on the landscape. Still, the unspoiled beauty of the Fraser Valley worked its magic on Moody, a man on his way to war.

"One can not write prosaically of such scenes as these, so pray make allowances when I get into rhapsodies at any time about this most beautiful country," Moody wrote his friend Arthur Blackwood of the colonial office. "The water of the deep, clear Frazer (such a name! the proper one is 'Tatouche') was of glassy stillness, not a ripple before us, except when a fish rose to the surface or broods of wild ducks fluttered away."[12]

The *Beaver* delivered Moody, Begbie and the rest of the expedition to Fort Langley the same day. There they met Captain Grant, whose force of Royal Engineers was known as the Columbia Detachment. It had arrived at the fort November 15, 1858, and was made up mainly of carpenters. Grant handed his commander, Moody, the letters that had been pouring in from Whannell demanding troops. The offended JP's prosings were "so alarming and so urgent in their nature that I had no option but instantly to go there and to take the detachment of R.E.'s with me."

In his letter to Blackwood, written in the safe afterglow, Moody

Fired by religious zeal, and a shrewd judge of character, Richard Clement Moody was already an old colonial hand when he arrived in British Columbia in 1859. Born in the West Indies, he'd been governor of the Falkland Islands by the time he was thirty years old, and he served in Malta. He cared deeply about his new colony and foresaw B.C.'s union with a confederated Canada.

makes light of the affair: "The notorious Ned McGowan, of Californian celebrity at the head of a band of Yankee Rowdies defying the law! Every peaceable citizen frightened out of his wits! Summons and warrants laughed to scorn! A Magistrate seized while on the Bench, and brought to the Rebel's camp, tried, condemned, and heavily fined! A man shot dead shortly before! Such a tale to welcome me at the close of day of great enjoyment."

Begbie was also affected by the letters, but was characteristically more restrained in his report to Douglas. "The loose rumor flying about Langley (but which was not credited) was that both Whannell and his constable had been shot by McGowan: and that the district was in open insurrection."[13]

Moody and Begbie decided to push on that very evening, taking Grant and his company with them. As a further precaution, Moody immediately sent a request to Douglas for reinforcements. The force Moody had at his disposal was pitifully small. Some of the sick had to be left behind, so even with Grant's twelve carpenters and sappers added to his own detachment of R.E.s, the colonel's military might numbered just twenty-five engineers and one chief justice who, thankfully, was not wearing his go-to-meeting clothes.

The winter night was bitterly cold, and the river was full of ice and flowing fast.[14] The *Beaver* was not suited for such conditions, so on the spot, Moody hired the *Enterprise* to undertake the journey for $1,000. The vessel was an American stern-wheeler, light-drafted, and could, with luck, make it as far as Fort Hope. From there it would be a short march to Yale and the source of the trouble. Curiously, the *Enterprise* was owned by the Wright Brothers; its captain, Thomas "Bully" Wright, was brother to George Wright who had given McGowan his free passage to Victoria. The Wrights were about to recoup that loss many times over thanks to Ned's undeserved reputation. The *Enterprise* steamed out on the frigid waters of the Fraser at about 11 p.m. on January 6, 1859.

Although small in number, the Royal Engineers were itching for action after a long passage from England and weeks of mundane tasks in Fort Langley. Moody, the grizzled veteran, watched as his red-jacketed men cheerfully prepared their revolvers and rifles. He spent his time inspecting these preparations with Begbie and attempting to look "grave and thoughtful." Moody found Begbie more "pugnacious" than himself, which amused him greatly.

"I seriously believe I was the most peaceable man on board," he wrote Blackwood and added, with italics for emphasis, "*Old Soldiers don't play at Soldiering.*"

Up the Fraser

Douglas received Moody's request for reinforcements the next day, the morning of January 7, and sent Captain Prevost and HMS *Plumper* to dispatch fifty marines and blue-jackets (sailors) as well as a field piece to Moody's aid. Among the force that left that day from Esquimalt naval base was a young naval officer, Lieutenant Richard Charles Mayne, the son of Sir Richard Mayne, chief commissioner of the Metropolitan Police of London. Mayne was only twenty-three at the time, but had already served in the navy for eleven years. He was well into a career that would end with his retirement as a rear-admiral in 1879. But first he would have to survive a harrowing adventure courtesy of Begbie, Moody and McGowan.

And where were those three key figures while Mayne was helping get the relief column mustered? Moody and Begbie were involved in a miserable slog up the icy Fraser. By January 7 the *Enterprise* had only made it as far as the mouth of the Harrison River, where the stern-wheeler ran into heavy ice. But they also ran into Billy Ballou coming downriver. The Wild French Waif of the Fraser told Begbie and Moody that, contrary to the outrageous rumours of murder and insurrection, things were quiet in Fort Yale, give or take the odd miners' meeting. In fact, nothing more violent than a series of strongly worded resolutions had passed on the gold fields since New Year's Eve. Moody was somewhat relieved. It appeared the matter might be settled without bloodshed if he acted quickly. He pressed on despite the ice.

They spent the entire day navigating the frozen channels of the river. Wright manoeuvred his 115-foot-long, 22-foot-wide steamer with all his considerable skill. He reached Umatilla Snag, a low point in the river named after the first steamer that managed to get as far as Fort Yale. It had also managed to become stranded on the snag. Try as he might, Wright could not get past the low water. Further attempts the next day were no more successful. Reluctantly, Wright backed the vessel into a small side stream where, overnight, the *Enterprise* was frozen in. The British expedition to put down the Yankee insurrection was well and truly stuck, unable to go up or down the river.

Begbie and Moody considered their options, which seemed limited. In their hour of need, the two officials of the new colonial administration were rescued by the agency they were supposed to supplant: the Hudson's Bay Company. Aboard the *Enterprise* was John Drummond Buchanan Ogilvy, factor for Fort Hope. Ogilvy was a consummate Company man; tough, hardy, quiet. He knew the country well and was in superb physical shape. He had climbed a peak in the Coquihalla range for a wager of five dollars and a champagne supper. A horseman, he had lived and ridden with the Prairie Indians. Moody was impressed by his "chieftain-like" manner and earmarked him as government material once the crisis was over.[15]

Ogilvy offered to go ahead of the expedition with two Native Indians and see if there was any trouble. Moody and Begbie agreed, and Ogilvy set off at once. In his letter to Blackwood, Moody gives a wonderful description of how "Ogilvie," as the colonel spelled his name, "tough and hardy by practice as a piece of whipcord or Mountain Ash," made his way to Yale and Hill's Bar.

"Ogilvie, in the dead of night, walked through and among what may be termed the rebel's camp, looked in at the windows of the huts, saw them gambling round the fires, heard their conversations, and was never questioned — The dogs bothered him most — They suspected him."

For four days, the expedition frozen aboard the *Enterprise* waited anxiously for word from their "young cavalier." As they waited, the weather moderated. The ice started to thaw and rain mixed with wet snow began to fall. When Ogilvy returned on January 12, he had both good and bad news. Yale was quiet, but with Whannell still in office, things were tense. "It was very probable an outbreak of a very serious nature might take place at any moment," wrote Moody. "In fact we had reason to believe that the turning of a straw might lead to his [Whannell's] being 'lynched.' He is a man overboiling with zeal, without the slightest personal fear, and raging under a sense of outraged dignity."

The *Enterprise* ploughed back into the Fraser River on January 13 with high hopes. Those hopes were dashed at Cornish (also known as Murderer's) Bar, just four miles below Fort Hope. The higher water had allowed the *Enterprise* to get past Umatilla Snag, but it had now swollen the Fraser's powerful current. Further progress was impossible, and once again Wright grounded his vessel. There they spent the night.

The next morning, an impatient Moody insisted he and Begbie travel the remaining four miles to Fort Hope. By eight o'clock in the morning, the judge and the colonel were in a whaleboat on the river, fighting the Fraser's tremendous current, a ferocious wind and blinding snow. It was nearly noon before they made it to the warm confines of Fort Hope. They were now just a few miles from Yale, but the morning's journey had been enough for Moody. He suggested they stay at Fort Hope for the night in Ogilvy's comfortable cabin. Begbie agreed. As for the troops, they would have to march through the snow to make it to the tiny Hudson's Bay Company outpost.

To make things look normal (although how the spectacle of a colonel and a judge parading through snow falling so thickly that visibility was near zero could be conceived as "normal" boggles the modern mind), Moody and Begbie went on a short tour of the fort, speaking with various miners and other citizens. Two were of particular interest: Robert Smith, the justice of the peace and revenue officer for Fort Hope, who would later become an MLA; and George Perrier, who had heard of Moody's approach and come flying downriver to give his account of the "incident."

It appears that Smith tried to be diplomatic, but he made it clear that Hicks was a man with manifold failings. He even passed on Ned McGowan's opinion of the assistant lands commissioner. According to Begbie:

Mr. Smith gave us a good deal of information as to Mr. Hicks, but in
a general way, which certainly confirmed every report which I have
heard of him from every body but himself. I can not get anybody to
speak up for him. Even Edward Macgowan [sic], who does him the
honour of preferring him to Capt. Whannell, alleges his reason to be
because he prefers dealing with a knave rather than a fool.

In particular, however, it appears to me that Mr. Hicks has been
probably exceeding any reasonable limits in granting and recording
rights of pre-emption and water privileges — having granted, I'm
informed, to one individual the exclusive water privilege of no less
than 7 streams which run into the Fraser between Hope and Yale.[16]

While Smith was helping to cement Moody and Begbie's opinion of
Hicks, Perrier was doing himself no harm by explaining why he'd
ordered Yankee desperadoes to arrest a fellow magistrate in his own
courtroom. He had already written Douglas on January 4, giving an
account that carefully avoided mentioning the name of McGowan,
but emphasizing Whannell's "*Insult* to me as a Magistrate and like-
wise a contempt of my court."

Begbie and Moody took an immediate liking to Perrier, deciding
he'd only acted after "the greatest provocation" from Whannell.
They had already decided to suspend Hicks for his alleged malfeasance, especially after Moody discovered the shady deal over the silver mine. It is clear from his writings that Moody was appalled, but
Douglas had not set a sterling example himself when it came to speculation. The governor was the largest landowner in Victoria, and
Lytton had already requested that Douglas relieve himself of his
shares in the Puget Sound Agricultural Society as well as his position
as chief factor of the Hudson's Bay Company, but Douglas had
dragged his feet over both. Hicks might have thought himself in
good company, but Moody thought otherwise, and it may be that
some of the poor relations between the colonel and Douglas had
their root here.

Mayne's Journey up the Fraser

Meanwhile, Mayne and the *Plumper* had reached Fort Langley, only to discover that Moody and Begbie had already departed in the only vessel capable of getting the reinforcements upriver. Even if they had abandoned the field piece, the marines and blue-jackets would have been obliged to travel by canoe: a dangerous prospect in such weather. Grant decided to keep the force aboard ship and send a messenger to overtake Moody. He chose Mayne for the assignment.

In his memoir, *Four Years in British Columbia and Vancouver Island*, Mayne describes how HBC chief trader James Murray Yale outfitted him with a canoe and arranged for a crew of nine paddlers ("four half-breeds and five Indians"). Mayne himself was given "a blanket, frock, and trowsers, a couple of rugs, two or three pipes, plenty of tobacco, tea, coffee, some meat and bread, a frying-pan and saucepan." It was Mayne's first canoe trip, and what with the weather and the ice, not to mention the urgency of his task, he can be forgiven for the "curious sensations" he felt at the prospect of making such a journey. He was grateful when Captain Herbert George Lewis of the HBC (who had been acting as pilot for the *Plumper*) offered to accompany him. Even so, it was an apprehensive Mayne who, at about 11 a.m. on January 13, climbed down from the *Plumper* into a ship's boat and set out for the shore, where his paddlers awaited.

"They were waiting on the beach, dressed in their best blankets, with large streamers of bright red, blue, and yellow ribbons, in which they delight so much, flying from their caps," wrote Mayne. "Mr. Yale had previously harangued them, and presented them with these streamers by way of impressing them with the importance of the service in which they were engaged."

The crew was lead by an experienced Kanakan hand named Myhu-pu-pu. With the crew singing, the wind shrieking and Mayne shivering, the fragile birchbark canoe set off up the river with the paddlers' streamers flapping in the breeze. At 5 p.m. they finally stopped for tea and supper. It was already dark and bitterly cold, but the crew set off once more. For Mayne, more than a decade in the Royal Navy had hardly prepared him for the miserable night ahead.

"Wet, cold, and tired, we rolled ourselves up in the rugs, and in time fell into a broken sleep, lulled by the monotonous rap of the paddles upon the gunwale of the canoe, the rippling sound of the water against its sides, the song of the men now rising loud and shrill, now sinking into a low, drowsy hum," wrote Mayne.

His fitful sleep was also disturbed by the mischievous nature of his crew. The Natives had no love for the white miners who had invaded their country and killed so many of their people. They were bent on disturbing their sleep as well as Mayne's.

"Whenever we passed a fire, or a boat drawn up ashore, or moored to the trees by the beach, in which miners might be sleeping, the Indians would commence singing at the top of their voices; and we often saw sleepers start up, in wonder no doubt, who could be traveling on the river at night at such a season — and some in fear perhaps, for several murders had been committed, which were attributed rightly or wrongly to Indian agency."

Scaring the bejesus out of the miners must have bolstered the paddlers' spirits. They continued up the river until four o'clock the next morning, an astonishing eleven straight hours of numbing exertion. Finally they beached the canoe, cleared some snow from the riverbank, lit a fire and rested. To Mayne's surprise, the break lasted just two hours. "At the end of that time we picked ourselves up, stiff with cold, and breakfasted, and by half-past seven were under weigh again and paddling up the river, the Indians, to all appearance, as lively and unwearied as if they had slept the whole night through."

For the next day the paddlers kept up this gruelling pace. Mayne and Lewis took their turns spelling off the Hudson's Bay men or huddled in rugs and blankets against the cold. The novelty for Mayne had worn off, and despite having experienced the rigours of life aboard ship, he was nearly spent. "I confess that the second night of my journey was one of unmitigated discomfort and weariness," he wrote.

Mayne sighted the *Enterprise* at about three o'clock that afternoon and must have been elated, thinking he was at the end of his harrowing journey. He climbed aboard, only to learn Moody was already at Fort Hope and the steamer was finally underway again after being trapped in the ice for three days. There was nothing for it but to take to the canoe once again. Myhu-pu-pu tried to cheer Mayne up by assuring him they'd reach Fort Hope before nightfall. The paddler was wrong.

As they neared Fort Hope, the river became more swollen and chunks of ice threatened to smash the canoe. Night fell while the paddlers were still a few miles from their goal. Mayne had fallen asleep by the time Myhu-pu-pu and crew reached the rapids at Cornish Bar. He was awoken by a sharp crack behind his head as the canoe smashed into a rock. The canoe had been stove in and was filling with water. Less experienced hands might have panicked, but Myhu-pu-pu and his veterans didn't. Several paddlers leapt out of the canoe and onto the slippery rock, lifting the craft off the stony surface against the full force of the current. The other paddlers churned the water furiously, making for the shore. A few yards from the bank, the entire crew, including Mayne and Lewis, jumped out and ran the stricken vessel ashore.

Though they were all soaking wet and freezing, there was still no respite. The men who had leapt out to save the canoe were still on the rock in the river, "the current sweeping by up to their knees and threatening to take them away." The canoe was hastily repaired and tied to a rope so it could be swept down to the stranded men. They were brought safely ashore, but it was clear the canoe, split fore and aft, would not be able to complete the trip to Fort Hope that night. Two paddlers were left in charge of it while the rest of the crew guided Mayne along a winding trail towards the fort.

Son of Sir Richard Mayne, commissioner of the Metropolitan Police in London, Charles Mayne was just twenty-three years old when he took part in McGowan's War. He had already served with the Royal Navy for eleven years by that time and impressed Moody with his stamina and courage. Both would be put to the test during McGowan's War, as Mayne accompanied the colonel and the judge into the heart of the trouble.

It was three miles to Hope and there were three feet of snow on the trail. Exhausted, his clothes frozen, Mayne stumbled forward. While crossing a river by a fallen tree, Lewis fell in and had to be rescued. The misadventure added another layer of ice to his already frozen clothes and body. In perfect misery, Mayne and Lewis finally reached the fort late in the evening. They were taken to Ogilvy's room, which served as his bedroom and sitting room. There Mayne and Lewis found Moody seated before a warm fire, Begbie beside him. Also gathered around the warmth of the flames were Captain Grant and the officers of the Hudson's Bay Company.

"We made our way [into their presence] looking, I dare say, pitiable objects enough," Mayne wrote.

Mayne gave his report. Moody was surprised and, according to Mayne, "perhaps a little embarrassed" that Douglas had sent the reinforcements so quickly. Troops and field pieces no longer figured in his plans. However, Moody liked the lieutenant and was impressed by his fortitude. He appointed Mayne his aide de camp and "confidential officer" on the spot. Mayne and Lewis were given dry, warm clothes and a hot supper. Moody wanted Mayne rested: he had plans for the young officer.

While Mayne was being paddled upstream, Moody and Begbie had been strategizing. Part of their design was born of necessity. They'd already seen how difficult it would be to move even a small number of troops up the Fraser given the weather conditions, so they decided the force would stay in Fort Hope. Moody suspected that McGowan's men had spied on their torturous journey upriver, and he received confirmation of the fact later. "Ned McGowan, I discovered afterwards has his scouts out and exact intelligence of all my movements from the very first," he confided to Blackwood. In fact, McGowan had an agent spying on the British at Fort Hope even as Moody and Begbie plotted their grand design. Alex Roberts, an American of English parentage, spent his time fraternizing with the Royal Engineers and sending messages to McGowan via Native couriers.

The other part of Moody's plan involved a bit of Victorian bluster. The colonel told Mayne to accompany him and Judge Begbie to Fort

Yale in the morning while the Royal Engineers and Grant stayed behind in Fort Hope. Instead of a show of force, which was impractical in any event, Moody and the judge would make a leisurely progress up the river pretending to take a civil survey of the diggings. It was a bluff. Begbie was very matter of fact when he wrote to Douglas that evening, detailing Moody's scheme. "He thought (in which I quite agreed) that it . . . would be more politic to treat the disputes at Yale as of secondary importance, place our passage up the country entirely to motives of civil survey, and proceed alone to Yale, taking me with him."

Moody was gambling that such nonchalance would impress McGowan more than parading two dozen half-frozen carpenters and sappers through the streets of Yale. Mayne was not just along for the ride, however. If things did get out of hand, it would be his job to slip downriver by canoe to Fort Hope and fetch Grant and the Royal Engineers. Captain Lewis was dispatched with the repaired canoe to Fort Langley to inform Captain Richards of the plan.

Meanwhile, Back on the Bar

It had been nine days since the expedition left Victoria and over two weeks since the abduction and the judicial humiliation of Whannell. What had transpired in Fort Yale and Hill's Bar in all that time? Newspaper accounts from Victoria to San Francisco were full of lurid, fictional accounts of murders and riots, but nothing more violent had occurred than a good old-fashioned American meeting.

On the very evening of the outrage, Dr. Fifer held a meeting of vigilance-minded citizens in Yale, which passed a series of resolutions supporting Whannell and condemning Hicks (who had been recalled to Victoria by Douglas and was allegedly on "official business"). Whannell was front and centre at the meeting and spoke in his usual blustery manner. Begbie, when he heard about the proceedings, dismissed them as a "multifarious conglomeration of heterogeneous nonsense." But the Californian Democratic refugees on Hill's Bar believed that Whannell was "endeavoring to excite this community in acts of violence,"[17] and it must have sounded to them like the next step in setting up a Committee of Vigilance. Even Begbie, after the troubles were over, came to see the Hill's Bar men's point of view and articulated them in his final report to Douglas.

"I believe that McGowan and his party had reason to believe that an attempt, at all events, was contemplated to construct something like a Vigilance Committee at Yale, directed against themselves . . . I believe that it was seriously apprehended by McGowan. They therefore resolved to anticipate violence by violence."[18]

During this period, Whannell and Dr. Fifer became close allies. Fifer enlisted the justice of the peace in his quest for government funding for the "indigent sick," January 3, 1859, producing a bill for the treatment of the sick for the month of December, which Whannell dutifully passed on to Douglas. Fifer had "furnished a great deal of medicine etc. without remuneration." In his accounts, Fifer lists medicines, splints, dressings and the like and gives details of the various illnesses afflicting the miners during that bitterly cold winter: mostly frostbite, but one case of gangrene and another of "accidental shooting (fracture of the radius)."

When he wasn't forwarding bills or issuing urgent pleas for troops, Whannell sat in his courthouse, anxiously waiting for his day of vengeance. On January 11 he received an unexpected visitor, John Ogilvy of Fort Hope, bearing a letter from Moody ordering the justice of the peace to find an appropriate billet for himself and Begbie.

Whannell immediately dashed off a quick response he hoped would impress Moody. "McGowan and their party have it all their own way at the present time, and are narrowly watching my actions. McGowan can at any time rally around him at least 100 desperadoes like himself, the greater part of them have been expatriated, and are one and all, the very *scum* of the Creation. They are all armed to the teeth, but I am very much mistaken if 25 British bayonets cannot route [sic] such a rabble."[19]

Whannell closed with a plea to Moody to have McGowan and several of his supporters shipped to a penal colony. But while he was brave in private, Whannell was positively timid in public. He had lost some of his old nerve. One by one, the saloons he'd closed began to reopen. The miners gathered to drink and talk, speculating on what would happen when Moody and the troops arrived. How would they deal with the Yankees who had dared to arrest one of the colony's officials in his own courtroom?

McGowan stated that during this interval, "order reigned in Warsaw." He paints a picture of Whannell as "crestfallen" and losing his "lordly pomposity."

> *He started out as a roaring lion, and fell down to a sneaking coyote ... Wannel [sic] was resting on his oars, and waiting for his day of revenge to come. He felt certain when the government troops arrived, he would 'snare his birds and spring the wire.'*[20]

McGowan himself got a chance to settle another score, this time with one of the top members of the Vigilance Committee, shortly after humiliating Whannell. Walking the streets of Yale with John Bagley, McGowan was surprised to see Jules David, a member of the executive committee of the purest and best, who had condemned Ned to death in absentia in 1856, by the boat landing. David had finished disposing of Fifer's property in San Francisco and had recently travelled to Yale to personally deliver the proceeds to his fellow committee member. McGowan appears to have attacked him without warning, grabbing David by the hair. To his astonishment, it came off in his hand — the Vigilante wore a wig. Versions of what followed differ. Some say McGowan was so amused, the fight ended then and there. He and Bagley allegedly went from saloon to saloon displaying the trophy until, at Bagley's suggestion, McGowan sent the wig via Ballou's express to William T. Coleman, former chairman of the Vigilantes in San Francisco, with a note saying the Ubiquitous had taken one scalp on the Fraser and would take others when he returned to California. But Fifer, who attended to David's wounds, said McGowan viciously beat the man with a wooden club. It took several stitches to close the wound.

Brawling and fighting was not confined to McGowan's enemies. Ned was having as much trouble with his own men as he was with the Vigilance Committee's supporters. He had to stop two of them from shooting each other even as Moody and his troops advanced painfully up the frozen Fraser. The pair were two of his key aides "While we were waiting the coming of the troops, I was called up early one morning by a friend, who informed me that Major Tom Dolan and Alex Roberts were going to fight a duel that morning. I arrived on the ground just in time. They had taken up their positions, pistols in hand. I said to them: 'You are engaged in a pretty piece of business, wanting to kill each other, when in a few days you will have an enemy to fight' — meaning the British soldiers."[21]

When not thwarting his lieutenants' plans to slaughter each other, McGowan would visit Ovid Allard, take a little of that dark brandy and try to learn as much as he could of Moody and Begbie and what their likely course of action would be. He hoped to get by using words alone. But if Moody insisted on an armed conflict, he had ambitious plans. Sometime during the approach of Moody's force up the Fraser, McGowan and Dolan held a council of war at Hill's Bar. They carefully laid plans that they hoped would end with the United States annexing British Columbia.

> We had arranged a plan, in case of a collision with the troops, to take Fort Yale and then go down the river and capture Fort Hope (they were only trading posts called forts), and retreat with our plunder across the country into Washington Territory — only twenty miles distant. This would, we supposed, bring on the fight and put an end to the long agony and the public clamor — that our boundary line must be "fifty-four forty or fight." This mode of procedure we held as a dernier ressort, in the event the military would adopt harsh measures towards us.[22]

Could McGowan have pulled off this audacious plan? Begbie and Douglas made light of the idea after the event, but there were several factors in McGowan's favour. First there were the numbers. There were about ten thousand Americans on the gold fields that winter, most of them currently unemployed due to the weather. Even a fraction of them rallying to McGowan's banner would have been enough to overwhelm Moody's small force. The Canyon War had shown they were capable of forming well-equipped military units with speed. McGowan had the unquestioned loyalty of his fellow Law and Order Party members, many of whom he had helped to return to San Francisco after they were sentenced to exile by the Vigilance Committee. McGowan also had experienced men like Dolan at hand to lead them, and like Dolan, many of the Americans were veterans of the Mexican-American War. By a curious coincidence, their old commander-in-chief, General Winfield Scott, had just been appointed the U.S. commissioner to the boundary dispute. Surely if the American miners rose up in the middle of a bitter feud over the final border between the United States and Great Britain, their old chief would come to their aid. Things might have been even more favourable had McGowan's old friend John Nugent still been at his post in Victoria.

Was McGowan capable of leading such an uprising? The answer is undoubtedly yes. McGowan has always been painted by most historians as a sort of likable rogue, full of mischief, bluff and bluster, but ultimately harmless. However, his unflagging, almost single-handed campaign against the Vigilance Committee at a time when the Stranglers were in the ascendancy is proof enough of McGowan's courage and determination.[23]

But as McGowan himself put it: "Fortunately, we fell into the hands of English gentlemen, and their presence and wise counsel saved many of us, no doubt, from a sad ending."

The English Gentlemen Arrive

The English gentlemen, Begbie, Moody and Mayne, left Fort Hope by boat on the morning of January 15, 1859. Moody took every opportunity to stop and chat with miners on the various bars along the way to show that spirit of grace and civility which comes with the certainty of power.

"We stopped at some of the Mining Bars," he wrote. "I conversed in a friendly way with all, asked about their prospects, wished them well and so on, scarcely alluded to the disturbances above and in fact acted in a manner to subdue all excitement and to allow information to go forward that I was coming up in this quiet peaceable way."[24]

Moody worked himself into that religious fervour peculiar to the Victorian colonial official who saw the empire as a manifestation of God's supreme plan to make a quarter of the world map pink. He waxed alternately poetic and mystic, comparing the Upper Fraser Valley and Little Canyon to the Tyrol and dubbing the area "Glen Albert." He wrote of cheerful miners working away as "the blue smoke from their log Cabins curled up among the trees and from the brink of the River when Fires were on the Bank. The trees being chiefly Cedar and Black Spruce contrasted with the dazzling Snow. The River was alternately 'Rapids' and 'Still-water' reflecting every thing — reflecting cottages, blue smoke, trees, mountains, and moving figures."

The mystic in Moody was moved by the sight of so many different races and nationalities all toiling away in the same spot. It was like a microcosm of Europe and the empire. Being a soldier, he didn't forget the task ahead of him, nor to put in a word with the Almighty for success.

It was impossible not to be deeply struck with the circumstances that our conversations all the way up were with ENGLISHMEN *(staunch Royalists)* Americans *(Republicans)* Frenchmen, *very numerous, Germans in abundance, Italians, several Hungarians, Poles, Danes, Swedes, Spaniards, Mexicans, and Chinese. As I sat in the boat the flood of thought that passed through my brain is not to be described. I was deeply moved that it pleased the Almighty Ruler of the Universe to bring these various nations together under the protection of our Queen, and you will readily believe that I prayed very earnestly for Him to endow me, for Jesus' sake with wisdom and prudence and to guide me in the matter before me. I prayed for His blessing on all our ways and for peace. My heart was overflowing with earnest love for all these manly energetic fellows.*[25]

The trio arrived in Yale at three o'clock in the afternoon. As they approached the sprawl of tents, log cabins and hovels strung along the river's bank and surmounted by the buildings of the tiny HBC post, Moody, Begbie and Mayne were greeted by a good part of the citizenry from Yale as well as the entire population of Hill's Bar drawn up along the shore. Among the crowd was McGowan himself, who had ignored messages from Roberts urging him to flee the country. As the three English gentlemen landed to face the crowd, the largely American gathering shouted and cheered enthusiastically. They also fired a six-shooter salute over their esteemed guests' heads. Moody took it very calmly at the time, but sounded a trifle nervous when writing to Blackwood about it after the fact.

"They gave me a Salute, firing off their loaded Revolvers over my head — Pleasant — Balls whistling over one's head! as a compliment! Suppose a hand had dropped by accident! If it was to try my nerves they must have forgotten my profession."

Moody, Mayne and Begbie waited for the acrid blue smoke of the gunpowder to clear. Then Moody raised his hat and thanked the miners in the name of the Queen. He received three cheers. From then on it was like a royal visit as they went down the lines of waiting men, "saying something friendly left and right." Rather than an unruly mob, the English gentlemen met a courteous crowd. Moody's strategy was working.

Moody and Begbie set up shop in Whannell's courthouse, with the justice of the peace doing everything he could to ingratiate himself with the two gentlemen. He spent the outrageous sum of $114 of his own money on the best wine, spirits, beef and potatoes he could obtain, bought new cutlery and crockery, and even hired a cook and an assistant at two dollars a day. Whannell was completely unaware that Douglas had already established a per diem, limiting travelling officials' expenses — but he would find out after submitting the bill.

Meanwhile, Moody started sorting out the civil service and defence end of things, interviewing his errant underlings and trying to determine to what extent they were to blame for the current situation. After speaking with Whannell, Moody described his "bold, insane, reckless zeal, and utter ignorance," declaring him "incorruptible [which would have surprised William Branson, who had just been released from an Australian penal colony, full of courage, and despotic as a Czar."

Begbie turned to legal matters. He discovered a jail full of men who had yet to be charged with any crime, including the wretched Allmeyer, who had been reincarcerated after his December 31 release by McGowan. The chief justice began to unravel the mess, while trying not to undermine Whannell's authority too much. He held a court session with Whannell beside him and had Allmeyer brought before the bench. Begbie knew the $1,500 bail Whannell had imposed on Allmeyer amounted to an indefinite imprisonment without trial and was not pleased.

> *Although when the man Allemeyer [sic] was brought before me I did not place much confidence in his looks or statements, I felt that it was impossible to condemn too seriously the course pursued: which amounted, the killer, Foster, having by this time absconded, to a sentence of perpetual imprisonment upon a witness of (as yet untried) murder: and which might turn out to be a case of even justifiable homicide. I therefore caused him to be brought up before Capt. Whannell and myself and we discharged him on his own recognizances in the sum of fifty pounds.*[26]

Begbie took similar steps to free a man named Compter, also imprisoned for the crime of being a witness in another case and unable to meet bail. Again, Begbie set the new bail at £50 and was seriously troubled by Whannell's conduct. "This man [Compter] when dismissed was in actual want of the commonest necessaries of food and clothing, and I only fixed the amount of his recognizances so high lest too great a contrast might be drawn between my proceedings and Capt. Whannell's."[27]

While Begbie was undoing Whannell's work, Moody had a personnel problem. The more he got to know Perrier, the more he liked him. It was readily apparent Perrier was popular with the Hill's Bar miners as well. But Moody had received explicit instructions from Douglas not just to fire Perrier pending the results of his investigation, but to post notices at Hill's Bar and Fort Yale advertising the fact. Moody was reluctant to carry out his orders. He discussed the problem with Begbie, who was also hesitant to execute the governor's instructions.

"It appeared to both of us a rather sharp proceeding, and I felt very much inclined to take on myself to postpone it until further inquiry," Moody told Blackwood. "But when I reflected he really was not fit for his post any more than Captn. Whannel [*sic*] I thought I had better do it at once and meet the storm. I did so immediately and the 'hubbub' began, and I felt I had to sit my micklesome steed warily — To rule a fierce democracy is no joke at any time be their numbers small or great."

Perrier was summoned to Fort Yale and interviewed by Moody and Begbie, but was not immediately told of his dismissal. That could wait for a day. Begbie had other business to attend to. McGowan had sent him a note promising to appear in court to answer any charges against himself, for the Ubiquitous was determined to see the business through.

"I was afraid of alarming some weak-kneed friends on the bar," wrote McGowan in his reminiscences. "I had made up my mind to stand trial, provided I was not sent to Victoria for trial."

McGowan had heard "a good account of Judge Bigbee" from Allard, and he had other reasons to submit. He'd heard that the ever-excitable Whannell had urged Moody to send the marines and sappers in full force to Hill's Bar to arrest him. McGowan didn't want to give Whannell any cause for satisfaction by running. He saw no need for an armed confrontation when some smooth legal manoeuvring might suffice. Ned promised Begbie he would appear at noon the next day. This suited Begbie perfectly. The notorious American rebel had come to heel without a show of force. Moody's plan had nearly succeeded.

After the meal prepared for him by Whannell's cook (which the colonel pronounced "very bad, indigestible food"), Moody settled down for the night on a bed made of three boxes in the post office hallway. At least he had a bed of sorts — Begbie and Moody's orderly slept on the floor on either side of the colonel.

There remained but one item of business to give the operation the appearance of complete serenity: a church service. Moody sent invitations to one and all to come and hear the liturgy of the Church of England in the Fort Yale courthouse. The next morning, Sunday, January 16, 1859, Moody read the sermon while Begbie "acted as clerk." Moody was characteristically carried away with religious fervour in describing the scene as miners packed the tiny courthouse. "It was the 1st time in B. Columbia that the Liturgy of our Church was read," he rhapsodized to Blackwood.

> *The first time that we know of that people had assembled together for Public Prayer of any kind in the Colony — To me God in His mercy granted this privilege. The room was crowded full of Hill's Bar men as well as others, old grey bearded men, young eager eyed men, stern middle aged men, of all nations knelt with me before the Throne of Grace. My heart was in the utterance I gave to the beautiful prayers of our Liturgy. When it was concluded, I gave them a few words in which I must have expressed my affections for them, and I prayed God to bless them and to prosper them in all their labours. Can anyone say how much this solemn meeting may have influenced their better conduct at the close of affairs. Let us hope it did!*

The religious spectacle had no edifying effect on McGowan's behaviour, but that would become apparent later. Next came the political aims of the gathering. Moody announced that he and Begbie would travel to Hill's Bar on Monday to investigate Whannell's arrest. Warrants had been issued for McGowan and a number of others to appear. Further, Perrier was taken aside and informed of his dismissal. Word spread quickly in the town and up and down the river. The "hubbub" Moody had anticipated began immediately. Despite what might have been seen as a provocation, however, McGowan did nothing to defend his erstwhile legal lieutenant. But it did put him in a foul mood.

So far, Moody and Begbie had worked a bit of colonial magic, but they could not account for all factors at play, and the deciding one in what happened next had nothing to do with warrants, policy or the law. It had everything to do with love and a personal vendetta. That afternoon, McGowan, still smarting from Perrier's sacking, wanted to drown his woes in a few drinks of good brandy at the Allard house, hard by the Hudson's Bay post where Moody and Begbie were continuing their investigation into Whannell and Hicks. Unfortunately, Fifer was already there, still wooing Allard's daughter.

"I saw Fifer there in full communion with my friend Allard. He stepped aside when I entered the house, and the daughter informed me he had been talking against me again."[28]

Fifer must have been in his glory, certain that McGowan was in for a long sentence from Begbie who would soon be known (unfairly) as "the Hanging Judge." He might have been emboldened by a bit of that fine, dark brandy. But whatever insult to McGowan's pride the member of the purest and best had inflicted this time, repeated as it was from the mouth of Allard's daughter, proved too much for the Ubiquitous. McGowan's temper once more got the better of him. He called Fifer out.

"I did not want to have any difficulty in the house, and I asked Fifer to step outside. I told him the reason I had submitted to his slanderous tongue as long as I had. We were both armed, but neither of us attempted to draw a weapon."

McGowan saw it as a good old-fashioned San Francisco street affray. Fifer was a slight, dapper man and not inclined to violence. McGowan was of average height and weight and had the edge in experience and nastiness. Once the fisticuffs started, it wasn't much of a contest.

"I commenced the affray, and Dr. Fifer was rather roughly handled," wrote McGowan. "I would not speak of the affair now, only it is a necessary prelude to my trial."

McGowan's sense of timing and place were superbly bad. He doesn't go into details in his own reminiscences, but various reports of the one-sided fight have him slapping Fifer with a ruler and spitting in his face. Whatever the details, McGowan committed his assault in broad daylight in front of a large crowd that included his friends and curious onlookers. No one lifted a finger as McGowan pummelled his foe less than one hundred yards from where Begbie and Moody were preparing for his trial. When Begbie heard of it, he was outraged. The majesty of the law was being openly flouted. And on the Sabbath!

"McGowan in the town of Yale assaulted one Dr. Fifer — it is true, without inflicting any personal injury, but with circumstances of great contumely, although he knew that the Lieut. Governor [Moody] was then residing within 100 yards of the spot where the assault took place. Under these circumstances it was considered right to proceed more formally."[29]

Begbie chose to interpret McGowan's actions not as a spontaneous outburst born of tensions that had simmered for months, but as a deliberate, premeditated insult to the British authorities. Why else would McGowan, who up to then had been remarkably cool, commit assault on one of Yale's leading citizens without apparent provocation? Clearly neither Moody nor Begbie were well-schooled in American fighting etiquette (although they were learning fast). Such a battle would hardly have raised an eyebrow in a community where revolvers and Bowie knives were the common instruments used to settle a dispute. Moody was given an insight into the American character of the age by none other than McGowan himself after the hostilities were over.

It requires to live among these people to understand them well — Their notion of what is loyal and our notion is rather different, and personal acts of violence even to murder are only called and only considered "difficulties." That is the word. When one man coolly shoots another in broad daylight, waylaying him for that purpose, and then finds it convenient to absent himself for a short time. The world says (I mean their world, their public society) "so and so" has gone, he has had a "difficulty" with "so and so." Ned McGowan himself told me afterwards in a general conversation that when on the point of leaving to come here, "a gentleman"! stepped up to him and said "I have a personal difficulty with you Sir" and fired at him when standing close to him.[30]

Unfortunately for McGowan, he was unable to provide this insight to Moody at the time. It would be three days before Ned got a chance to speak with Moody, and on that day he was in court before Judge Begbie. Those were three eventful days in which the future of British Columbia hung in the balance.

SEVEN

McGowan's War

The one-sided fight between McGowan and Fifer provoked a series of arguments, brawls and bullying between the Law and Order faction from Hill's Bar and Yale's Vigilance Committee supporters. One man sent word to Moody that he was "besieged in his house" by an ugly-looking crowd.

"Many persons were in evident terror. The language of the Town was violent and these excitable fellows were getting their blood up," Moody wrote to Blackwood.

Concerned that arguments would escalate into "difficulties," Begbie and Moody decided to take no chances. If a leading member of the Vigilance Committee faction could be beaten with seeming impunity under their very noses, then the Yankees from Hill's Bar were certainly capable of causing a riot if they didn't like the verdict in McGowan's trial. Begbie moved McGowan's hearing from Hill's Bar to Yale and scheduled his appearance for Wednesday morning. The two English gentlemen also decided a show of force would be necessary after all.

Call for Reinforcements

"I knew that no indignity would be offered to either Judge Begbie or myself," wrote Moody. "But from the intelligence we received from all quarters it was very evident that to go on with the legal proceedings in a way to ensure the Peace not being broken it was necessary to bring up the detachment of R.E.'s from Fort Hope, and I was most anxious that not even a spark should get alight, that all should be at once crushed, and an example be shown at [*sic*] to what we could do."

Moody wrote orders for the marines, blue-jackets and artillery at Fort Langley to proceed to Fort Hope and be ready if needed. The Royal Engineers under Grant already at Fort Hope were to proceed to Yale immediately. It was now time for Moody to cash in his insurance policy: Mayne would take two Native paddlers and a light canoe and, under cover of darkness, slip downriver to Fort Hope to deliver the orders.

Mayne's first canoe trip had been exciting enough. Now he was being asked to run a gauntlet on a frigid, black night, passing Hill's Bar itself in order to reach his goal. And all without a soul knowing. "The utmost precaution was taken about my journey," he wrote.

Utmost precautions did not include a thorough security screening of all Hudson's Bay personnel, however. The man assigned to provide Mayne with canoe and paddlers was none other than Ovid Allard, McGowan's good friend and drinking companion. As Mayne and his crew pushed off and headed downstream, there were many eyes watching.

"As we dropped down the stream I was afraid even to light a pipe lest we should be stopped at Hill's Bar," wrote Mayne. "Absurd as all this now seems — especially as I heard on my return that the miners knew perfectly well of my starting."

Mayne's second canoe trip turned out to be dull compared to his first. He reached Fort Hope at 8:30 that evening and told a surprised Grant he was to gather his troops and start for Yale at once. Moody's orders were carefully detailed, taking into account all the difficulties of bringing even a small force up through such dangerous territory. Moody also instructed Grant to bring with him "a few picked Cornish Miners on whom I knew I could depend." Moody had met these staunch defenders of the Crown at Cornish Bar. Some two hundred had volunteered to fight the American menace, and Moody selected a dozen of the more experienced men as "special constables" for a reserve in the event of hostilities.

Grant's force was to travel by boat, landing just below Hill's Bar, on the opposite bank of the river from McGowan's stronghold. They could not take the boats any farther because the river narrowed at Hill's Bar, and a strong, rapid current made paddling almost impossible. The only channel available was right next to the bar itself, and Moody did not want to risk having his troops fired on in their small, slow-moving craft as they passed the American positions. The reliable John Ogilvy was sent ahead in a canoe to act as a scout in case of an ambush. Moody considered this assignment a compliment, confiding in his letter to Blackwood: "You may imagine how much I thought of Ogilvy, to give him the post of honour, viz. the post of danger."

Grant roused his troops at once and prepared to move out. Mayne, however, had to relay Moody's orders for further reinforcements to Fort Langley. It was once again into the canoe and off. The passage down the river was much faster than struggling up against its considerable current, and by midnight Mayne reached the *Enterprise*, which was supposed to immediately take him to Fort Langley and embark the reinforcements. But Tom Wright would not risk his vessel in any nighttime journey, no matter how urgent the message from Moody. The steamer didn't start for Fort Langley until dawn, and it was afternoon before Mayne could hand over Moody's orders. By the time the *Enterprise* had loaded both troops and fuel, it was 6 p.m. If there was any trouble with the Yankees at Yale, Grant was on his own.

Unaware of the delay, Grant followed Moody's orders to the letter. In the darkness, the R.E.s and the Cornish volunteers set out in a flotilla of small boats. Ahead of them went Ogilvy with two Native paddlers and another Hudson's Bay man named MacDonald (possibly Ranald MacDonald, son of Archibald MacDonald, a long-time HBC employee). These two men were also in charge of the Cornish "special constables," who acted as a vanguard because of their experience on the river. Also accompanying the force was Chartres Brew.

Everyone knew the hazards of the journey. Moody was frank in his assessment of the area he called "Glen Albert," telling Blackwood: "To a military advance, if opposed, Glen Albert is full of danger."

The night was intensely cold and clear. Moonlight helped the small force see, but also lit them up for anyone interested in using them for target practice. Ogilvy, MacDonald and their paddlers proceeded slowly, landing occasionally to get their bearings. The journey took all night, and it was first light by the time they landed on the shore opposite Hill's Bar. With MacDonald and Ogilvy leading, the Royal Engineers and special constables began their march towards Yale, just a short distance from McGowan's forces. Wrapped in their dark greatcoats, the engineers stood out against the white snow. Despite the cover of trees along the riverbank, they were easily spotted by sentries at Hill's Bar, who had anticipated their arrival.

This was the moment of truth. If McGowan and Dolan were to oppose Grant's passage and fall back on their "dernier ressort," now was the time. And as rifle balls and bullets hurled overhead, it must have seemed, at least for a moment, that the Yankees had chosen to fight.

"At Break of day the Hill's Bar Men saw the detachment filing past between the trees on the opposite bank and they ran down shouting and firing their rifles," wrote Moody. "It might have been and probably was only a bravado."

Luckily for Grant and his men, it was. The shots came nowhere near the British force. Grant said he heard no bullets, but Ogilvy and the Cornish special constables did. Even then, things might have gotten out of hand had anyone returned fire, especially the Cornish volunteers. But Moody had picked his men well.

"The Cornish men did not even turn their heads or utter a syllable, they just marched steadily on but with a look of very determined character, while on the opposite side of the River all was shouting and excitement. With respect to my own good fellows I have only to say they are '*Royal Engineers*' that is surely enough."[1]

The shouting and confusion died down as the troops disappeared up the river. As dawn broke fully over the Cascades, Ogilvy and MacDonald led the way into Yale, grinning and enjoying themselves as Moody raced out to greet them. Guided by the Native men and the Hudson's Bay Company employees, the Royal Engineers and Cornish volunteers had made it to Yale intact.

After breakfast, Moody paraded his small but impressive-looking force in front of the fort and in full view of "Heaps of Rowdies." With their red uniform jackets and pillbox hats, the Royal Engineers helped set the style for the future Northwest Mounted Police. The people of Yale and a good number of McGowan's agents watched Moody inspect his troops. The display of force was small, but had its calculated effect.

"From the moment of their arrival, everything began to change and brighten up," wrote Moody. "Alarm vanished and Hill's Bar Men were full of assurances to everybody that they were and always had been loyal men and to say otherwise was to libel them."

With the troops in town, Begbie felt confident enough to send a single constable to Hill's Bar to serve McGowan with a summons. Also summonsed was Terence Kelly, McGowan's assistant during Whannell's arrest. McGowan dutifully promised to appear and the stage was set for a legal showdown in Yale that Wednesday.

Moody felt the Americans had, up to then, not really appreciated how seriously the British took the concept of "the Law" with a capital L. "After the Sappers came one constable was quite sufficient to execute the summons anywhere, not I believe from fear exactly, but because their eyes were open for the first time to see that in the Queen's dominions an infringement of the Law was really a serious matter, and not a sort of half joke as in California," he wrote to Blackwood.

Speechifying ... without the Adjectives

The Americans had been thwarted in getting their way by force, so now they resorted to their other great weapon — speechifying. The situation called for a meeting, with yet more resolutions designed to show the English gentlemen just how things sat. That evening of Tuesday, January 18, 1859, with the sappers in town and everyone full of British patriotism, Moody and Begbie received a delegation of three miners who invited them to a meeting of "citizens of Fort Yale" at Bennet's Gambling House.

"They had a meeting and *respectfully* and earnestly invited me to be present as they wished to address me," wrote an amused Moody. "After telling them I should make no reply to their address, and that the Law should have its course and their declaring that all who had offended the law would be present to stand their trial at the hour at which they had been summoned before Judge Begbie ... After declaring the above I went to the Meeting accompanied by Judge Begbie."

Moody and Begbie took Whannell along for their first taste of American-style democracy. Although billed as a local gathering, there were but six residents of Fort Yale present and about two hundred from Hill's Bar. After three cheers for Governor Douglas, the Americans launched into a bitter attack on Whannell, using what Begbie delicately described as "a good many epithets." Moody had in fact just officially rapped Whannell's knuckles for posting his $100 reward for Foster's capture, something the colonel reminded the JP he had no authority to do. But Moody was mindful of preserving the dignity of Whannell's office, so he interrupted the first speaker and ordered him to omit the insults and stick to the facts. This threw the Americans for a loop.

"This produced a very bald reading," Begbie wryly noted. "I took the liberty of suggesting a short adjournment in order to re-draw the resolutions with an eye to the adjectives."[2]

After the adjectives were adjusted, the meeting resumed. This time, the Hill's Bar men trotted out Chas Wilson, a former San Francisco commissioner and their best speaker. Dressed in a red flannel shirt and jeans, Wilson might have looked like any other miner, but he certainly didn't sound like one. He commenced "pitching heavily into Whannell" and praising the absent Hicks. One can only imagine how Whannell felt, receiving such a dressing down in front of his superiors. It was likely only Moody and Begbie's calming influence that prevented him from attempting a mass arrest.

The list of resolutions passed by the gathering included a mixture of toadyism, veiled threats and, adjectives or no, vicious criticism. Begging Douglas to "remedy the evils which we now so grievously suffer from," the miners passed resolutions condemning "the tyrannous conduct of P.B. Whannell, a Magistrate in Her Majesty's service, in arresting persons without cause, without issuing warrants and for imprisoning persons merely to gratify his own caprice, and in refusing said persons an examination, as the law directs, and also for levying fines in violation of the Statutes, deserves the severest censure, and we earnestly pray that His Excellency Governor Douglas will remove said Whannell from his present position, and appoint a gentleman possessing sufficient knowledge of the duties of his office as will meet the confidence of this community."[3]

Wilson and the miners, including McGowan's good friend P.J. Cassin, a Yale saloon keeper who signed the resolutions, certainly had a case against Whannell. They went a bit far, however, in defending Hicks as "a gentleman" and an officer of the Crown who had "always been fair and honourable," although the praise might have been thrown in just to see if it would give Whannell an aneurysm. Begbie and Moody already had a wealth of information to the contrary, and it amused them to listen to yet another American "multifarious conglomeration of heterogeneous nonsense." Moody, however, was impressed by Wilson, although he was less moved by the formal resolutions.

"In addition, one man in a red shirt, formerly an Alderman of San Francisco made me an admirable speech, extremely clever and in the *best possible taste and feeling* — They all cultivate the art of speaking, and SOME speak very well — The address was a long defence, explanation and apology, nothing particularly clever in it."

Begbie and Moody listened to everything "in solemn silence." After the rhetoric concluded, Moody refused to comment on the contents of the resolutions, but "merely gave answer that his ear and his heart were open."[4] However, they made no attempt to defend Whannell, who had to sit there and suffer. Both Moody and Begbie did reply to Wilson's clever address, and both sought out the well-spoken miner after the meeting to assure him his fine words would have no effect whatsoever in the Queen's dominion, where judges did not have to face the electorate and governors didn't have to worry about winning the next election or, in Douglas's case, worry overmuch about popular sentiment.

"In answer, however, to a previous very excellent (but superlatively humbugging) address from a red-shirted miner named Wilson," wrote Begbie,

> *both Col. Moody and myself had given a few words, not above 5 minutes apiece, expressive of the general intention of the Government to carry out the laws without fear or favour: And in conversation with Wilson and a very fine young fellow, not more than 21 or 22, who has already the distinction of being Ned McGowan's lieutenant, we had both impressed them with the fact that His Excellency could make no answer to the address: that the mere fact of our presence here, in such weather, our proceeding to action, and quite alone (in the first instance) shewed our resolution to examine into matters, and that whatever might be the particular terms of the address, the line of action ultimately adopted would be utterly irrespective of their views and sentiments and would be guided solely by the facts.[5]*

The meeting broke up with three cheers for the Queen. As an attempt by the Hill's Bar men to sway Begbie while he was sitting in judgment over McGowan the next morning, the meeting had failed pointedly. As the miners left, they hotly debated what the morrow would bring. It would not bring any blue-jackets to bolster the Royal Engineers: Moody had ordered them back to their base. If reinforcements were required, he decided he would do fine with just the marines, still struggling up the river with Mayne aboard the *Enterprise*.

Day of Judgment

On Wednesday, January 19, 1859, the day of judgment dawned. It was in the cramped confines of the log-cabin courtroom that the principal battle of McGowan's War would be fought. At the front of the room was Begbie in his magistrate's robes. On the judge's left was Whannell; to his right, Moody and Brew. The tiny courtroom was packed with miners from both Law and Order and Vigilance Committee factions.

As Moody surveyed the crowd, he did not fail to note that every

man in attendance was "armed to the teeth." He had taken the precaution of stationing his troops in and around the courthouse in case
of trouble. If Moody was anxious, he had a right to be. His entire
force was sick and worn from their exposure in the cold trip upriver.
Many, including Moody and Begbie themselves, were suffering from
diarrhea. If the Yankees chose to make trouble, they might easily
overwhelm his tiny, weakened force.

McGowan made his entrance, dressed, as he put it, in "a full suit
of the Hudson Bay rig, with a thick blue shirt outside." He was also
packing a pistol. There was a nervous pause as the court awaited the
arrival of Fifer. When the doctor finally pushed his way inside, Begbie called the proceedings to order and the business began in earnest.
It was to be an education in American politics and political invective,
for there were some "adjectives" with which Begbie was not familiar.

First McGowan had to answer to a charge of assault on Fifer.
McGowan pleaded guilty, but gave, as Moody put it, "an exquisitely
beautiful speech, so neat, such few words, all to the point, nothing
discursive, no 'bunkism,' no nonsense of any kind, admirable for
what *he left out* as well as for what he said — It was in fact a very
clever and very gentlemanly speech — dignified and yet respectful."

In the speech, McGowan placed his reasons for assaulting Fifer in
the context of the struggle between the Democrats / Law and Order
faction and the Vigilance Committee.

*I made a statement to the court, giving a short history of my
persecutions and trials in my own country; that I was driven from
mine by a mob, who, had they caught me, would have hanged me;
when the people came to their sober second senses I went back and
stood my trial, and was honorably acquitted; that I had now left my
own country, and sought a domicile on British soil and protection
under the British flag. I added that I knew the complainant, Fifer, in
San Francisco, where, although a foreigner himself (a Dane), he then
belonged to a party who were against all foreigners, called the Know
Nothings; that he was also a strangler . . .*[6]

Begbie did not know what the term "strangler" meant and interrupted McGowan. The Ubiquitous obligingly explained the apt nickname he had given Fifer and the other members of the committee who lynched their victims. Begbie does not mention if he considered this an "epithet," but McGowan resumed his attack on Fifer.

> *... and one of the parties who had been instrumental in making me an outcast from society and a wanderer ... that he now claimed to be a British subject, and how he had slandered me to the authorities, etc.*

McGowan did not forget to apologize personally to Moody for giving Fifer a thrashing in such close proximity to the lieutenant governor. As he wrote later, "I then apologized to the court, and to His Excellency Lieutenant Governor Moody, for having committed the offense, as it were, in their very presence, and hoped they would take into consideration the great provocation I had had, as I did not want them to place me in the category of either an outlaw or a desperado."[7]

McGowan finished with a promise to Begbie that he would obey British law in future. Begbie was grateful to hear it and considered it sincere. "On the summons for the assault on Fifer, McGowan pleaded guilty, expressed his regret and his intention to observe the laws strictly for the future — expressions which I was very glad to hear, as coming from a man reputed to be of violent character, and made without any compulsion whatever, and in the presence of a large crowd of men over most of whom he exercises a very considerable influence, and therefore possessing much more weight with these bystanders than any words of mine."[8]

Finished for the time being, McGowan sat down. Fifer sprang up to make a statement, but was stopped by Begbie: McGowan had pleaded guilty and there was no need to hear from the victim. At this point the San Francisco *Bulletin*, which printed a florid account of McGowan's trial, has Begbie gravely stating, "You shall have justice, Mr. McGowan, here; Justice which I fear, even after having heard your own story, you have not often met with." Begbie doesn't mention it, and even if he did say something akin to this, it was no prelude to a sympathetic sentence.

"Begbie inflicted the greatest fine he could [£5] and caused him [McGowan] to enter into recognizances to keep the peace," wrote Moody to Blackwood. "He also delivered a very manly address what you might expect from an Englishman who has high courage — He gave it to McGowan very heavily, and stripped bare all their false definitions of right and wrong."

As harsh as he was in condemning McGowan's assault, Begbie was obviously swayed by McGowan's tale of flight from the clutches of an avenging mob, for while the British held a generally low opinion of American "democracy" in general and American politicians in particular, the one thing they abhorred more than anything else was mob rule. In their eyes, McGowan might be a cad and a ne'er-do-well, but he deserved a fair trial. He also did not deserve a prison sentence, though Begbie's order that he keep the peace was a sort of unofficial probation.

McGowan went to the clerk's desk to pay his fine, and, according to his reminiscences, "a dozen buckskin bags with gold dust were offered to me by miners present in court to pay the fine and costs." Gold dust was the currency of necessity in Yale's saloons, but in Begbie's court, fines had to be paid in coin. McGowan had none on him, but his friend Cassin, the saloon keeper, came to the rescue.

A Clever Yankee Trick

McGowan was over his first legal hurdle, but when the court settled down, Begbie proceeded with the more serious charges against McGowan and Kelly of falsely arresting Whannell, taking possession of the jail and freeing prisoners of the Crown. McGowan and Kelly pleaded not guilty. Then McGowan pulled a legal trick out of his hat: instead of proceeding immediately to trial, he asked if Begbie would be prepared to hear McGowan's evidence first, weighed against Whannell's, and decide if there was a case. Although he found the idea "irregular," Begbie agreed to what we would now call a preliminary hearing.

Whannell took the stand and gave an account of his arrest, transportation to Hill's Bar, trial and conviction for contempt of court. According to McGowan, "I observed the Judge smiled several times as he [Whannell] gave his evidence." Whannell wasn't much of a witness, but he was a justice of the peace and an officer of the Queen, and there was no doubt he'd been arrested and fined. It appeared an open-and-shut case. However, though McGowan may not have practised law for years, he was still a shrewd lawyer. He knew something of Begbie's mind and now he went to work on it. He knew he had to ruin what little credibility Whannell had left with Begbie. He also had to prove provocation.

"I asked Wannel [*sic*] only a few questions — about the illegality of his official acts," wrote McGowan. "He was surprised that any official act of his should be considered in that light. I could see by the manner of the Judge, however, that he coincided in my view of the matter, as far as the illegality was concerned."[9]

McGowan was right about that, as Begbie had spent his first afternoon in Yale freeing an entire jail full of innocent men put there by the over-ardent magistrate. Whannell stepped down and Wright the jailer took the stand.

"He detailed the facts as they occurred, with a slight exaggeration of the amount of bravery he had exhibited in his resistance — drawing his pistols etc. I did not cross-examine him, but admitted the facts as the witness had stated them," wrote McGowan magnanimously.

Begbie had evidently heard enough. He asked McGowan if he wanted to be bound over for trial. McGowan reminded Begbie he'd agreed to hear evidence for the defence as well as the prosecution.

"Oh yes, yes," said Begbie. "Go on."

McGowan called to the stand the only witness he needed: George Perrier. The former justice of the peace for Hill's Bar was sworn in, and McGowan pulled out his trump card.

"Judge, will you be kind enough to tell His Honor whether or not I acted under your instructions?" McGowan asked.

Perrier testified that McGowan had been deputized to do his court's bidding. McGowan then produced the warrant for Whannell's arrest issued by Perrier, the order deputizing him as a special constable and the transcript of the proceedings that he had instructed Perrier to have drafted. The lot was entered in as evidence. Perrier went on to testify that McGowan had acted "with great moderation" and was about to launch into a litany of Whannell's shortcomings when Begbie stopped the proceedings.

The judge conferred with Brew and Moody. McGowan had turned Begbie's strongest weapon, the law, against him. It was instantly apparent to the Equity Court-trained mind of Begbie that there was no way to legally convict McGowan of anything other than having a bad reputation. A trial would just give McGowan a soapbox from which to preach about the blatant injustice being done to him, an American citizen. It could become a rallying point for Americans who, contrary to their express opinions in the saloons of Yale, still harboured Manifest Destiny sentiments in their hearts. After a short conversation, the three wise Englishmen (or two Englishmen and one Irishman, to be precise) realized their desperado was about to slip from their grip.

"On the whole, Mr. Brew and I were both of opinion that no jury would have convicted on an indictment for the alleged misdemeanour in assaulting the Justice and forcing the gaol," wrote Begbie in explaining the trial to Douglas. "It appeared, indeed, to me that if the matter had gone to trial I should have been bound to direct an acquittal. With the concurrence of the Lieut. Governor, therefore, Mr. Brew and myself directed the defendants to be dismissed."[10]

McGowan records that Begbie was somewhat less formal and distressed in the courtroom than the tone in his final report to Douglas implies. After Begbie stopped Perrier from attacking Whannell, McGowan wrote: "The judge . . . conferred for a few moments with Lieutenant Governor Moody, when both of them laughed. Judge Bigbee then turned to me and said: 'A clever Yankee trick!!' and added: 'Mr. McGowan, you are discharged.'"

The Hill's Bar men burst into cheers. Whannell's reaction is not recorded. As they had done after their first great victory over Whannell, McGowan and his party adjourned to a saloon, this time Cassin's. It was not a private party for the Law and Order faction. There were in attendance "citizens and soldiers, who thought the 'Yankees' a lot of good fellows."

A Grand Reception

To show just how good a fellow he was, McGowan was prepared to go to extraordinary lengths. At Moody's request, McGowan provided the colonel with a copy of his account of his adventures at the hands of the San Francisco Vigilance Committee, and the two men had a pleasant chat. But McGowan had something other than reading in mind for Moody.

> *As soon as Colonel Moody had retired to his quarters, I went to the store of my friend, William Woodcock, Esq. (still up in that country), and purchased two baskets of wine at $50 a basket, the only champagne that had ever reached that part of the mines, and indicted the following note:*
>
> > *Judge McGowan presents his compliments to Lieutenant General Moody, Commander-in-Chief of Her Britannic Majesty's forces in Vancouver's Island and British Columbia, and begs his acceptance of the accompanying basket of wine, that he may drink Her Britannic Majesty's health, this being his first visit to British Columbia.*

McGowan dispatched his right-hand man, Tom Dolan, with the wine. Dolan employed a Native bearer to carry the stuff and arrived at the post office, where Moody had set up his headquarters. Dolan presented McGowan's note to Moody's orderly, and in a few minutes the colonel greeted the American adventurer. Dolan related the following conversation to McGowan, who recorded it in his "Reminiscences."

"Ah," said Moody. "Major Dolan. Of what army, Major?"

"Nicaragua, Colonel," said Dolan, saluting.

"Why, you are a blasted filibuster," cried Moody. "Tell Judge McGowan I have not drunk Her Majesty's health in a glass of wine since I have been in British Columbia, and I will do so tomorrow with him at his hut."

Moody doesn't mention this incident specifically, but he did tell Blackwood that, after the trial, he told the men of Hill's Bar he "would now come and see them and go over their works and make their acquaintance, on the distinct understanding there should be no demonstration of any kind whatsoever (I now feared their excess of loyalty, they are so impulsive)."

An excessive display is just what McGowan had in mind. Dolan returned to Hill's Bar with the champagne and Moody's reply. Here, Ned knew, was a perfect opportunity to show what a loyal British subject he had become. The Boatmen set about throwing a first-class bash for Moody and his suite: a "grand reception." McGowan gives a vivid description of the Hill's Bar men scrambling to find all the delicacies needed to put on such a display in what was to them the wilderness.

> We hired a baker at Fort Yale to work all night and make us a sugar-crusted poundcake — reserved both baskets of wine. Borrowed an English and a French flag (we had the stars and stripes), and a number of the miners remained up all night decorating the San Francisco Boatmen's Company's cabin ... We decked our cabin with evergreens, and arranged the American flag in the center, the British and French flags on the right and left sides. This was in honor of the French being the allies to the English troops in the Crimean War. The victories won by the United French and English troops in those terribly fought battles were still green in the memories of the British soldiers; some of those present were heroes of the Redan and the Malakoff.
>
> The table was arranged in capital style. We had borrowed all the crockery, tumblers and table linen in the Bar. We could not boast of having all the "delicacies of the season," but we had the substantials

and an immense sugar-crusted poundcake and two baskets of genuine Heidsieck.[11]

At noon on Thursday, January 20, 1859, Begbie, Brew and a few officers arrived at Hill's Bar. Also present was Mayne, who had reached Fort Yale with the reinforcements after two hideous days of battling ice and the river's current, only to find the campaign over. He was on time to taste the fruits of victory, however.

McGowan records that Moody and a force of twenty-five sappers and miners were in attendance, but this is a case of the Ubiquitous's memory playing him false. Moody would drink champagne with McGowan, but only a few days later, on his way back to Victoria. On this day he was in Yale, sick as a dog. He'd collapsed that morning, due, he told Blackwood, to the "excessive cold the daily wet feet, cold up to my knees in snow and sludge, sleeping on all manner of things ... very bad indigestible food, etc. etc." Moody "almost fainted and became vulgarly sick," but he records that "Begbie, Mayne (who had returned to me) and Brue [*sic*] who had come up country went to Hill's Bar and were very well received."

It is interesting that Begbie makes no mention of this visit in any of his official reports to Douglas. Perhaps he thought what the governor didn't know (that his top officials were fraternizing with an American desperado who, even if he had been found not guilty, had still cost the new colony a pretty penny) wouldn't hurt him. But Mayne described the event enthusiastically in his memoirs.

"Next day, upon Hill's Bar being visited by Mr. Begbie (the Chief Justice) and myself, he [McGowan] conducted us over the diggings, washed some 'dirt' to show us the process, and invited us to a collation in his hut," wrote Mayne.

"Collation" is the word used by several writers who were present — including Perrier — to describe the event, and it was the perfect word to use, given the circumstances. According to the *Oxford Concise Dictionary* it means "a light meal (usu. cold ~) often at an exceptional time" and refers to the Benedictine monks' practice of a collatio (a reading of the Lives of the Fathers, or *collationes patrum*), followed by a debate and a light repast. "Pipe of peace" might also have been an appropriate description.

"Well received," Moody wrote, and well received they were. Begbie and party entered a rude miners' cabin transformed into a ballroom, decorated with evergreen bows, flags and in the middle, a table of food and drink unrivalled on the B.C. mainland. A dozen or so of McGowan's friends were inside, and the old Ubiquitous himself was in his glory.

"As soon as they placed themselves on each side of the festive board, the band played 'Rule Britannia' and 'Hail Columbia,'" wrote McGowan.

The music ceased. McGowan rose and gave a brief speech of welcome and asked pardon of his refined English guests as "we were American miners from California, unaccustomed to the etiquette of society, and that any errors that might occur on this festive occasion must be attributed to the 'head and not to the heart.'"

"I ventured further to say 'that our status of yesterday looked dark, but to-day the horizon was bright; that all of our difficulties had been settled to our entire satisfaction, and I hoped, also, to the satisfaction of the authorities.' The prediction of the press of San Francisco and Victoria to the contrary notwithstanding, our fight had been a bloodless one — a legal fight — which leaves no one killed or wounded to be carried off the field — instead of a funeral we were to have a feast."[12]

McGowan was deafened by cheers and cries of "hear hear!" It quite unnerved him, and for a moment he lost his place. But recovering quickly, he ordered the glasses be filled with champagne and proposed a toast to the Queen, knowing it would have the desired effect on his guests. "When the health of his Queen is drunk an Englishman is always proud," wrote McGowan. "And the three or four hundred miners on the outside made the welkin ring with loud cheering."

The excessive display of courtesy worked. Any fears Begbie may have had of Yankee insurrection or further trouble from McGowan fizzled like the bubbles popping in his glass. The band played "God Save the Queen," and Begbie stood to give his response. He praised James Buchanan, whom he had met when the American president was a young diplomat in London. He downplayed the boundary dispute and, according to McGowan, said, "the good feeling — the intente cordial [*sic*] — of the two great powers would not be disrupted by a question of such minor importance." Begbie also laid on thick the theme of England as the Mother Country and the ties of language and heritage between the U.S. and Great Britain. McGowan, at least, was captivated by the performance.

"I cannot do justice to the great speech the Judge made, after a lapse of twenty years. He was a fine actor and an accomplished gentleman, and a scholar. Our glasses were again filled, and Judge Bigbee toasted 'The President of the United States.' (Cheers and 'Yankee Doodle.')"

After a few more speeches, including another vintage performance from the well-spoken Wilson, it was Begbie's turn to be impressed. McGowan states Begbie asked him if all the miners present were of Wilson's wit and education.

"I replied, 'Oh yes.' He then said: 'What a wonderful nation you Yankees are. I thought the French were vivacious, but you beat them all to pieces.'"

Begbie asked McGowan if he would swear allegiance to the Queen, since he was now an exile from the United States. McGowan cheerfully told Begbie his "difficulties" were limited to the city of San Francisco, not the United States generally, and "that, in my defense, all my talk before the court about the British soil and protection of the flag was bosh. I was only 'playing' for the sympathy of the Judge; and also, that nine-tenths of the men on the Bar were Irishmen or the sons of Irishmen, all of them Catholics and enemies of his country, and the very moment I became a subject of Great Britain my influence with them would cease."

Begbie politely changed the topic to the charming scenery and natural resources of the United States. There followed a short tour of the diggings, which impressed Mayne. In fact, everything about the event, including McGowan, impressed Mayne, who wrote:

We drank champagne with some twelve or fifteen of his Californian mining friends. And, whatever the opinion the Vigilance Committee of San Francisco might entertain of these gentlemen, I, speaking as I found them, can only say that, all things considered, I have rarely lunched with a better-spoken, pleasanter party.

The word "miner" to many unacquainted with the gold-fields conveys an impression similar, perhaps, to that of "navvy." But among them may often be found men who, by birth and education, are well-qualified to hold their own in the most civilised community of Europe. Here, for instance, I was entertained in the hut of a man who — by virtue of his rascality, no doubt — had been selected to fill the office of judge among his fellows in California; while one of my neighbors had taken his degree at an American university, and may since, for aught I know, have edited a Greek play and been made a bishop.

After a final toast of champagne, Begbie and his party departed for Yale before nightfall. McGowan had reason to congratulate himself. He'd won a considerable legal victory, which had derailed Fifer's plans to establish a local Vigilance Committee. He'd impressed B.C.'s top legal officer and, for good measure, he would entertain the recovered Moody a few days later. The colonel confided in his letter to Blackwood (and, like Begbie, *not* to Douglas) that he was enchanted by McGowan's blarney, but still wary.

"So much disappointment was expressed at not seeing me that I determined to call on my return down river," wrote Moody.

I now ordered the Marines up to relieve the R.Es, and sent the latter down to Langley to their work. The Marines I thought it prudent to leave for a short time. The following day in dropping down the River I called at Hill's Bar and was very properly received everywhere. The men all busy at work. Ned McGowan pressed me to enter his Hut gave me an excellent Glass of Champagne! The best I have almost ever tasted, and with me drank Her Majesty's health! He gave me a very great deal of useful information and I seriously entertain the hope that I may convert him into a valuable subject of the Crown eventually, but he needs watching.

It was during this visit that McGowan explained the American meaning of the term "difficulties" to Moody. The colonel passed down the river the same day. McGowan's War was over, fought and won in the courts and formally ended by a glass of champagne. The humiliation of Richard Hicks, however, had just begun.

Hicks's Humiliation

Hicks knew the game was up and begged for clemency by appealing directly to Douglas even before Moody and Begbie arrived in Yale. In a desperate letter penned aboard the *Otter* on January 11, 1859, Hicks asks for Whannell's job as justice of the peace for Fort Yale, "should Your Excellency *make any alterations, as is generally expected.*" Douglas, however, left Hicks's fate in the capable hands of Moody and Begbie.

Moody continued his investigation into the suspended assistant commissioner's affairs. By February 1, 1859 (the date of his letter to Blackwood), he was able to confide to his friend in England: "there can be no doubt of the gross corruption and pusillanimous conduct of a Mr. Hicks, a Gold Commissioner and Magistrate, a miserable creature."

Begbie was also on the case. Together, the two men grilled Hicks in Yale. Hicks suddenly developed amnesia about almost all his business affairs, and even the details of his most recent transactions slipped his mind. Did he own part of a sawmill? Ferry at Spuzzum? What ferry? It took some time, but the English gentlemen finally extracted from Hicks a fair semblance of the truth. And what an astonishing catalogue of bribery, extortion, embezzlement and speculation it was. On February 3, 1859, Begbie reported to Douglas that Hicks was "totally unworthy of serving Her Majesty in any capacity whatever" and recommended criminal charges be laid against him.

I am sorry to have to report, as the result of those inquiries, throughout which the Lieut. Governor bore a patient and laborious part, Mr. Hicks appears wholly to have neglected his duties as far as

*keeping any records: the imperfect entries which he has kept being
such as to invite doubt and investigation only, and being apparently
incapable of proper explanation even by himself — that he appears
wholly to have neglected any attempt to collect the revenue which it
was his duty to have collected, and which to some extent at least
might have been collected, whereas it is now more than probable
that much of the arrears will be lost; that he has on many occasions
by his own admission taken unauthorized fees from miners or others
for recording or pretending to record their claims; that he has in
several instances, on granting or pretending to grant privileges
connected with the land, reserved or obtained for himself an interest
in the profits; that he, being authorized to grant liquor licenses, has
in particular granted to one Kingham an exclusive wholesale liquor
license at Yale in which he is allowed a third or a quarter share on
the express stipulation that no other person shall be allowed a
wholesale license there, and has refused to grant such other license
accordingly; and that he has brought the whole administration of
justice into contempt. It is scarcely possible to arrive at an accurate
knowledge of his misconduct, as we found by experience that no
reliance is to be placed on his most distinct assurances on subjects
which must be within his own personal and very recent knowledge;
e.g., an interest reserved to himself in a sawmill and a ferry, as to
which he admitted on the last day we were at Yale that he had told
us clear and repeated falsehoods.*

*The whole of the leases in the Yale town district are, moreover, so
far as I have seen them, void, in consequence of his having without a
pretense of authority very materially altered the terms of the printed
forms which he had furnished by Your Excellency; in fact, omitting
the principal stipulations in the lease introduced on the part of the
Crown. I am therefore of the opinion that Mr. Hicks is totally
unworthy of serving Her Majesty in any capacity whatever, and that
it would be extremely proper that criminal proceedings should be
instituted against him.*[13]

As a result of Hicks's malfeasance, the question of who owned what
in Yale was completely tangled. Begbie recommended wiping the

slate clean and starting over. Nor did Begbie content himself with merely cataloguing Hicks's iniquities. He went further, placing the blame for "McGowan's" War squarely on the collective shoulders of Hicks, Whannell and Perrier.

> *It is easy to conceive what a ready opening there was for disturbance in a district where a weak and corrupt magistrate like Mr. Hicks, having thrown men's minds and titles into discontent and confusion, was succeeded by two magistrates like Captain Whannell and Mr. Perrier, alike ignorant of the law, surrounded by evil counsellors, and carried away with the most unbounded ideas of the dignity of their offices and themselves. It appears very providential that no more serious consequences took place.*

Of all the charges against Hicks, the one taken most seriously was his manipulation of the Yale town survey. The initial evidence of wrongdoing was so extreme that Douglas handed the case over to yet another newly arrived official, George Hunter Cary, B.C.'s first attorney general. Cary landed in Victoria in early 1859 carrying only "six law books, a carpetbag and a toothbrush." According to Dr. Helmcken, he drank too much, was conceited, irritable, untruthful, unscrupulous and "shallow beyond belief." Cary's habit of riding his horse at breakneck speed along Victoria's sidewalks got him arrested in September 1859 for "furious riding" on James Bay bridge, but the case was dismissed. In January 1860, Cary was again arrested for riding his horse on the footpath on Fort Street and had to pawn his gun to pay the $10 fine. Prior to this he had been thrown in jail for accepting a challenge to duel with David Babbington Ring, an Irish lawyer, in October 1859. Cary was charged with intention to commit a breach of the peace and ordered to pay a bond of $500 to keep the peace for one year or face twelve months' imprisonment. When Cary refused to post the bond, he was thrown in the Victoria jail. He spent the next few hours alternately raging and crying until he was released later in the day on a writ of *habeas corpus*. Helmcken said that "genius and madness in him were closely allied."[14]

Hicks somehow had to convince the unstable Cary he had not conspired with the surveyor he hired, a Mr. Lammott, to illegally obtain three prime waterfront lots in Yale, on which he planned to build a waterfront hotel. He claimed he was only following Douglas's personal order to have the town laid out forthwith. Cary wasn't convinced and demanded Hicks's correspondence and records. Hicks responded by asking Douglas to confirm that the governor himself had promised the lots to him the previous spring to "compensate me for the laborious work I performed." Douglas did not reply. He had his secretary, Young, send Hicks a letter demanding written proof of his claim.

"I have to acquaint you that no record is found of any grant of land having been made to you in May last, nor does His Excellency remember the transaction to which you allude," wrote Young.[15]

Unofficially, however, Douglas appears to have acted in concert with Moody and Begbie to find a way to make Hicks go away quietly. Douglas felt it best to let the matter be forgotten rather than display the new administration's initial incompetence and corruption in an open trial. In fact, Hicks threatened to go public with his side of the story. "I would at all times sooner complain to you right out than through Newspapers — this at all times is the proper course," Hicks wrote to Douglas. In the end, the deal Douglas struck with Hicks was a simple one: sell off your ill-gotten goods, leave quietly, and you won't go to prison. It was the sort of discreet Victorian arrangement common at the time. In March, Douglas officially fired the "respectable" Richard Hicks.

Hicks received the not-unexpected news and at once penned a letter to Moody. As an apologia, it is somewhat lacking. After declaring he is "not for a moment going to defend my conduct in any one respect," Hicks proceeded to do just that, severally.

I performed the duties of every office in my district for about five months with no one to advise or assist me. My pay was very small and I thought it not more than just that I should enter into some speculations, that I may make a little money as well as others in a Country like this and where Americans were grasping at every thing.

*I see that I was wrong in doing so and admit my error and having
relinquished every undertaking I embarked in after you left Fort
Yale, I am now nearly five hundred dollars worse than I was when I
accepted office and taking my age into account its sure hard upon
me, not being able to do much hard work.*

Hicks begged for another job in government, assuring Moody he
would conduct himself in the future in a manner which "shall merit
your esteem." Moody did not even dignify this suggestion with a
reply. Hicks hired a lawyer and hinted at a lawsuit. But with Cary
making his life miserable, he finally capitulated. Despite having
proudly told Douglas he was "an Englishman, pure bred, and born,
never having foresaken myself from my Queen and always proud of
my country," Hicks abandoned Queen, country, everything (including his wife, Orinda) and returned to San Francisco in the autumn of
1859.

George Perrier, on the other hand, had to force a reluctant Douglas's hand before being officially removed from his post. Moody
had told him he would be dismissed, but it had to come from Douglas in writing, and the confusion around Hicks had occupied almost
the whole of the officials' attentions. On April 1, 1859, Perrier
handed in his resignation before he could be officially fired.

"Having waited some time for your final decision, and thinking
that such an humble individual as myself might be forgotten in the
press of Executive duties, I therefore take this missive to recall your
excellencies' attention and pray you receiving my resignation," Perrier wrote in his letter to Douglas.

Perrier gave the letter, as well as the handwritten commission
Douglas had given him the previous year, to Moody, who conveyed it
to the governor without further comment. It was a classy move that
served Perrier well. Unlike Hicks, he was not blacklisted from government work. In November 1861, Perrier wrote a letter to Arthur
Birch, an official in Victoria, thanking him for employing him on a
public project. Having completed his task, Perrier was headed to the
Salmon River to prospect for gold.

"Acquaintances have already taken up a Claim for me with an Interest in a Ditch that they intend to bring on to the diggings this winter," Perrier wrote happily.

At this point, Perrier fades into official silence, still searching for his pot of gold.

Freezing out Whannell

Douglas, Moody and Begbie did manage to find time to deal with Whannell, who, contrary to many accounts, was not fired as justice of the peace for Yale as a result of his part in McGowan's War. Instead, Douglas decided to restrict Whannell's powers and placed another official at Yale to oversee him. Gold Commissioner Edward Howard Saunders was appointed justice of the peace and acted as Whannell's overseer and nursemaid.

Saunders was a bit of an eccentric. He kept a bear cub, nearly an adult, as a pet. The morning of his wedding, Saunders went to feed the animal as usual and, being hard of hearing, did not pick up on the not-so-subtle verbal clues that the animal was in a foul temper. Instead of the food, the bear grabbed Saunders and bit off part of his nose. Fifer sewed it back on, but the bridegroom made a sorry spectacle at the altar with sutures securing his nose to his face. The bear was killed the same day as the nuptials. Saunders' deafness didn't disqualify him for office in Douglas's eyes, however, and he was given judicial authority for the whole of British Columbia, while the scope of Whannell's jurisdiction was restricted to Yale itself.

Whannell characteristically failed to understand the arrangement and was slow to realize how close he'd come to dismissal. As the excitement over McGowan's War faded, Whannell amused himself by tormenting Richard Hicks until the assistant commissioner was officially fired. In a freezing February, with the snow lying deep and dark shadows of the mountains chilling everyone in Yale, Hicks begged Whannell to let him back into his house.

"The stove in the room at the back of my office belongs to me," wrote Hicks on February 2, 1859. "I would like to have the use of it."

Whannell not only refused to allow Hicks to set foot inside the house, but he also threatened to throw the stove out into the snow. Only his suspicion that Hicks didn't own it prevented him from carrying out his threat. There was no depth to which Whannell would not sink in his efforts to ensure Hicks was fired. However, when Douglas asked him to give specific information to back his allegations of Hicks's wrongdoing, Whannell discovered he could actually prove nothing. Given a chance to help kick Hicks out the door, the best Whannell could do was show that the assistant commissioner had misused government mail by sending two personal letters to Fort Langley in the colonial service bag. Total cost to the government: two, two-cent stamps. It was extremely petty, but then, that was Whannell's way.

Hicks behaved no better in his efforts to discredit Whannell. After the stove incident he stopped addressing Whannell by name, referring to him as "the Postmaster." He resorted to delivering mail to people behind Whannell's back and wrote to Douglas that the post office was only open between 11 a.m. and 2 p.m. Whannell retaliated by posting a policeman to patrol the office after it closed. This went on, tit for tat, until Hicks left for San Francisco.

As winter loosened its grip and spring arrived, new problems presented themselves. Georgina was pregnant. Whannell was stuck in a job paying £200 a year, a totally inadequate sum given the exorbitant prices charged for basic necessities in Yale. He was jealous of William Dounellar, the Yankee chief of police in Yale, who was paid $150 a month (and constantly released people Whannell had arrested for no good reason). Promotion also seemed very slow in coming. Whannell could not imagine why his requests for a new job — any job, anywhere else — were turned down. He was passed over for the position of justice of the peace for Fort Langley, for a magistrate's job in Queensborough, for a deputy sheriff's job (which he desperately wanted because sheriffs collected fees and fines that would "increase my present miserable income"), and the real plum: the captaincy of the Gold Escort.[16] Men Whannell considered lesser mortals filled all these vacancies.

When a case he'd made a ruling on was referred to Chartres Brew for a final decision in May 1859, Whannell's considerable magisterial pride was wounded and he finally started thinking that perhaps he wasn't held in the esteem he had always believed he was. In a confidential letter to Moody on May 4, the slow dawning of suspicion is evident. "I sense a want of good feeling and confidence on the part of Mr. Douglas," he wrote. Whannell poured out his soul to Moody, asking where he stood in the civil service, wondering what his future prospects were, asking why Begbie seemed to mistrust him. He even threatened to resign.

"I am the hardest worked official in Yale and least paid. I am pretty well disgusted," he concluded.

Whannell developed an obsession with capturing Foster, possibly seeing the American's escape as the cause of all his woes. Certainly he felt if Foster could be brought to trial, he would be able to prove that his nemesis, McGowan, had sheltered the saloon keeper, which might allow him to bring charges against the Ubiquitous. He entered into a considerable correspondence with the constables and other officials in Lytton and Lillooet, where Foster was sighted in May, but the fugitive escaped capture. The problem, as Whannell saw it, was that his powers were limited to Yale and he needed Saunders' signature to carry force outside the district. Whannell wrote to Douglas, demanding that he be given colony-wide powers. This was the last thing Douglas had in mind and Whannell was politely but pointedly rebuffed.

Spring gave way to a summer of discontent. As the time for Georgina to give birth drew near, Whannell brooded in his office, watching as special constables earning $100 a month strolled through the town, smoking cigars and, in his eyes, doing nothing for their wages. He considered himself "nothing more or less than a slave, tied almost the whole day in the Post Office." Water running off the slope behind the house had washed under the foundation, forming a stagnant pool with a breathtaking stench.

Once again, in June, Whannell came close to quitting. He was upset when he discovered that the town's constables, which he had been in charge of, were now under Saunders' control. Saunders had fired two of them without even telling him. Presumably, Whannell would have relished carrying out that task. He complained to Young in Victoria that he had so little power he was "looked upon as a mere puppet, not only by the officials here, but by the public generally." Whannell said if he was not considered fit for office, he would cheerfully resign. He backed down after Young said he would just as cheerfully accept.

Whannell contented himself with tending to the post office. He wrote to Attorney General Cary in Victoria, asking what he should do with confiscated property piling up in the jail (mostly rifles, revolvers and other weapons used to commit various murders and assaults). He held an inquest into the death of two murdered men fished out of the river. With no sense of loyalty, he hired Dr. Crane instead of Fifer to do the post-mortem examination. He squawked when Crane presented him with a bill of $50 for the service, but the gin-soaked doctor insisted that Fifer would have charged the same fee. Besides, Crane pointed out, the corpses had been rotting.

On August 23, 1859, Whannell wrote Young to inform the secretary that he'd had to have a drainage ditch dug at the side of his house because of "the unbearable smell." It was a vintage day for bad aromas, for on that date Douglas also received a letter from Sir Henry Barclay, governor of the Colony of Victoria, Australia. Sir Henry had enclosed a letter sent to him by James Ross, Whannell's old commander from the Victoria Yeomanry Cavalry, which had just received permission to add the title "Royal" to its name. Ross had read in a Melbourne newspaper about "Captain" Whannell's appointment as justice of the peace and was astounded. He immediately went to see Barclay, who he knew personally, and urged the governor to let Douglas know that his "Captain" was really a cad: a disgraced trooper who had been struck off the regimental roll. Barclay agreed and asked Ross to put his concerns on paper. On May 9, 1859, Ross did so.

I have now the honor of acquainting you that a person of the name of Whannell, who for some time held a situation in the customs department here, absconded from this Colony in the month of

November, 1856, accompanied by the wife of a resident in
Melbourne whose name I have not learned, leaving his own wife and
family behind.

Whannell was a private trooper in the Victoria Volunteer
Yeomanry Corps under my command, and at the time of his
enrollment represented himself as having been formerly in a light
cavalry regiment in India, as to which I had some reason afterward
for expressing my doubts in consequence of his ignorance of
ordinary Cavalry exercise and field movements.[17]

Ross explained that Whannell may have been aided in perpetrating "a deliberate falsehood" on Douglas by virtue of the corps uniform, "which is a very expensive one, that of the ranks being mounted with gold lace precisely the same as a commissioned officer, and I have no doubt that this has assisted Whannell in some measure, if he appeared in that uniform, in imposing upon the Governor with the tale of being a commissioned officer.

"I deem it my duty, as commanding officer of the Royal Victoria Yeomanry Corps, that some steps for the purpose of making known to Governor Douglas that Whannell is an absconder, and that if he has represented himself to His Excellency Governor Douglas as having held a Commission in the Victoria Yeomanry Corps (now called 'Royal' by Her Majesty's permission) he [Whannell] has been guilty of falsehood and willful imposition."

Ross finished by mentioning that Whannell had been dismissed from his customs job in absentia and his name erased from the roll of the members of the Royal Victoria Yeomanry Corps. He also sent a copy of the letter to the Melbourne chief of police, who was presumably still keen to have a little chat with Whannell in regards to his role in the Branson affair.

The news presented Douglas with a problem. These were extremely serious allegations, and it would take a great deal of time to investigate them thoroughly. If they were true, Whannell, who had been personally appointed by Douglas, would have to be fired, the second handpicked official in Yale to be dismissed under a cloud in less than seven months. The government's critics would have a field day. The Duke of Newcastle, now running the colonial office in London, would frown.

Fortunately, Whannell solved the problem for the governor. On August 26, 1859, another legal decision Whannell had made (fining a husband-and-wife bootlegging team from Emery's Bar the sum of £12 10 shillings) was referred to Saunders for final decision. This indignity was the final straw. Whannell resigned his position with the government, penning a furious letter to Young.

> *This, I beg to observe, is the second instance of a similar act of discourtesy being shown to my present position in this district, clearly convincing to me that I do not possess that confidence in the Government which it has been my most anxious and earnest wish and ambition to secure for myself, and which my faithful, zealous and indefatigable Services and strictest integrity have merited at their hands.*
>
> *Under those circumstances, and although I am in no position to throw up the Government Service, still I feel it to be incumbent upon me in justice to myself to resign my present appointment, which I now do, with all due deference and respect for His Excellency the Governor of British Columbia.[18]*

If Douglas felt anything but relief, his handwritten note in the margin of Whannell's letter doesn't show it. Right next to the reference to Whannell's "due deference" to himself there is a small, neat notation on the paper: "resignation accepted. JD."

Whannell, unaware that Ross had exposed him, was stunned that his resignation was actually accepted. He appears to have hoped his gesture would finally spur Douglas to give him a better job, seeing as he had suffered so much in the governor's service. Bewildered, he was forced to hand over to a new postmaster the house he had gone to such lengths to evict Hicks from. He was now nearly penniless, marooned in Yale with a wife and newborn infant, with no job and no prospects. Whannell had to sell off most of his possessions to buy a passage back to Victoria for himself and his family.

Once in the capital, Whannell petitioned Douglas, Young and

Moody for another government job. He was mystified when he received the bureaucratic cold shoulder. His confusion turned to alarm when in early October he began to hear the rumours about his past making the rounds in Victoria's parlours and saloons. Whannell demanded an explanation from Young and on October 13, 1859, received copies of both Ross's and Barclay's letters. The reason for the official silence towards him was now clear. Since he could not deny the basic facts of the matter, Whannell seized on small errors and semantics to refute Ross and Barclay, adding a healthy dose of character assassination.

"I totally deny ever having imposed upon Your Excellency by stating that I had been a *captain* in that volunteer regiment," Whannell wrote to Douglas the same day he received Ross's letter. "Neither have I ever represented myself to that effect to any other person in creation."

Whannell also took great offence at the accusation that he had stowed away aboard the *Zaboah* in 1856.

"I left Australia *freely* and *openly*," Whannell fumed. "I went aboard the ship *Zaboah* in Hobson's Bay in broad daylight, and sailed openly from Melbourne on that vessel, remaining on the deck the whole time and not stowed away in the hold . . . From the above, your Excellency and others who are aware of the meaning of the word 'abscond' will plainly see that I have not '*absconded*' from Australia."

Whannell failed to mention that he had boarded under an assumed name, using Branson's money and carrying Branson's belongings. But he did his best to discredit Ross, denouncing him as "a drunken debauchee and libertine" and branding his information "false fabrications" of a "distorted, malicious, vindictive and wicked mind." He also took the last resort of all disgraced officials facing an unpleasant truth who wish to discourage further public debate: he threatened a lawsuit, followed by a complaint to London.

"It is my fixed determination, so soon as I shall obtain the necessary letters and documents from Melbourne and the East Indies, to forward them and the whole matter to the authorities in Downing Street," Whannell concluded.

He tried every means possible to gain access to either Douglas or Moody so he could personally refute the charges against him. He ranted and railed in letters; he entreated and whined for an interview with Douglas. He even used the considerable charms of his wife, Georgina, writing to Moody to inform him that "Mrs. Whannell wishes an interview" on business of "vital import to the both of us." Moody respectfully declined. Douglas pointedly refused, having Young inform the disgraced magistrate that the governor "considers the matter closed."

Humiliated, Whannell changed his tactics. It was clear he would never work for the colonial government again. Instead of restoration, he now sought restitution and revenge. In early 1860, using money obtained from Georgina's family, the Whannells opened a rooming house, Clifton House on Broad Street. Here, Whannell played the gracious host while waging a grim war against the civil service. Anyone who has ever tangled with a bureaucrat would wince at the record of petty claim and counterclaim from both sides as Whannell tried to squeeze every cent he could out of an unyielding Young. Whannell billed the government for every conceivable expense, including a week's wages owed, he said, between the period of his initial appointment by Douglas and the time he actually set out for Yale. Total amount: just under four pounds. He tried to get reimbursement for more of the money he'd spent entertaining Moody, Begbie and Mayne during McGowan's War: grand total, $150. He even claimed the sum of two dollars and eighty cents for "two Hudson's Bay blankets, for use in Fort Yale jail."

Young retaliated politely but firmly, accusing Whannell of stealing stationery from the post office when he vacated the building, and demanded an inventory of every article in the place. And what of the property confiscated from criminals locked up in the jail? Was it all accounted for? An infuriated Whannell accused Young of leaking the contents of Ross's letter to certain people in Victoria to discredit him.

The only request for compensation Young granted Whannell was perhaps the least valid: remission of the fine levied on him by Perrier for contempt of court. That had been paid by Dr. Fifer.

By April, Clifton House had to close its doors for lack of customers. Even in this, Whannell saw the hand of the government. His was the only English-owned and -operated house in Victoria, yet no government official would stay there.[19] Even Chartres Brew, who Whannell counted as a friend, preferred the French and German hostelries. Broke, Whannell, the loyal son of England, abandoned the empire and moved to the disputed San Juan Island, where he and his wife obtained a 160-acre pre-emption. Grandly titling his holding Glenlivat Farm, Whannell led "a miserable existence." Georgina was reduced to taking in sewing to supplement their meagre income.

The hard life of a farmer didn't prevent Whannell from finding time to continue his campaign to clear his name, which had by now degenerated into a vendetta against Douglas. Gone were the warm regards to His Excellency. In their place were threats to expose "government imbeciles" to the press in Victoria, San Francisco and London. In his letters he paints a picture of a hard, cruel Douglas not accepting his resignation, but dismissing him summarily from the service, casting his wife and infant daughter adrift.

"My integrity has never been questioned, corruption and malpractice of any kind have never been so much as breathed about me," Whannell wrote in 1860. "Discharged from office, and thrown upon the wide world with a wife and new born infant without my money (a fact *well* known to the governor of B.C.) except a few, a very few dollars which I raised by the sale of a few articles to some of the officials and others at Yale."

Whannell threatened in 1860 to launch a wrongful dismissal suit, arguing that only "the house authorities" — i.e., the home government in London — could dismiss him from a "magistrate's" job. He warned he had sent a report of his dismissal to the colonial office and to a "Man of influence in Downing Street, who will prosecute the matter."

In 1861 the Whannells abandoned Glenlivat Farm and moved to San Francisco. By now the U.S. was embroiled in the Civil War. Sensing an opportunity, Whannell scouted about for a commission in a war-torn nation that was too busy to ask many questions. He organized a volunteer company of cavalry in Oregon and placed it at the disposal of Governor Addison Gibbs. The governor wrote General

Alvord of Fort Vancouver, Washington Territory, asking that "Captain" Whannell's detachment be placed under the command of the Oregon Cavalry. Whannell was given a commission and finally became a bona fide captain. The volunteers were sent to Alcatraz Island in California in October 1862, which is about as close to prison as Whannell ever got. His mounted troop was rolled into the 6th Infantry Regiment, California, with Whannell commanding Company A. His duties left him enough time to harass Young with yet another letter promising retribution and demanding back pay from August 31, 1859, the date of his "dismissal," to the present.

On June 12, 1863, Whannell was mustered out of the 6th Infantry to the 1st Cavalry Regiment, California, and put in command of Company G. Transferred to Camp Stanford in Stockton, California, Whannell had a quiet war, getting nowhere near the front lines. Instead he guarded the Presidio in San Francisco, attended social functions and raised volunteers for the Union cause. When the war ended he decided to make a go of it in San Francisco, becoming a naturalized citizen of the United States in 1867.

But in keeping with his character, Whannell was unable to stay in America for long. By 1868 he was back in Australia, this time in Sydney, where he styled himself a "master mariner." His final attempts to have London review his "dismissal" failed. In 1870 he returned to Madras to spend his final years with his family. Georgina died in 1877. Peter Brunton Whannell, former bank clerk, customs official, saloon keeper, justice of the peace, Union officer and raconteur, died on March 26, 1878, having outlived Sir James Douglas by nearly eight months.[20]

Fifer and McGowan Depart

Long life was to elude Dr. Max Fifer, who soon got over his failure to set up a Vigilance Committee at Yale and his defeat at the hands of McGowan. Dogged and determined, with a caseload grown to twelve government patients, who he tended for ailments like hypothermia, frostbite and malnutrition-related diseases, the doctor switched to a third horse in his quest to get recompense for treating sick prisoners and performing post-mortems. With Hicks fired and Whannell in disgrace, Fifer applied to Chartres Brew for justice. He could not have chosen a worse champion, as Brew was disfavoured and distrusted by Douglas as Lytton's man in the gold fields.[21] Brew's petitions to Victoria on Fifer's behalf were ignored. Finally in March 1859, Douglas directed his secretary, Young, to inform Brew: "Dr. Fifer has no claim against the government generally. If Mr. Brew is employing him to attend prisoners, he is at liberty to pay the bill." Brew was not inclined to reimburse Fifer out of his own pocket and there the matter finally died.

Fifer turned his attention to civic politics and became chairman of the Yale town council. Soon he was busy with trail- and road-building projects, freight rates, opening the river to steamboat navigation and other municipal concerns. Fifer brought some of his Know-Nothing sentiments to the job, for on August 11, 1860, he and his council wrote to Douglas complaining about "Chinamen" (or "Celestials," as he also called them) not paying their fair share of taxes.

Their principle articles of consumption are brought direct from China, consigned to China houses, distributed through the country to Branch houses. With the exception of opium, and Brandy, they use none other of the luxuries from which the principal portion of the revenue is derived. For instance, Our Tobacco costs Us in addition to first cost and freight 12-½ cents per pound duty; Our Cigars $1.00 per box. Now the first of their luxuries: Opium could not be successfully taxed, as the bulk of a valuable invoice is so small, the facilities for smuggling — wide, wide trousers, etc. — so great that no revenue could be derived from that source. The second article, Brandy, is a vile concoction manufactured here expressly for them.

We would therefore suggest specific duty on all articles imported for the exclusive use of the Chinese, embracing such articles as: Opium, Rice, Fried Fish, Oil, etc. etc. etc. together with many articles too numerous to mention. Taxing the Celestials is a subject which has already excited considerable discussion, but any direct tax

on them to the exclusion of all other foreigners would appear unjust;
but an indirect tax as We have suggested would not only be just and
equitable, but prove a source of revenue to the Colony from a now
barren and unprofitable soil.[22]

Fifer and the good burghers of Front Street also urged Douglas to
relocate the Yale Indian reserve because of "the evils flowing therefrom to the detriment of the morals of the White Inhabitants." Further, the council wanted to "recommend such municipal regulations
as will restrict the Indians from visiting the town after certain hours
of the day." In other words, implement a curfew.

Had he lived longer, Fifer might have become an MLA or even an
MP. He had the credentials and the experience, but never got the
chance. It was his long-running feud with Dr. Silas Crane, not
McGowan, that proved to be Fifer's undoing. In 1861, Robert Wall,
a young miner, came to Fifer with a serious sexual problem. Basi-
cally, he was unable to keep his hands off himself. Fifer prescribed
wolfsbane to "deaden his sensibilities." The treatment worked, but
when the prescription ran out, Wall didn't have the money for
another dose, so he called on Crane. The gin-soaked quack told Wall
that he didn't need any more wolfsbane, claiming Fifer's treatment
had rendered him impotent. Wall tracked Fifer down and shot him
on July 5, 1861. Begbie presided over Wall's trial, wearing his cus-
tomary judge's robes and wig, and swiftly found him guilty. As was
his custom when pronouncing the sentence of death, Begbie placed a
black cap on his head as he condemned Wall to be hanged. In a
macabre twist, the gallows were built on top of Fifer's freshly dug
grave, and when Wall dropped to his death, his feet danced just
above the dirt covering the doctor's remains.[23]

McGowan was not present at Fifer's funeral. He stayed at Hill's
Bar only a short time after his legal victory over Whannell. His
acquittal by Begbie had hit the Vigilance Committee press in San
Francisco hard. The *Bulletin* rather spitefully described Ned's dinner
with Begbie and Mayne in its February 28, 1859, edition, insinuating
that the colonial administrators attended out of fear, not fellowship.

"Ned is lord of the manor, and of the 'colony.' He entertains, on behalf of his subjects, all distinguished strangers, and these public hospitalities can no more be civilly declined by British officials than a public dinner given in the United States (by the b'hoys) to a distinguished statesman — personal like or dislike of the host is not considered. McGowan on such occasions, drinks the Queen's health in champagne with high gusto," reported the *Bulletin*, in obvious reference to the "collation."

It was clear that as long as Ned resided at Hill's Bar there was potential for trouble. The differences between the Vigilance Committee supporters and the Law and Order boys had not been settled, merely contained. They may have been under some constraint due to the show of force, but Moody and his Royal Engineers couldn't be everywhere, nor could the marines remain in Yale indefinitely, so Moody set Chartres Brew the task of watching McGowan. Brew didn't like McGowan, writing Moody on February 4, 1859, that Ned was spending his time drinking and gambling. "I think he is a bad fellow who can only be restrained by fear," Brew reported.

Ironically, McGowan's next battle would be (as was so often the case among Democrats) with one of his own friends and would occur on no less an occasion than George Washington's birthday.

On February 22, 1859, McGowan and the Hill's Bar boys decided to do up Honest George's birthday right proper. They obtained permission from Brew to fly the Stars and Stripes over the bar and fire a salute in Washington's honour. They didn't have a cannon, so they resorted to using a pair of anvils and a judicious amount of gunpowder. One hundred charges were set off in a display of patriotism aided by the obligatory over-indulgence in alcohol. Mining had not yet resumed due to heavy snowfall and frost, so the event was well attended. The anvil cannonade was but an appetizer to the main course: a dinner, fancy ball and dance set for that evening.

Brew had specifically requested the Americans for once go to the festivities unarmed in an attempt to keep the peace. But some revellers didn't need guns and knives to make trouble. One of these was McGowan's long-time associate John Bagley. It was five years since Bagley had tangled with and been wounded by Casey, and perhaps McGowan remembered how that indiscretion had helped make him

Vigilance Committee Enemy Number One. Or it may have been that McGowan received the signal honour of being seated next to the few ladies in attendance. At any rate, as the soup was being served, Bagley said something to McGowan. The official version recorded by William George Cox, a gold commissioner, has Bagley calling McGowan "an old grey-haired scamp." Doubtless that was a euphemism for an American "epithet." Whatever it really was, the caustic comment infuriated McGowan and his temper got the better of him. He broke a plate over Bagley's head. In the ensuing melee, soup and plates flew.[24] There was a general rush for the door, where the guns had been deposited, as McGowan and Bagley stared each other down.

Bagley called McGowan out and Dolan, not to be outdone in backing his ancient chieftain, challenged a friend of Bagley named Burus. McGowan refused to fight a duel in a British colony and suggested he and Bagley fix a date for the affair south of the border. The insult could then be settled at forty paces using rifles, which were considered more sporting than revolvers. Failing a fatal wound on either side, final resolution was to be by Bowie knives. Dolan and Burus agreed to revolvers at thirty paces, each man advancing one pace after each shot. Burus later insisted if there were no hits after their six-shooters were empty, they should "finish the business with Bowie knives." Dolan refused because of an arm wound and the matter was postponed indefinitely.

The duel between McGowan and Bagley was set for March 2, 1859. They never settled their affair of honour. McGowan himself makes no mention of these difficulties. He wrote that he wished to see his son James in Mexico and that he was tired of the cold weather in B.C. Whether that was the real reason or it masked his fear of Bagley's marksmanship (which, given his encounter with Casey, appears to have been questionable at best), or whether he simply knew he could not make a fresh start in B.C. because of the Vigilance presence on the gold fields, McGowan decided to pull up stakes. He gave away all his goods as presents to his friends, sold his claim for $500 and left Hill's Bar on February 26, 1859, with nearly $5,000 in gold dust, accompanied by his friends Dolan and Banta.

The Boys crowded the riverbank, and the few ladies from the bar waved their handkerchiefs. As McGowan doffed his hat one last time, the crowd cheered and shouted "God speed!" He would never see British Columbia again. McGowan went home to California via Victoria on the same steamer that had brought him to the Glorious River of Gold just months before. There would be no peace for the Ubiquitous, however. Nor would there be for James Douglas.

EIGHT

To the Victors, the Spoils

McGowan's flight from the gold fields was an omen. By the time of his departure, many of the richest bars on the Fraser were swiftly being played out. Rumours abounded of even richer strikes upstream, and many miners, like the ever-roving James Moore, had already departed for a distant country known as the Cariboo. Soon the Fraser Canyon was nearly deserted. The miners who stayed the longest were Chinese, patiently extracting every trace of gold on their claims before drifting away. The Sto:Lo, the Nlaka'pamux and other B.C. First Nations were visited by a smallpox epidemic in 1862 that killed an estimated one-third of B.C.'s Native population.

Moody's Prophecy

Farther down the river, Moody left his mark on the mainland in the form of roads, bridges, buildings and his crowning achievement, the city of New Westminster. It rose above the banks of the Fraser, a citadel of red brick and the surest sign that a new age was dawning. Life along the great river would never be the same again. But none of this was achieved without fighting with James Douglas.

Moody and Douglas did not get along well, likely because Douglas wanted to control every aspect of the new colony and Moody, who had been governor of a far-flung colonial outpost himself, had his own idea of how to run things. Most of their quarrels were over

An idealized portrait of Moody and Douglas on the scene of B.C.'s first megaproject. In reality, the two men never got along, and Moody's career in the new colony was short. He was recalled to England in 1863. Douglas never completed his term as governor of British Columbia, retiring a year early in 1864, showered with good wishes, honours and a knighthood.

money. Douglas was aghast at the cost of the expedition to put down "McGowan's" rebellion, which had all but exhausted the colony's treasury. The Royal Engineers were a continual strain on British Columbia's resources, since the colony had to pay for their presence. Douglas estimated the cost at £11,000 a year. The governor's complaints received a sympathetic hearing from the Duke of Newcastle, who had replaced Lytton as colonial secretary following Palmerston's restoration to power in June 1859. Newcastle didn't envisage the "second England" on the Pacific that Lytton did, nor could he see why the empire was wasting a detachment of elite troops like the

Royal Engineers on British Columbia. Moody and his men were recalled to England in 1863.

Before he left, Moody made an uncanny prophecy about the future of B.C. and even foretold the establishment of the Commonwealth. It was in that first magnificent letter to his friend Blackwood, when the events of McGowan's War were still fresh in his mind and the problem of building a capital for B.C. defensible against the Americans was his next great task. Moody also hit upon the peculiarly Canadian dynamic that united the British North American colonies, yet threatens to divide the modern nation of Canada.

> *I hope it may be united some day for Canada as a great nation forming in some federal manner an integral portion of the whole empire of which it is now a Colony — Say what we may and explain away as we please, politically Colonies do not FEEL as if they were integral portions of the empire. I have lived a great portion of my life among Colonies and know the feeling which (perhaps insensibly) moves them at that disagreeable phrase to them 'Dependency' — Colonists are sensitive people — I don't despair after a Federal Union of the North American Colonies should have been brought to pass, to see a very satisfactory sort of Federal union of all the British Empire. It may appear to be only a name, but names and words are things of tremendous force at times, dis[s]olving or uniting Policies with extraordinary power — Sometimes slowly, sometimes explosively.*[1]

Moody lived long enough to see the federal union of the Canadian colonies, including the reluctant entrance of his godchild, B.C., into Confederation. Fortunately, Moody was long gone before those explosive things, words and names, started tearing at the fabric of that union, with premiers and would-be presidents of portions of our nation haggling over words like "distinct" and "unique." Moody eventually achieved the rank of major-general before retiring to Lyme Regis, England, in 1866. He lived a life of seclusion, returning to public office only once, in 1868, as a municipal boundary commissioner. On March 31, 1887, while visiting one of his daughters in

Bournemouth, Moody suffered a stroke and died within hours, leaving a wife and eleven children, two of them sons who were officers in the British Army.

The Decline of James Douglas

Moody's departure from British Columbia brought little relief for Douglas. He had won a great victory for the empire by saving the mainland from possible annexation, but it had come at a huge personal cost. He had been forced to exchange his cherished title of chief factor for that of governor. He had to forfeit his pension, which entitled him to 1 / 85 share of the Company's profits for the first six years of his retirement.[2] Lytton had forced him to divest himself of some other potentially profitable holdings — most notably his shares in the Puget Sound Agricultural Society — to prevent accusations of a conflict of interest. And he was also involved in a bitter dispute with Alexander Dallas, his own son-in-law and successor as chief factor of the HBC, over the negotiations to end the Company's ownership of Vancouver Island. In this, Douglas largely took the side of the colony, while Dallas tried to get every cent he could for the HBC. It wasn't until 1867 that the matter was settled and Vancouver Island was formally reconveyed to the Crown. The HBC managed to wangle £57,500 compensation for its claims to property and other expenses.

Douglas's greatest victory also proved his social undoing. A new elite above that of the Company he had cherished sprang up as the colony grew, one based on political power and legitimate connections to the Old Country. Begbie, Moody, Cary, Joseph Trutch and Joseph Pemberton were the heads of this new circle. Also muscling their way into the new circle were people like Amor De Cosmos, an upstart colonial from Nova Scotia, to be sure, but considered of a better pedigree than the illegitimate son of a Scottish plantation owner and a black woman. While Douglas was still the governor, he preferred to stay at home and not attend parties where he knew he and Amelia would be the target of polite, middle-class English ridicule behind their backs.

The gold rush and the establishment of British Columbia were the high points of Douglas's career. He had finally won a round with the Yankees, but he would strike out in his next two at-bats against Uncle Sam. During "The Pig War," over San Juan Island in July 1859, Douglas wanted to use force against the Americans, but was thwarted by (among other people) Admiral Baynes. Just how deeply Douglas resented the loss of the Columbia territory and the humiliating climbdown at San Juan Island would be revealed two years later. In late 1861, when it looked like Britain and the U.S would go to war over the Trent affair,[3] Douglas proposed an audacious plan to recover the lost Pacific Northwest empire for Britain.

In such circumstances, I conceive that our only chance of success will be found in assuming the offensive, and taking possession of Puget Sound with Her Majesty's ships, reinforced by such bodies of local auxiliaries as can, in the emergency, be raised, whenever hostilities are actually declared, and by that means effectively preventing the departure of any hostile armament against the British Colonies, and at one blow cutting off the enemy's supplies by sea, destroying his foreign trade, and entirely crippling his resources, before any organization of the inhabitants into military bodies can have effect.

There is little real difficulty in that operation, as the coast is entirely unprovided with defensive works, and the Fleet may occupy Puget Sound without molestation.

The small number of regular troops disposable for such service would necessarily confine our operations onto the line of the coast; but should Her Majesty's Government decide, as lately mooted, on sending out one or two regiments of Queen's troops, there is no reason why we should not push overland from Puget Sound and establish advanced posts on the Columbia River, maintaining it as a permanent frontier.

A small naval force entering the Columbia River at the same time would secure possession and render the occupation complete — there is not much to fear from the scattered population of settlers, as they would be but too glad to remain quiet and follow their peaceful avocations under any government capable of protecting them from the savages.

With Puget Sound and the line of the Columbia in our hands, we should hold the only navigable outlets of the country, command its trade, and soon compel it to submit to Her Majesty's rule.

This may appear a hazardous operation to persons unacquainted with the real state of these countries, but I am firmly persuaded of its practicability.[44]

The British government chose a diplomatic solution to the crisis, and Douglas's dream of regaining the Columbia Territory died. He would never again face the kind of crisis presented by the Fraser River gold rush and McGowan's War, in which he had thrived. The remainder of his term as governor of both B.C. and Vancouver Island was plagued by a series of embarrassing scandals, and he was personally savaged by a hostile press. The ambitious De Cosmos feasted on the frailties of Douglas's underlings, including Jeremiah Nagle, who had brought that first, fateful shipload of blacks and miners to Victoria aboard the *Commodore* in 1858. In October 1861, Douglas was forced to dismiss Nagle as acting harbour master of Victoria after "discovering irregularities in his accounts" that showed £100 missing. John D'Ewes, the acting postmaster for Victoria, absconded with as much cash as he could get his hands on and later committed suicide in Germany. These were nothing, however, compared to the sensation caused by Captain George Tomline Gordon.

Gordon was "an English gentlemen" who arrived in Victoria during the gold rush with his wife on one arm and impeccable letters of recommendation in his hand. Tall, bearded, well-dressed, Gordon had polish and style. Once, while Gordon was walking down the street in Victoria with Helmcken, the doctor remarked on how everyone they passed waved or tipped their hats respectfully. Gordon told Helmcken: "Do you know why these people salute? I owe every one of them money! If I did not, they would not be so damned polite! The only way to gain the respect of people is to be in debt to them!"[5]

Gordon was the MLA for Esquimalt Town from March 1860 to

December 1862. Given his idea of how to gain "respect," he was, perhaps, not the natural choice for Douglas to appoint as treasurer for Vancouver Island in 1860 — an appointment approved in London while Newcastle was on vacation. Gordon's money problems soon caught up with him. He defaulted on a loan of £600 and helped himself to the colony's money to make up the shortfall. In late 1860, Newcastle finally learned of Gordon's appointment and was appalled. The Duke personally knew Gordon to be a cad. He immediately fired off a letter to Douglas, who was mortified to learn that Gordon had fled England after raping a friend's wife and absconding with a considerable amount of cash.

"I fear he may be led into some serious fraud upon the Colonial Revenue and the sooner you can get rid of him, the better for all concerned," wrote Newcastle, who also ordered a thorough review of the colony's books.[6]

Gordon was subsequently charged with embezzling colonial funds. Although acquitted, he was sent to debtor's prison. Locked up in the Victoria jail, Gordon escaped in May 1862 by using a skeleton key to unlock the gate between the barracks and the kitchen. He was seen fleeing through Beacon Hill Park, but managed to elude capture and board a ship for the U.S. side of the Strait of Juan de Fuca and freedom.[7]

Douglas faced further controversy over the construction of the Cariboo Road, which was supposed to open up the mainland to a flood of riches. Instead it was a fiasco that ended up costing the truly astronomical sum of $1 million, far exceeding its original budget and saddling B.C. with a debt the contemporary economists claimed it would never be rid of. Fairly or unfairly, Douglas was blamed for all this and more. De Cosmos had a field day with the scandals, decrying "the vice of embezzlement and corruption which seem almost chronic in certain other quarters, and we have well nigh exhausted our patience."

De Cosmos's *British Colonist* changed the face of newspapers in B.C. Fiercely partisan and anti-Douglas, the *Colonist*'s editorial assault on the governor started in December 1858 and did not cease until Old Square Toes retired from office in 1864. De Cosmos's scandal rag and muckraking sheet forced Douglas to issue a proclamation in spring 1859, requiring all newspapers to post bonds for payment of fines or civil damages in case of a libel conviction. The bonds were set at £400 per newspaper proprietor and two sureties of £400 each, for a total of £1,200. De Cosmos held a public meeting that helped raise the necessary funds.

In an issue withheld from publication because he could not find anyone to pay the bonds to, De Cosmos denounced Douglas's administration. "We must be rid of the present government, with its lick-spittle characteristics, its crawling and evil proclivities, its thousand and one faces, and all the corruption which it has engendered; they must curb its profligate extravagance ... they must show it to the world in all the hideousness of sin, that honesty may blush and bow the head," he thundered.[8]

Douglas finally did strike a blow that hurt De Cosmos and mortally wounded his competition, the *Gazette*, which had supported the American side during the San Juan Island Pig War. Douglas founded an official government propaganda newspaper, the government *Gazette*. To this official organ went all the government advertising that, until then, had propped up Douglas's opponents. The Yankee-backed *Gazette* folded within weeks.

Douglas also got back at De Cosmos in a way that hurt even more than pulling government advertising. He helped the blacks he'd encouraged to move to Victoria form B.C.'s first special-interest voting block. The election of 1860 (held after Helmcken *finally* convinced Douglas to dissolve the first assembly) was a typical B.C. campaign, with two bitterly opposed factions scrapping for power. The anti-HBC interest was led by De Cosmos, who ran for one of two seats in Victoria. He was opposed by George Cary, the attorney general, and Selim Franklin, an auctioneer and independent candidate. The black community wanted the vote, something De Cosmos looked on with suspicion. The law stated that only citizens of the empire could vote. As former U.S. citizens, the blacks would have to wait seven years to be "naturalized" before being able to cast ballots. But Cary, a cunning lawyer, used his office to find a loophole to tip the scales in his favour. He ruled that since the U.S. Supreme Court

Dred Scott decision of 1857 had held blacks were property and not citizens of the United States, they were therefore citizens of no nation at all. That being the case, all that they needed to do to become citizens of the empire and be eligible to vote was to take the oath of allegiance to the Queen. The black community did so, and when the votes were counted, Cary and Franklin had beaten De Cosmos.[9]

De Cosmos never forgot, nor did he forgive, that result. Blacks would soon be disenfranchised. After the Union victory in the Civil War, many blacks, frustrated by the discrimination they faced in British Columbia, returned to a changed America where there was more opportunity than existed in a colony dominated by De Cosmos and his kind. A keen observer of B.C.'s early political process was none other than Isaac Dixon, who moved his barber shop from Yale to Barkerville during the Cariboo gold rush. Dixon, who had experienced the "fierce democracy" firsthand during his incarceration by Whannell, wrote regular missives to the *Cariboo Sentinel* from his "Shampooin' Stablishmen." On June 10, 1865, Dixon penned the following letter to the editor, writing in his "cracker" voice to sum up his views on B.C.'s somewhat Californian style of democracy.

> *I hear de boys say dere's to be a 'lection at de Mouth soon, I hope, sar, yer goin' to put de bes man in, de culed genelmen de best, but as de 'jority ob de boys is not culed genelmen, best for de country's good to put in de white man, assiss de subjecs, mister editer, ob dis loyal counry to get good representatives . . . P.S. I's most forgot to add, on behaf ob de 'tilligent culed population on dis crek, days 'pointed me de litary cracker to send 'butions to yer valable jernel. Dixie.*

Dixon's 'butions castigated the pompous and the proud. Overzealous preachers, bellicose warriors of the gold fields (who boasted of personally "whuppin' the Czar" and taking "Sabastepol" singlehanded during the Crimean War) and many of the other asses who filled his shop with their nonsense were skewered by his fearless pen.

By the time Dixon was starting his career as a newspaper columnist, Douglas had said good-bye to public life. He left office with one year remaining in his term. The decision was a joint one. Douglas did not get on well with Newcastle, and for his part, Newcastle was concerned with the unending complaints about Douglas's rule and the record of what was, up to then, B.C.'s most scandal-ridden government. He suggested in 1863 that Douglas retire. To ensure that Douglas's enemies could not boast they had driven him from office, Newcastle softened the blow by arranging a knighthood for Old Square Toes. The offer couldn't have come sooner for Douglas, who, concerned as he was about the optics of leaving before his term was over, confessed he was "nearly worn out with the toils and incessant cares of my present position." In early 1864, Sir James Douglas, sixty years old, having served his two masters in the New World for forty-four years, retired.

Douglas enjoyed his new freedom, doing a grand tour of Europe, visiting England (where he gazed upon the graves of Wordsworth and Coleridge) and playing *pater familias* as his children married and had children of their own. When he died in 1877 at the age of seventy-four, the outpouring of grief was genuine and universal. Even the *Colonist* wrote: "Today, a whole Province is in tears. The flags droop sadly."

Douglas was laid to rest on August 7, 1877. Virtually everyone in Victoria took part in the official mourning in some way.[10] Schools and businesses closed. The funeral cortege stretched for over a mile behind his coffin. Church bells tolled, HMS *Rocket* fired a continuous salute from the harbour, and many of the city's buildings were covered in black crepe. Among the pallbearers were Begbie, symbol of the new order, and former MLA Roderick Finlayson, Douglas's good friend and fellow Hudson's Bay employee. Douglas was buried in Ross Bay Cemetery, having rightly earned the title of the Father of Modern B.C.

One task Douglas left unfinished was a comprehensive treaty with B.C.'s First Nations. Although he set things in motion by having initial surveys of claims taken, the job was incomplete by the time he retired. It soon fell to Joseph Trutch, who considered B.C.'s aboriginal population "savages" who had no concept of land ownership. He had the Douglas-commissioned surveys of Native lands revised.

Under Trutch, the Sto:Lo lost over 90 percent of their land base. Other B.C. First Nations suffered similar fates, and to this day, aboriginal leaders compare how badly they got "Trutched" in the 1860s. Trutch and his kind believed the aboriginal population would die off, naturally replaced by the superior white man, and decided there was no need to make treaties with a dying race. Douglas's land claims process was abandoned, and the question has yet to be settled.

Ned's Golden Years

And what of our hero / villain, the Ubiquitous, Judge Edward McGowan? No easy life of luxury awaited Ned in his golden years. His Confederate heroics turned out to be more of a liability than an asset, as backing the wrong side during the Civil War proved a fatal blow to his political career. He did manage to enter Congress, but not in the manner he had hoped. Instead of representing Arizona in the House or Senate, he had to rely on the patronage of a friend to get him the post of assistant sergeant-at-arms for the House of Representatives in Washington, D.C. When the job ended, McGowan once again drifted west. He was sighted in Arizona under curious circumstances in early 1881, as a witness in a murder case in the legendary mining town of Tombstone, home of the O.K. Corral and Wyatt Earp. McGowan had acted as the lookout for a faro game in the Oriental Saloon, which ended with one of the gamblers shooting a fellow player. William Hunsaker, a Los Angeles lawyer, put McGowan on the stand as a witness for the defence.

Even in his seventies, McGowan was an impressive figure and still had his undeniable charm. "McGowan ... was of prepossessing appearance, probably 5 ft. 7 inches in height, weighing not over 160, had clear blue eyes, his hair, chin beard and mustache were white," wrote Hunsaker.[11]

Ned made one last attempt to clear his name in 1888, when he sued Bancroft for $50,000 for libel after the publication of *Popular Tribunals*, a history of California that had a decidedly Vigilante slant to it. McGowan got an admission of error and a retraction from Bancroft, but never collected a cent.

McGowan tried his hand at journalism once more, writing his invaluable accounts of the war that bears his name for the San Francisco *Argonaut* and the *Saturday Evening Post*. But it didn't pay the bills and he spent his final years in poverty. His last weeks were spent in a bare room in the Commercial Hotel, paid for by an admirer. His endgame was made slightly more comfortable by a gift of twenty dollars from William T. Coleman, once head of the all-seeing Vigilance Committee, who died two weeks before the Ubiquitous. McGowan died on December 8, 1893, in St. Mary's Hospital at age eighty-four. He would have received a beggar's burial in Potters' Field had another acquaintance not donated fifty dollars for a decent grave and a headstone. The funeral cortege to Holy Cross Cemetery consisted of two very old friends, and there was but a single floral memorial on the grave.

McGowan had outlived almost all his friends, most of his enemies and the era that had spawned him. Had he remained in British Columbia, who knows: he might have become premier — even De Cosmos managed that. His philosophy can perhaps best be summed up in his own words:

> *When fortune smiles, we ride in chaises;*
> *When she frowns, we walk by "Jasus."*

McGowan might have added that, on occasion, he had not only walked, but got out and pushed.

The fortunes of the gentlemen involved in birthing British Columbia were mixed, but McGowan, Douglas, Begbie and Moody were all godfathers, in their own ways, to a unique political entity that baffles pundits, politicians and plain folks from Cornerbrook to Comox. Part of Canada, and yet somehow not. Yearning to be American in its politics and British in its allegiance. All four of these men left their mark on the "distinct society" called British Columbia.

Notes

One: Idylls of the Mulatto King

1. John Helmcken, *The Reminiscences of Doctor John Sebastian Helmcken*, ed. Dorothy Blakey Smith (Vancouver: UBC Press with the Provincial Archives of B.C., 1975), page 154. Helmcken was very close to Douglas. He was married to Cecilia, Douglas's eldest daughter. One of their sons was named James Douglas Helmcken. Helmcken himself outlived a number of B.C. leaders — Douglas, Amor De Cosmos, even Richard McBride. He died in Vancouver in 1920 at the age of ninety-six.

2. Peter C. Newman, *Caesars of the Wilderness*, vol. 2 of *The Company of Adventurers* (Markham, ON: Penguin Books of Canada, 1987), page 400. Newman goes on to recount how Douglas once "wrote a long letter to his London outfitters instructing them to ship his clothes in as small a package as possible because local customs officers judged parcels by size rather than by weight."

3. According to Peter C. Newman, the seven members of the London Committee were equivalent to a board of directors that ran the Company from London's financial district. From *Company of Adventurers* (Markham, ON: Penguin Books of Canada, 1985), page 5.

4. Peter C. Newman explains that chief traders were responsible for the actual bartering for furs within a fur post. They usually served an apprenticeship of between thirteen to twenty years as a clerk first. Chief factors were in charge of the Factory or fur trading area. The title was to some extent interchangeable with "Governor," such were the chief factor's powers, although there was only one real governor of the HBC, and he was in London. From *Company of Adventurers*, page 226.

5. As Margaret Ormsby so aptly put it in *British Columbia: A History* (Toronto: Macmillan Canada, 1958), page 135.

6. See Terry Reksten's *More English Than the English* (Victoria: Orca Book Publishers, 1986), page 15.

7. Helmcken, *Reminiscences*, page 150.

8. Ibid., page 151.

9. At first there were no colonists, so there was no pressing need for representative government. As the number of settlers grew, so did the demand. Matters came to a head when Douglas appointed David Cameron, his brother-in-law, as chief justice. His opponents sent a petition to England, outlining their grievances, but in one of those remarkable cases of bad timing, a small matter called the Crimean War diverted the government's attention. Eventually, in late 1855, under pressure from Gladstone and other anti-HBC critics, the colonial office reluctantly sent word to Douglas to proceed.

10. Douglas to Henry Labouchere, colonial secretary, July 22, 1856, Colonial Correspondence, B.C. Archives. (All letters quoted are from the Colonial Correspondence unless otherwise noted.)

11. Helmcken, *Reminiscences*, pages 333 – 334. In fact, in its first year of operation the assembly did so little it cost the princely sum of $25 to run and was noted ironically in *The Times* for its frugality.

12. Ibid., page 333.

13. Ibid., page 338.

14. Reksten, *More English Than the English*, page 84.

15. The phrase was first used to describe southern Vancouver Island by legendary journalist Bruce Hutchison in *The Unknown Country* (New York: Coward McCann, 1942). Hutchison described the Island south of Nanaimo as "a happy never-never land."

Two: The Glorious River of Gold

1. Averill Groeneveld-Meijer makes a convincing case that Douglas planned the Fraser River rush in order to sell supplies and town lots in Victoria in "Manning the Fraser Canyon Gold Rush" (master's thesis, University of British Columbia, 1994).

2. In a letter to Henry Labouchere, dated October 29, 1856, Douglas described "persons presently engaged in the search of gold" as "chiefly of British origin and retired servants of the Hudson's Bay Company, who being well acquainted with the natives, and connected by old ties of friendship, are more disposed to aid and assist each other in their common pursuits."

3. James Moore, "The Discovery of Gold on Hill's Bar in 1858," *B.C. Historical Quarterly*, 3, no. 3 (July 1939), page 217. Moore's reminiscences are in the B.C. Archives.

4. Douglas to Labouchere, July 15, 1857.

5. Frederic W. Howay, *The Early History of the Fraser River Mines* (Victoria: King's Printer, 1926), page 25, footnote 13.

6. The fullest account is in Helmcken's *Reminiscences*, page 154.

7. Formed in 1854, ostensibly because of the threat of Russian invasion during the Crimean War, but in reality for defence against attacks by Natives, the

Voltigeurs at first numbered only ten men — eight privates, a corporal and a sergeant — though this volunteer militia was later expanded.

8. Notable and excellent exceptions to the rule of excluding the arrival of the black delegation are Crawford Kilian's *Go Do Some Great Thing* (Vancouver: Douglas and McIntyre, 1978) and James William Pilton's master's thesis, "Negro Settlement in B.C., 1858 – 71" (University of British Columbia, 1951).

9. Nagle was soon afterwards appointed acting harbour master of Victoria by Douglas.

10. Pilton, "Negro Settlement in British Columbia."

11. Moore, "Discovery of Gold," page 219.

12. This scene is wonderfully re-created in Chapter Sixteen of *Fur and Gold* by Roderick Haig-Brown (Toronto: Longmans Canada Ltd., 1962).

13. Douglas to Lord Stanley, colonial secretary, June 15, 1858.

14. Ibid.

15. The Hudson's Bay Company had long had a post on San Juan Island, which it considered to be British soil. American squatters on the island, however, knew that San Juan and the rest of what was then referred to as the "Arrow Archipelago" sat south of the 49th parallel. They felt the land should be part of the United States, not the Crown colony of Vancouver Island. Tensions mounted, and in the summer of 1859 a pig owned by the HBC wandered into the garden of Lyman Cutler, an American settler. Cutler promptly shot the intruder (the pig was, apparently, a repeat offender), enraging HBC officials, including Douglas's son-in-law, Alexander Grant Dallas. A few days later, Dallas was among a delegation that arrived at Cutler's door to demand payment for the pig. Cutler refused, and the commander of the Oregon Military Department, General William Harney, seized upon the issue as a pretext to occupy the disputed island.

On July 27, 1859, George Pickett landed on San Juan Island with sixty soldiers, touching off what came to be known as the "Pig War," which very nearly escalated into a real war between the United States and Great Britain. Douglas was all in favour of sending in the Royal Marines, backed by the Royal Navy, to expel the Yankees, but was restrained by Rear-Admiral Robert Baynes, commander of the Pacific Squadron, who felt it was ridiculous "to go to war over the shooting of a pig." A joint occupation by British and U.S. troops followed while sovereignty of the islands was decided by an arbitrator, Kaiser Wilhelm I of Germany. In 1872 he decided the San Juan Islands belonged to the U.S.A.

16. Although one, Lorne Lewis, served for several years as the constable for the Songhees Reservation.

Three: The Iniquitous Ubiquitous

1. The truth about McGowan is recorded in loving detail by John Myers Myers in *San Francisco's Reign of Terror* (Garden City, NY: Doubleday &

Company, 1966). Bancroft's *Popular Tribunals,* published in 1887, has coloured many a historian's view of McGowan, even Derek Pethick's, who described McGowan as "an American with a long criminal record" (*James Douglas: Servant of Two Empires,* page 177).

2. Part of a letter to McGowan from his friend Judge Alexander Wells of San Jose, quoted in Myers, *San Francisco's Reign of Terror,* page 84.

3. The closest B.C.'s elected members came to such mayhem was in 1902, when Richard McBride and "Fighting" Joe Martin had a fistfight during prayers over who would be the leader of the Opposition.

4. Myers, *San Francisco's Reign of Terror,* page 32.

5. For example, McGowan's friend and political patron, Broderick, was gunned down in a duel with a fellow Democrat, David S. Terry, chief justice of the California Supreme Court. They broke over the issue of slavery. Broderick opposed the expansion of slavery into the west. Terry, a former Kentuckian, didn't. The September 12, 1859, duel was fixed. Terry had earlier got hold of the pistols to be used and found one had a hair-trigger. He made sure Broderick received that weapon. During the duel, Broderick's gun misfired, missing Terry completely. Terry very coolly took aim at the defenceless Broderick and shot him right in the chest. It took several days for Boss Broderick to die. Terry himself had almost been lynched in 1856 when he stabbed a member of the Vigilance Committee while rescuing an accused felon from a bloodthirsty mob.

6. Myers, *San Francisco's Reign of Terror,* page 83.

7. The parallels between the Vigilance Committee's tactics and those of some anti-crime crusaders of our own time are uncanny. First create the perception of a rising tide of murder and mayhem. Then undermine the credibility of the current legal code and law system in order to supplant it. In 1850s San Francisco, as in Canada in the 1990s and the early twenty-first century, the real facts were that violent crime was on the decline when the cry to "Hang 'em!" went up.

8. Most of them were Whigs in 1851, but became Braves in the American Party's Wigwams in 1854.

9. Myers, *San Francisco's Reign of Terror,* page 64.

10. The editor added the "of William" to his name to differentiate himself from all the other James Kings. William was his father's given name and was apparently unique among the Kings of the time.

11. Originally, a filibuster or freebooter was a pirate. The word later came to mean someone who engages in unauthorized warfare against a foreign state.

12. William Tecumseh Sherman, commanding general of the San Francisco division of the California state militia, tried to oust the committee by force, but was foiled when the U.S. Army's Pacific Department commander, John Wool, leery of the military interfering in civilian affairs, refused to issue him the weapons he needed. Another hero-to-be who might have acted was Captain David Farragut, who was in charge of the Pacific Squadron at the time. Although he showed remarkable courage during the Civil War and gained immortality for his battle cry of "Damn the torpedoes! Full speed ahead!" he

didn't lift a finger to fight the lawlessness running rampant right outside his naval yard.

13. There was a huge eye on the outside wall of Fort Gunnybags, just like the eye of the Holy Spirit on the U.S. dollar bill. The "all-seeing eye" of the committee had a far-reaching and penetrating gaze.

14. It's interesting that the Vigilantes would not even credit the Democrats as a "party," but referred to them as a "gang," which is a game played in today's geopolitics, where one nation's "freedom fighters" are another country's "terrorists."

15. Myers, *San Francisco's Reign of Terror*, page 209.

16. Ibid., page 214.

17. Boyce was arrested and charged, but in the end was only fined $300 for careless use of a firearm.

18. Edward McGowan, "Reminiscences," San Francisco *Argonaut*, May 18, 1878.

19. Ibid.

Four: The Canyon War

1. See Cole Harris, *The Resettlement of British Columbia: The Fraser Canyon Encountered* (Vancouver: UBC Press, 1997) for a wonderful discussion of how the Sto:Lo and Nlaka'pamux world views differed from those of the European-American newcomers, as well as for a description of the impact of the gold rush on the canyon.

2. Keith Thor Carlson, ed., *You Are Asked to Witness* (Chilliwack, BC: Sto:Lo Heritage Trust, 1997), page 54.

3. Douglas to Lord Stanley, June 15, 1858.

4. Douglas was also indirectly helping the Yakima alliance via the Hudson's Bay Company. The U.S. military complained bitterly that HBC gunpowder and musket shot were being found in Native camps and on the battlefields of Washington Territory. As well, the HBC was accused of buying U.S. Army horses stolen by the Yakima and other First Nations, thus helping to finance the war. See Colonel E.J. Steptoe to Douglas, July 22, 1858.

5. The defeat marked the end of Steptoe's career. He was forced to take sick leave for the next three years. His health failed and he resigned his commission on November 1, 1861. He died in 1865 near Lynchburg, Virginia, aged forty-nine. The defeat prompted the U.S. to launch an all-out assault on the Yakima in the fall of 1858. It forced the Yakima's allies to surrender, one by one, until Kamiakin fled to the safety of the lands owned by the Kootenai in what had just officially become British Columbia.

6. From D.B. Nunis Jr., ed., *The Golden Frontier: The Recollections of Herman Francis Reinhart, 1851–1869* (Austin, TX: University of Texas Press, 1962).

7. Ibid.

8. Ibid. Nicola died in 1859 and was temporarily buried at Kamloops near the Hudson's Bay Company fort until his people removed his body to Nka-ma'peleks.

9. Ibid.

10. H.M. Snyder, Captain of the Pike Guards & Commander of Company, to James Douglas, Governor of Vancouver Island, Fraser River, Fort Yale, August 28, 1858.

11. Ibid.

12. *Victoria Daily Gazette*, August 24, 1858.

13. Snyder to Douglas, August 28, 1858.

14. This point is made convincingly by Andrea Laforet and Annie York in *Spuzzum: Fraser Canyon Histories, 1808 – 1939* (Vancouver: UBC Press, 1998). Miners like Graham were following the same script as they had in the California rush of 1849, right down to the language used to describe Native villages: "rancherie" being a Californian term.

15. Snyder to Douglas, August 28, 1858.

16. Ibid.

17. Ibid.

18. This was a common conspiracy theory of white miners both in California and B.C. See Dan Marshall, "Rickard Revisited," *Native Studies Review* 11, no. 1 (1996), pages 92 – 108.

19. Snyder to Douglas, August 28, 1858.

20. Laforet and York, *Spuzzum*.

21. Snyder to Douglas, August 28, 1858.

22. Richard Bocking, *Mighty River: A Portrait of the Fraser* (Vancouver: Douglas and McIntyre, 1997), page 134.

23. Snyder to Douglas, August 28, 1858.

24. Snyder in a letter to the *Victoria Daily Gazette*, August 24, 1858.

25. Snyder to Douglas, August 28, 1858.

26. Ibid.

27. Ibid.

28. Ibid.

29. Donald Fraser, *The Times*, November 30, 1858.

30. McGowan, "Reminiscences," May 25, 1878.

31. Ibid.

32. Ibid.

33. Donald Fraser, *The Times*, December 24, 1858.

34. T.W. Patterson, *Fraser Canyon*, British Columbia Ghost Town Series 3 (Langley, B.C.: Sunfire Publications, 1985).

35. Laforet and York in *Spuzzum*, as well as Dan Marshall in "Rickard Revisited," paint a grim picture of Rouse's campaign. Kowpelst survived the Canyon War and was a chief at Spuzzum until the late 1890s.

36. Douglas recorded this meeting in "Diary of Gold Discovery on Fraser's

River in 1858," a copy of which is in the Bancroft Library, University of California, Berkeley.

37. Snyder's practice of giving the Nlaka'pamux white flags had a totally different symbology for the Natives than it did for the Euro-Americans. To the First Nations of the canyon, white symbolized death and ghosts, from which sickness came. Laforet and York, *Spuzzum.*

38. James Alexander Teit, *Mythology of the Thompson Indians* (New York: AMS Press, 1975). This scene is also described in Harris, *The Resettlement of British Columbia,* page 112.

39. Teit, *Mythology.*

40. Douglas, "Diary of Gold Discovery on Fraser's River in 1858."

41. William Yates, "Reminiscences," B.C. Archives.

42. Ibid.

43. Ibid.

44. One version of Graham's death states the captain, in his haste to arm himself for the fight, leapt from his bedroll, fumbled with his revolver in the darkness and somehow managed to shoot himself. See G.P.V. Akrigg and Helen B. Akrigg, *British Columbia Chronicle, 1847 – 1871: Gold and Colonists* (Vancouver: Discovery Press, 1977), page 133.

45. Yates, "Reminiscences."

46. Baynes finally arrived aboard the eighty-four-gun *Ganges* in October. Douglas breathed a sigh of relief, believing he would have no further worries about being able to assert military authority over the bands of American miners. For the Sto:Lo and the Nlaka'pamux, however, the point was rather academic.

47. The "stump speech" was a dangerous thing during the gold rush. Yates recalled "a fir stump which stood about sixty feet in front of the company's store here," which was a popular, natural, speaking podium and may have been the same one used by Douglas. If so, he had better luck than some speakers. Yates recalled that in 1859 a Hill's Bar miner climbed the stump and boasted of the fabulous success he'd had at the diggings. "Somebody in the crowd called out that he was a dam [*sic*] liar and a shot was fired which killed him instantly . . the next day there was another stump speech in the same place and another miner was shot." See Yates, "Reminiscences."

48. The entire text of Queen Victoria's letter can be found in Frederic W. Howay and E.O.S. Scholefield, *British Columbia: From the Earliest Times to the Present* (Vancouver and Chicago: S.J. Clark Publishing Company, 1914).

49. Douglas's address is also found in Howay and Scholefield, *British Columbia,* pages 1-3.

Five: Putting the Pieces in Place

1. McGowan, "Reminiscences," June 1, 1878.

2. Fifer's enlistment papers record his name as "Max Wilhelm Pfeiffer," so presumably, the doctor anglicized his name once he reached the Golden State. McGowan stated Fifer was originally Danish. It is interesting to note that Stevenson's regiment brought one of McGowan's bitterest enemies (Fifer) as well as one of his saviours (Jack Power) to the West Coast.

3. Dr. Carl Friesach was an Austrian soldier, academic and astronomer who toured the Fraser River during a sightseeing trip in September 1858. Friesach was clearly not taken with Allard. He put the trader's "decline" down to his nationality. "It is a matter of common experience that Frenchmen and Irishmen become almost entirely savage when living with the Indians. In the case of men belonging to the Teutonic races this process encounters stronger obstacles. The Yankee and the Scotchman seem to resist best." See Friesach's *Ein Ausflug nach Britisch-Columbien im Jahre 1858* (Gratz: The Philosophical Society, 1875). Also see Robie L. Reid, "Two Narratives of the Fraser River Gold Rush," *B.C. Historical Quarterly*, July 1941, pages 221 – 228.

4. McGowan, "Reminiscences," May 25, 1878.

5. Gallagher won his suit, but lost his life. Awarded $3,500 in damages, Gallagher was killed in a drinking argument with a Vigilance Committee member named Roach. The money was eventually paid to Gallagher's widow.

6. McGowan, "Reminiscences," June 8, 1878.

7. Fifer was not the first choice of the young woman's mother, Mrs. Allard, who blamed the doctor for the death of her youngest daughter, Sara. The little girl had eaten a potato contaminated by mercury. Not knowing the cause of her illness, Fifer gave Sara laudanum, a mercury compound, and bled her. The girl died, and in her grief, Mrs. Allard beat the doctor, who offered no defence while being thrashed. I am indebted to Dr. Gerd Asche of Hope, the foremost authority on Fifer's life, for these and other details.

8. Roberta L. Bagshaw, ed., *No Better Land: The 1869 diaries of the Anglican colonial bishop George Hills* (Victoria: Sono Nis Press, 1996).

9. Hills went on to write: "She spoke of her unhappiness as to her own state of life. She once lived, she said, a Christian life and was happy and every day her resolutions were good. She was surrounded by profanity which her heart condemned." Orinda Hicks was "glad" of the sermon Hills delivered that stormy night. The rest of the audience was polite, but unenthusiastic. From Bagshaw, *No Better Land.*

10. Richard Hicks, assistant commissioner for Crown lands and district revenue commissioner, to Douglas, October 3, 1858.

11. Ibid.

12. See Dr. Gerd Asche, "Government says 'no' to medicare (1858)," *B.C. Medical Journal* 37, no. 5 (May 1995), pages 367 – 370.

13. Young was related to Douglas by marriage, having taken the hand of Cecilia Cameron, the governor's niece.

14. Hicks to Douglas, October 12, 1858.

15. Ibid., October 28, 1858.

16. Ibid.

17. Hicks, on paper at least, seems to have been more concerned that his deeds to various claims in which he had an interest look impressive (and legal) than he was worried about criticism from Douglas. He went so far as to ask the governor to send him an official seal and some sealing wax.

18. Hicks to Douglas, October 3, 1858.

19. Nugent's career was, from Douglas's point of view, mercifully short. His appointment was terminated on November 13, 1858.

20. Hicks to Douglas, November 17, 1858.

21. Maria Jane bore Whannell ten children. Six survived infancy: Maria Lily, 1841; Catherine Margaret, 1843; Peter George Alexander Samuel, 1844; Laura Adelaide, 1851; George Arthur, 1854; and Harriet Annie, June 15, 1856 (Victorian Pioneers Index, Marriages, Public Records Office, Victoria, Australia).

22. Maria Jane Blake didn't mourn her lost husband long. In 1858, lacking a divorce, she married again. There was no divorce in the state of Victoria until the 1860s, but such legalities were seldom observed. She claimed she'd been widowed in January 1856 and said the father of her children was Peter Whannell's deceased father, Thomas. She had at least two children by her new husband and died in South Yarra, Victoria, in 1898 at the age of seventy-six.

23. The letter was published in the *Argus* newspaper of February 27, 1857. The original of the letter is in the Public Records Office of Victoria, Australia.

24. Ibid.

25. Gordon J. Smith, "Some Biographies of Colonial Days of British Columbia," MS-0383, B.C. Archives.

26. Yates, "Reminiscences."

27. The B.C. Provincial Police, officially founded in 1858, was a rather informal affair until 1923, when the force was reorganized and, for the first time, uniforms were issued. Its ranks swelled to nearly 500 officers at its peak in 1950, when it merged with the RCMP.

28. See Sydney G. Pettit, "Dear Sir Matthew: A Glimpse of Judge Begbie," *B.C. Historical Quarterly*, 11 (1947).

29. Cameron received his appointment from Douglas in 1853. A cloth merchant from Perth, he had no legal training at all, but he did have one vital qualification for the job: he was married to Douglas's sister, Cecilia.

Six: To Rule a Fierce Democracy

1. Richard Hicks to Peter Brunton Whannell, justice of the peace for Yale, December 3, 1858.

2. Which shows that the controversy over B.C.'s tortured liquor laws has its roots much farther back than W.A.C. Bennett, who gets the blame from most modern journalists for the difficulty of buying a bottle of scotch on a Sunday.

3. Whannell to Douglas, n.d.

4. McGowan, "Reminiscences," June 1, 1878.

5. Estimates differ, but between 7 and 40 percent of Californians came from slave-holding states.

6. Although later, when he moved to Richfield during the Cariboo gold rush, he became a correspondent for the local newspaper and signed his missives "Dixie."

7. Patterson, *Fraser Canyon*, page 211.

8. The following exchange is based on the court documents regarding the case filed before Begbie, as well as on the reminiscences of several of the parties involved. The scene is vividly recreated in *Ned McGowan's War* by E.F. Miller (Toronto: Burns and MacEachern, 1968).

9. McGowan paints an interesting picture of this moment in his "Reminiscences," June 1, 1878.

10. Whannell to Douglas, December 31, 1858.

11. Edward Bulwer Lytton, colonial secretary, to Douglas, September 2, 1858.

12. Willard E. Ireland, ed., "First Impressions: Letter of Colonel Richard Clement Moody, R.E., to Arthur Blackwood, February 1, 1859," *B.C. Historical Quarterly*, 15 (January-April 1951), pages 85 – 107.

13. Matthew Baillie Begbie, chief justice of B.C., to Douglas, January 14, 1859.

14. These extreme conditions may seem surprising today, but the weather on the Fraser was colder in 1858, and the river's current was much stronger prior to the damming of some of its main tributaries, most notably the Nechako. The flow of that river into the Fraser has been checked by 30 percent, and with the once-pristine forests of the Fraser Valley now gone — not to mention the effect of air pollution by industry and car — the average temperature of the Fraser Basin has risen two degrees in the last century. See Bocking, *Mighty River*.

15. Ogilvy met a tragic end and was never to fill the high office Moody envisioned for him. He joined the colonial service and became the customs officer at Bella Coola. There he was shot by a Swedish bootlegger on April 11, 1865. His corpse wasn't found for months.

16. Begbie to Douglas, January 14, 1859.

17. Ibid.

18. Begbie to Douglas, February 3, 1859.

19. Whannell to Colonel Richard Clement Moody, R.E., lieutenant governor of B.C., January 11, 1859.

20. McGowan, "Reminiscences," June 8, 1878.

21. Ibid.

22. Ibid.

23. Certainly his later career proved Ned capable of damn near anything. In 1860, to the express displeasure of the U.S. federal government, McGowan was elected as a congressman representing Arizona, then a slave-territory desperate to join the Union (something the government in Washington was loathe to

grant on the eve of the Civil War). At the outbreak of the war, McGowan was supposedly too old for military service, but he helped raise the Arizona Battalion of the Confederate Army. He drove cattle from Texas to Louisiana and Mississippi for the Confederate cause. But his finest hour under fire came when he joined the Confederate Navy as a purser.

McGowan was assigned to the gunboat CSS *Diana*, defending Bayou Teche near New Orleans. Shortly after his appointment, the Union Navy attacked, and in the ensuing battle of Bisland Island, McGowan found himself one of the few surviving officers on the lone defending vessel, facing overwhelming odds. With half the crew dead, McGowan rallied the survivors to continue the defence. Colonel Tom Ochiltree of the Arizona Battalion was sent as a messenger to the ship and reported later to the San Francisco *Examiner*: "The boat was absolutely riddled with shell and shot. The boiler had been smashed, and the escaping steam mingled with the smoke of battle. But above all else was heard the voice of Ed McGowan calling upon his men to continue the fight" (quoted in Carl I. Wheat, "Ned the Ubiquitous," *California Historical Society Quarterly* 6, no. 1 [March 1927], pages 2 – 36).

When it was obvious the Confederate land forces had been defeated, McGowan and the surviving crew blew their vessel up in mid channel rather than surrender. Attempting to escape, they were surrounded and captured by Union soldiers. That might have been the end of the Ubiquitous. He and the few remaining men of the *Diana* were placed aboard the steamer USS *Catawba* to be shipped to the forbidding Fortress Monroe. The prisoner ship left New Orleans and was rounding the tip of Florida when the captive Confederates, under McGowan's leadership, rebelled and seized control of the vessel, taking the Union crew prisoner. McGowan planned to sail the ship to Nassau as a Confederate prize, but discovered the steamer was dangerously low on coal. Undaunted, McGowan and company ran the ship on shore near Cape Henry and made their way to Richmond, the Confederate capital, where Ned was hailed as a hero.

A swashbuckler capable of such a feat later in life was certainly up to raiding a couple of lightly defended Hudson's Bay Company posts and creating an international incident before scampering home.

24. Ireland, "First Impressions."
25. Ibid.
26. Begbie to Douglas, February 3, 1859.
27. Ibid.
28. McGowan, "Reminiscences," June 8, 1878.
29. Begbie to Douglas, February 3, 1859.
30. Ireland, "First Impressions."

Seven: McGowan's War

1. Ireland, "First Impressions.

2. Begbie to Douglas, 18 January, 1859.

3. Begbie enclosed a copy of the resolutions in his despatch to Douglas on January 18, 1859.

4. Begbie to Douglas, January 18, 1859.

5. Ibid.

6. McGowan, "Reminiscences," June 8, 1878.

7. Ibid.

8. Begbie to Douglas, February 3, 1859.

9. The following exchange is based on McGowan's "Reminiscences" June 8, 1878.

10. Begbie to Douglas, February 3, 1859.

11. McGowan, "Reminiscences," July 13, 1878.

12. Ibid.

13. Begbie to Douglas, February 3, 1859.

14. Helmcken, *Reminscences*, pages 176 – 177.

15. W.A.G. Young, Douglas's secretary, to Hicks, May 18, 1859.

16. Whannell claimed that Douglas promised him this position during their first interview in August 1858. He lobbied hard for the job, writing endless letters, and even provided his own design for the stables and guard house.

17. Ross's letter is quoted in Howay, *Early History of the Fraser River Mines*, page 58-59.

18. Whannell to Young, August 26, 1859.

19. Of course, if Whannell ran his hotel the way he ran his courtroom / post office, it would been like staying with Basil Fawlty, with house rules like: Wipe your feet, Take off your hat, and Address the owner as "Your Honour."

20. I am grateful to Nola Buzza, who is married to one of Whannell's descendants, for details of Peter Brunton's last years.

21. Douglas deliberately foiled all of Brew's attempts to organize a truly colony-wide police force, which had been his mandate, and saddled him with every petty administrative job he could. Brew petitioned both Douglas and Moody, to no avail. He died in the Cariboo on May 31, 1879, having been appointed gold commissioner for the district (another job he didn't want). He is buried in Barkerville.

22. Dr. Max William Fifer to Douglas, August 11, 1860.

23. Dr. Gerd Asche, "On the Trail of Dr. Fifer," *Canadian Medical Association Journal* 154, no. 9 (May 1, 1996), pages 1397 – 1399. Additional information was provided in e-mail correspondence.

24. D.W. Higgins, who was present, has an amusing version of this brawl in *The Mystic Spring*, claiming that Whannell hid under his wife's hooped skirt during the scrap.

Eight: To the Victors, the Spoils

1. Ireland, "First Impressions."

2. See Derek Pethick, *James Douglas, Servant of Two Empires* (Victoria: Mitchell Press Ltd., 1969), page 182.

3. In 1861 a Union warship stopped the British steamer *Trent*, and men went aboard to seize two Confederate diplomats. It was a clear violation of British neutrality and it took all the considerable diplomatic skill of Lincoln and his secretary of state, Seward, to prevent war between Britain and the United States. It was settled by a non-apology and honour was satisfied.

4. Douglas to Duke of Newcastle, colonial secretary, December 28, 1861.

5. Helmcken, *Reminiscences.*

6. Newcastle to Douglas, December 31, 1860.

7. Gordon later joined the Confederate Army, serving with distinction from 1862 to 1865 as a captain. He survived the war and died in 1868.

8. See Hugh Doherty, "The First Newspapers on Canada's West Coast," a 1973 research paper from the University of Victoria. Retrieved from http:// members.tripod.com/Hughdoherty/victoria.htm#vancouver.

9. One member of the black community, Jacob Francis, was elected to the legislative assembly in 1861 during a byelection. However, the authorities broke the rules in order to give his seat to Joseph Trutch, who, since he wasn't even in the colony during the election and could not have taken the oaths legally required of a candidate, should have been disqualified. Mifflin Wistar Gibbs succeeded in becoming a city councillor in Victoria in 1868. He returned to the United States to become both a judge and an American consul: offices he would never have held in B.C.

10. In contrast, when Amor De Cosmos died in 1897, mad, shunned and repudiated at the polls, few attended his funeral. De Cosmos is also buried in Ross Bay Cemetery.

11. Carl I. Wheat, "Ned the Ubiquitous," *California Historical Society Quarterly* 6, no. 1 (March 1927).

Bibliography

Books

Adams, John. *Old Square Toes and His Lady*. Victoria: Horsdal and Schubart, 2001.

Akrigg, G.P.V., and Helen B. Akrigg. *British Columbia Chronicle, 1847 – 1871: Gold and Colonists*. Vancouver: Discovery Press, 1977.

Bagshaw, Roberta L., ed. *No Better Land: The 1869 diaries of the Anglican colonial bishop George Hills*. Victoria: Sono Nis Press, 1996.

Bocking, Richard C. *Mighty River: A Portrait of the Fraser*. Vancouver: Douglas and McIntrye, 1997.

Carlson, Keith Thor, ed. *You Are Asked to Witness: The Sto:Lo in Canada's Pacific Coast History*. Chilliwack, BC: Sto:Lo Heritage Trust, 1997.

Friesach, Carl. *Ein Ausflug nach Britisch-Columbien im Jahre 1858*. Gratz: The Philosophical Society, 1875.

Gregson, Harry. *A History of Victoria, 1842 – 1970*. Vancouver: J.J. Douglas Ltd., 1977.

Haig-Brown, Roderick. *Fur and Gold*. Toronto: Longmans Canada Ltd., 1962.

Harris, R. Cole. *The Resettlement of British Columbia: The Fraser Canyon Encountered*. Vancouver: UBC Press, 1997.

Helmcken, John Sebastian. *The Reminiscences of Doctor John Sebastian Helmcken*. Edited by Dorothy Blakey Smith. Vancouver: UBC Press with the Provincial Archives of B.C., 1975.

Higgins, David W. *The Mystic Spring and other Tales of Western Life*. Toronto: William Briggs, 1904.

Howay, Frederic W. *The Early History of the Fraser River Mines*. Victoria: King's Printer, 1926.

Howay, Frederic W. and E.O.S. Scholefield. *British Columbia: From the Earliest Times to the Present*. Vancouver and Chicago: S.J. Clark Publishing Company, 1914.

Hutchison, Bruce. *The Unknown Country: Canada and her People*. New York: Coward McCann, 1942.

Kilian, Crawford. *Go Do Some Great Thing: The Black Pioneers of British Columbia.* Vancouver: Douglas and McIntyre, 1978.

Laforet, Andrea, and Annie York. *Spuzzum: Fraser Canyon Histories, 1808 – 1939.* Vancouver: UBC Press, 1998.

Langston, Laura. *Paydirt! The Search for Gold in British Columbia.* Victoria: Orca Book Publishers, 1995.

Mayne, Richard Charles. *Four years in British Columbia and Vancouver Island: An Account of their forests, rivers, coasts, gold fields and resources for Colonization.* London: John Murray, 1862.

McGowan, Edward. *The Narrative of Edward McGowan, Including a Full Account of the Author's Adventures and Perils While Persecuted by the San Francisco Vigilance Committee in 1856.* San Francisco: no publisher, 1857.

Miller, E.F. *Ned McGowan's War.* Toronto: Burns and MacEachern, 1968.

Myers, John Myers. *San Francisco's Reign of Terror.* Garden City, NY: Doubleday and Company, 1966.

Newman, Peter C. *Company of Adventurers.* Vol. 1 of *The Company of Adventurers* Markham, ON: Penguin Books of Canada, 1985.

——. *Caesars of the Wilderness.* Vol. 2 of *The Company of Adventurers.* Markham, Ontario: Penguin Books of Canada Ltd, 1987.

Nunis, D.B. Jr., ed. *The Golden Frontier: The Recollections of Herman Francis Reinhart, 1851 – 1869.* Austin, TX: University of Texas Press, 1962.

Ormsby, Margaret. *British Columbia: A History.* Toronto: Macmillan Canada, 1958.

Pethick, Derek. *James Douglas: Servant of Two Empires.* Vancouver: Mitchell Press, 1969.

——. *Victoria: The Fort.* Vancouver: Mitchell Press Ltd., 1968.

Pierce, J. Kingston. *San Francisco, You're History!* Seattle: Sasquatch Books, 1995.

Reksten, Terry. *More English Than the English.* Victoria: Orca Book Publishers, 1986.

Rutland, Robert A. *The Democrats from Jefferson to Carter.* Baton Rouge, LA: Louisiana State University Press, 1979.

Sterne, Netta. *Fraser Gold 1858! The Founding of British Columbia.* Pullman, WA: Washington State University Press, 1998.

Teit, James Alexander. *Mythology of the Thompson Indians.* New York: AMS Press, 1975.

Ward, George F. *Victorian Land Forces, 1853 – 1883.* Victoria, Australia: Croydon, 1989.

Articles

Asche, Dr. Gerd. "Government says 'no' to medicare (1858)." *B.C. Medical Journal* 17, no. 5 (May 1995), pages 367 – 370.

——. "On the Trail of Dr. Fifer." *Canadian Medical Association Journal* 154, no. 9 (May 1, 1996), pages 1397 – 1399.

Dixon, Isaac. Letter to the Editor. *Cariboo Sentinel*, June 10, 1865.

Doherty, Hugh. "The First Newspapers on Canada's West Coast." Based on a research paper done for the University of Victoria graduate history department, 1973. Revised January 28, 2001. Retrieved from http://members.tripod.com/Hughdoherty/victoria.htm#vancouver.

Ireland, Willard E., ed. "First Impressions: Letter of Colonel Richard Clement Moody, R.E., to Arthur Blackwood, February 1, 1859." *B.C. Historical Quarterly* 15 (January-April 1951), pages 85 – 107.

Law Report, "Embezzlement," *The Argus* (Melbourne, Australia), February 23, 1857.

Lugrin, N. de Bertrand. "Policing in B.C." *Maclean's Magazine*, February 1, 1935.

Marshall, Dan. "Rickard Revisited." *Native Studies Review* 11, no. 1 (1996), pages 92 – 108.

McGowan, Edward. "Reminiscences." San Francisco *Argonaut*, May 11 to July 13, 1878.

Moore, James. "The Discovery of Gold on Hill's Bar in 1858." *B.C. Historical Quarterly* 3, no. 3 (July 1939), pages 215 – 220.

——. "Story of the Great Cariboo Gold Rush Is Told By One of Those Who Took Part In It." Vancouver *Province*, March 26, 1918.

"Ned M'Gowan is Dead." *San Francisco Chronicle*, Dec. 9, 1893.

Pettit, Sydney G. "Dear Sir Matthew: A Glimpse of Judge Begbie." *B.C. Historical Quarterly* 11 (1947).

Reid, Robie L. "Two Narratives of the Fraser River Gold Rush." *B.C. Historical Quarterly*, July 1941, pages 221 – 228.

Rickard, T.A. "The Fraser River Gold Rush." *The Beaver* September 1942, pages 32 – 34.

Wheat, Carl I. "Ned, the Ubiquitous: Soldier of Fortune par Excellence, Being the Further Narrative of Edward McGowan." *California Historical Society Quarterly* 6, no. 1 (March 1927), pages 2 – 36.

Unpublished Material

Colonial Correspondence, B.C. Archives, including the correspondence of Judge Matthew Baillie Begbie, Isaac Dixon, Sir James Douglas, Dr. Max Fifer, Richard Hicks, Colonel Richard Clement Moody, George Perrier, H.M. Snyder, Peter Brunton Whannell.

Douglas, James. "Diary of Gold Discovery on Fraser's River in 1858." Bancroft Library, University of California, Berkeley.

Groeneveld-Meijer, Averil. "Manning the Fraser Canyon Gold Rush." Master's thesis, University of British Columbia, 1994.

Moore, James. "Reminiscences." B.C. Archives.

Pilton, James William. "Negro Settlement in British Columbia, 1858 – 71." Master's thesis, University of British Columbia, 1951.
Smith, Gordon J. "Some Biographies of Colonial Days of British Columbia." MS – 0383. B.C. Archives.
Yates, William. "Reminiscences." B.C. Archives.

Additional Research

Dr. Gerd Asche, on Dr. Max Fifer, Edward McGowan and Richard Hicks.
Nola Buzza, on Peter Brunton Whannell.
Helen D. Harris, on Peter Brunton Whannell.

Index